The Artist Explorers

The Artist Explorers

Painting The New World

John Fairley

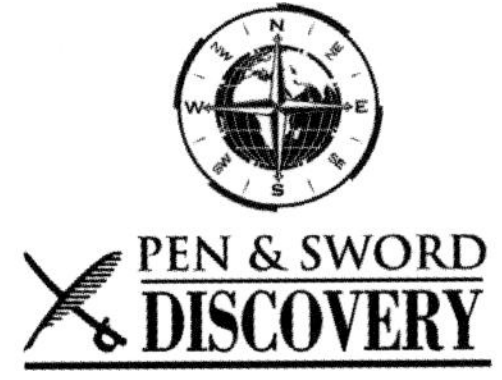

PEN & SWORD
DISCOVERY

First published in Great Britain in 2024 by
Pen & Sword Discovery
An imprint of Pen & Sword Books Limited
Yorkshire – Philadelphia

Copyright © John Fairley 2024

ISBN 978 1 39904 711 1

The right of John Fairley to be identified as
Author of this Work has been asserted by him in accordance
with the Copyright, Designs and Patents Act 1988.

A CIP catalogue record for this book is
available from the British Library

Typeset by Mac Style
Printed and bound in China by 1010 Printing International Limited

Pen & Sword Books Limited incorporates the imprints of After the Battle, Atlas,
Archaeology, Aviation, Discovery, Family History, Fiction, History, Maritime,
Military, Military Classics, Politics, Select, Transport, True Crime, Air World,
Frontline Publishing, Leo Cooper, Remember When, Seaforth Publishing, The
Praetorian Press, Wharncliffe Local History, Wharncliffe Transport, Wharncliffe
True Crime and White Owl.

For a complete list of Pen & Sword titles please contact

PEN & SWORD BOOKS LIMITED
47 Church Street, Barnsley, South Yorkshire, S70 2AS, England
E-mail: enquiries@pen-and-sword.co.uk
Website: www.pen-and-sword.co.uk
or
PEN AND SWORD BOOKS
1950 Lawrence Rd, Havertown, PA 19083, USA
E-mail: uspen-and-sword@casematepublishers.com
Website: www.penandswordbooks.com

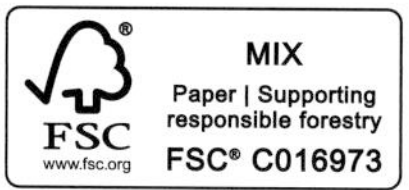

Contents

Preface

The great explorer Captain James Cook insisted on taking artists on his voyages. He wrote: 'This is for the express purpose of supplying the unavoidable imperfections of written accounts, by enabling us to bring home the most memorable scenes of our transactions.'

And, indeed, his artists fulfilled his vision. John Webber was able to exhibit fifty paintings at the Royal Academy after Cook's fateful third voyage. William Hodges on the second voyage had been similarly prolific.

This was to be the way, for the centuries before photography, that the European public first came to view these new worlds that their intrepid seafarers were discovering. Their work, the authentic depicting of places and sights that Europeans had never dreamt of, was to shape the imaginations and aspirations of many future adventurous generations.

This book seeks to display not only the beauties and dramas of the scenes and landscapes which the artists found around the globe, but above all, to convey the wonderment which these works evoked in the public back home.

It is not hard to imagine the astonishment of Europeans when they first saw the paintings which artists brought back from the new worlds of the South Seas.

From Captains Cook's first voyage William Hodges returned with his picture of the mountains of Tahiti and the cascade at Dusky Bay in what was to become known as New Zealand. Charles Heaphy painted the extraordinary white mountain which became known as Mount Egmont. John Buchanan painted what became known as Milford Sound. William Fox gave us his 'Bird's Eye View of Waitoi', and Alfred Sharp's beguilingly fertile view of 'The Landing Place at Takapuna' might have tempted any potential traveller.

Inevitably it was the landscape which appealed first to the European eye, but then there was the intriguing question of who peopled it. The artists were soon fascinated. They tried to portray the exotic strangeness as well as the human qualities they discerned in their first encounters.

There are Māoris, as they became known, even in some of Hodges' earliest paintings, such as 'Dusky Bay'; and the death of Captain Cook at the hands of the Hawaiians was dramatically painted by John Webber, the *Resolution*'s artist.

And across the world, the mysteries of Australia, the long exploration of Africa, the slow and careful venture across what became Canada, were brought to Europeans most vividly by the artists. It is through their work that the modern mind can perhaps best hope to rediscover the excitement and wonder of two or three centuries ago, sensations which were, for sure, as acute as those provoked by our own exploration of the moon, the planets, and who knows what lies in the universe beyond.

Acknowledgements

The paintings in this book are scattered across the world – many of them in the countries which they were among the first to depict. The staff of the galleries and museums and the individuals who take care of these works have been enormously helpful. They are credited in the captions and picture lists.

Felicity Page has been the most determined ally in successfully seeking out these works of art. George Chamier has been the most helpful and creative of editors. And Matt Jones at Pen & Sword has seen the project through from its earliest concept to the finished article.

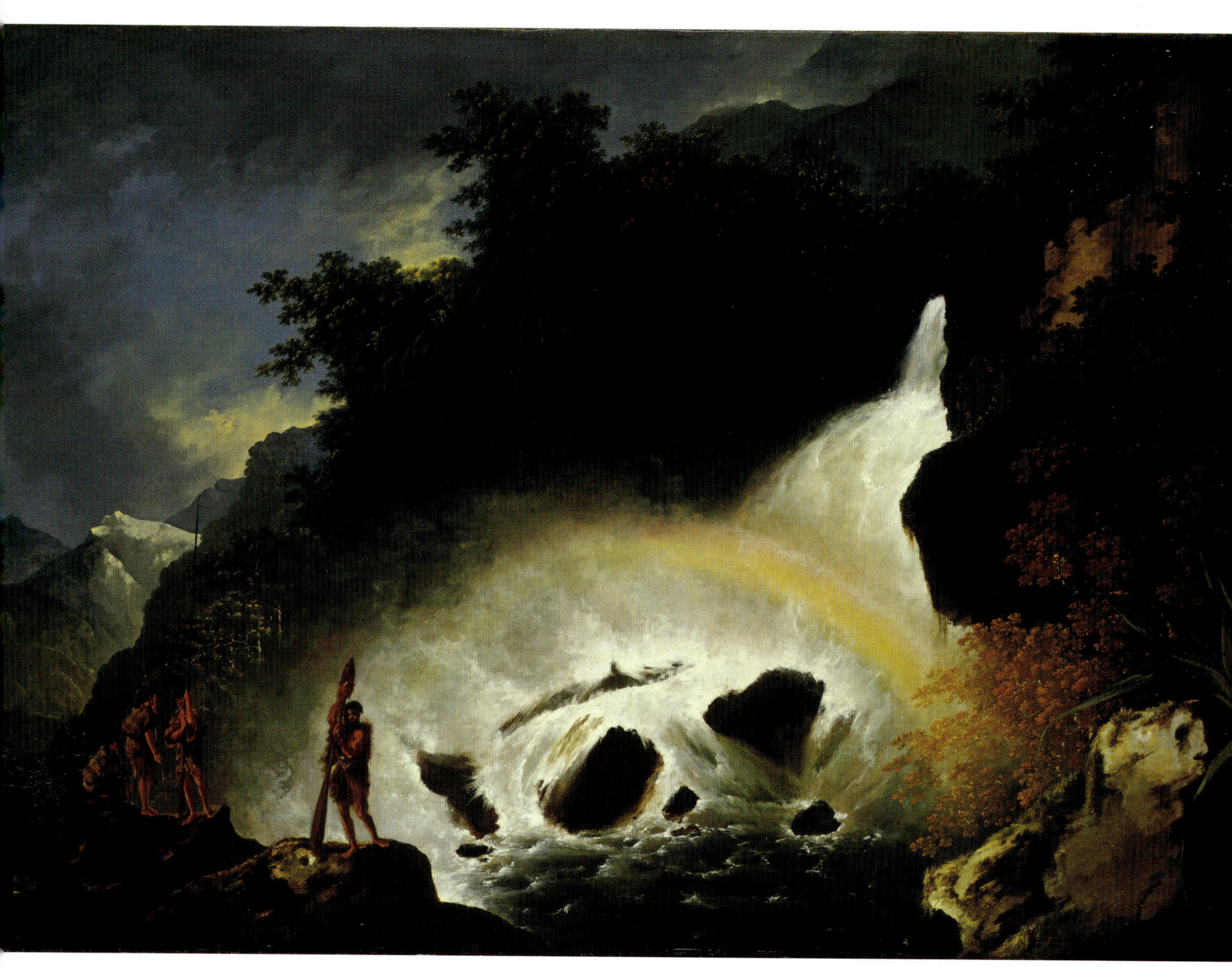

William Hodges – [Cascade Cove] Dusky Bay.

Charles Heaphy – Mount Egmont from the southward.

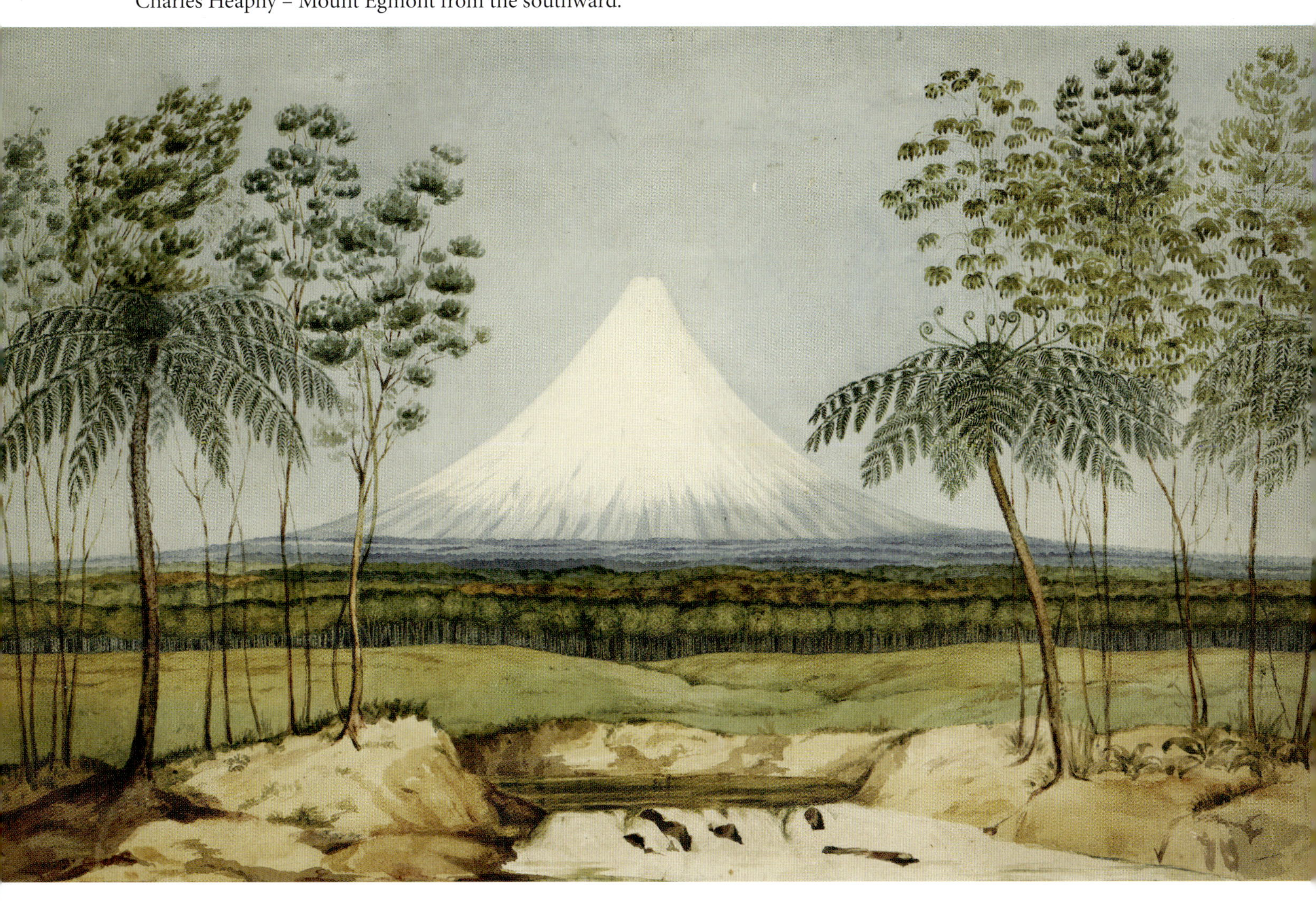

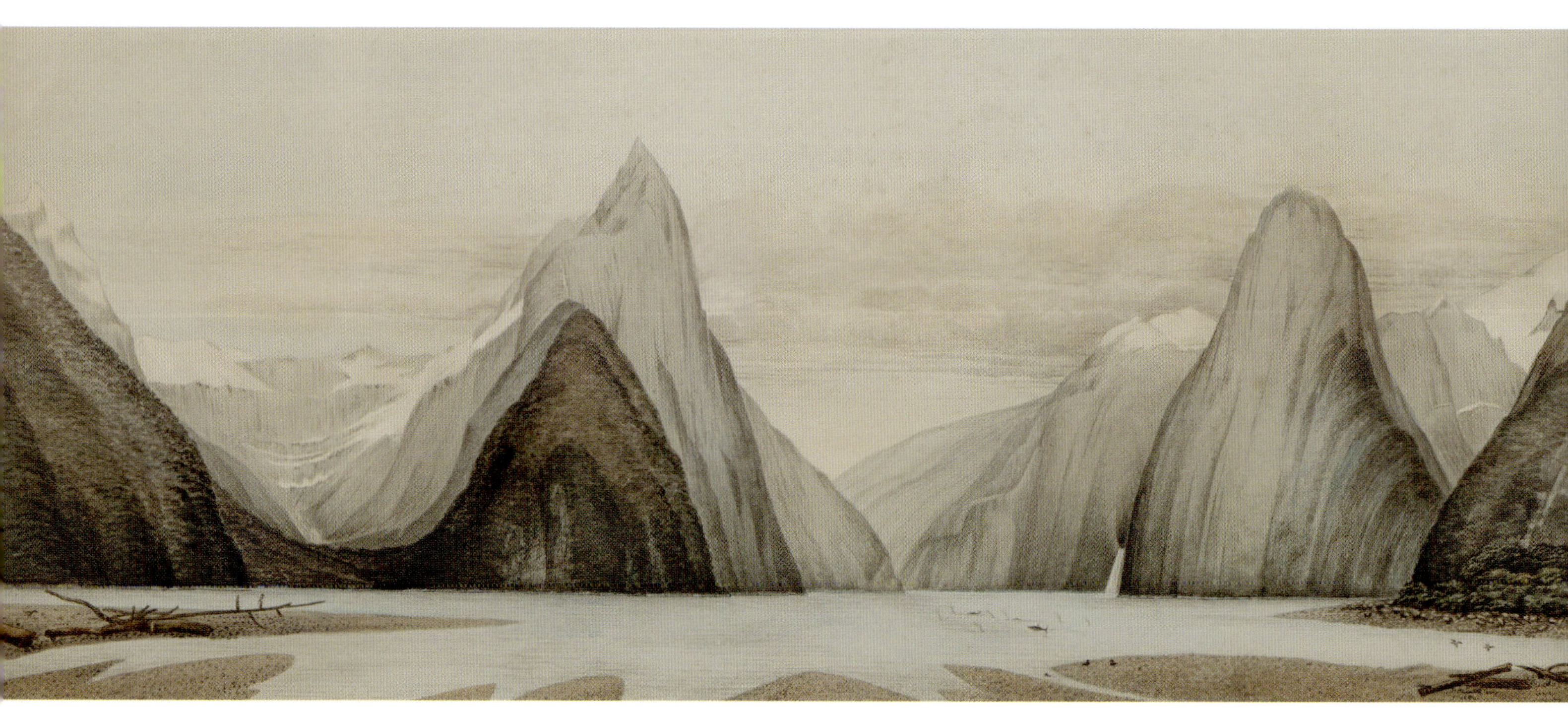

John Buchanan – Milford Sound, looking north-west from Freshwater Basin.

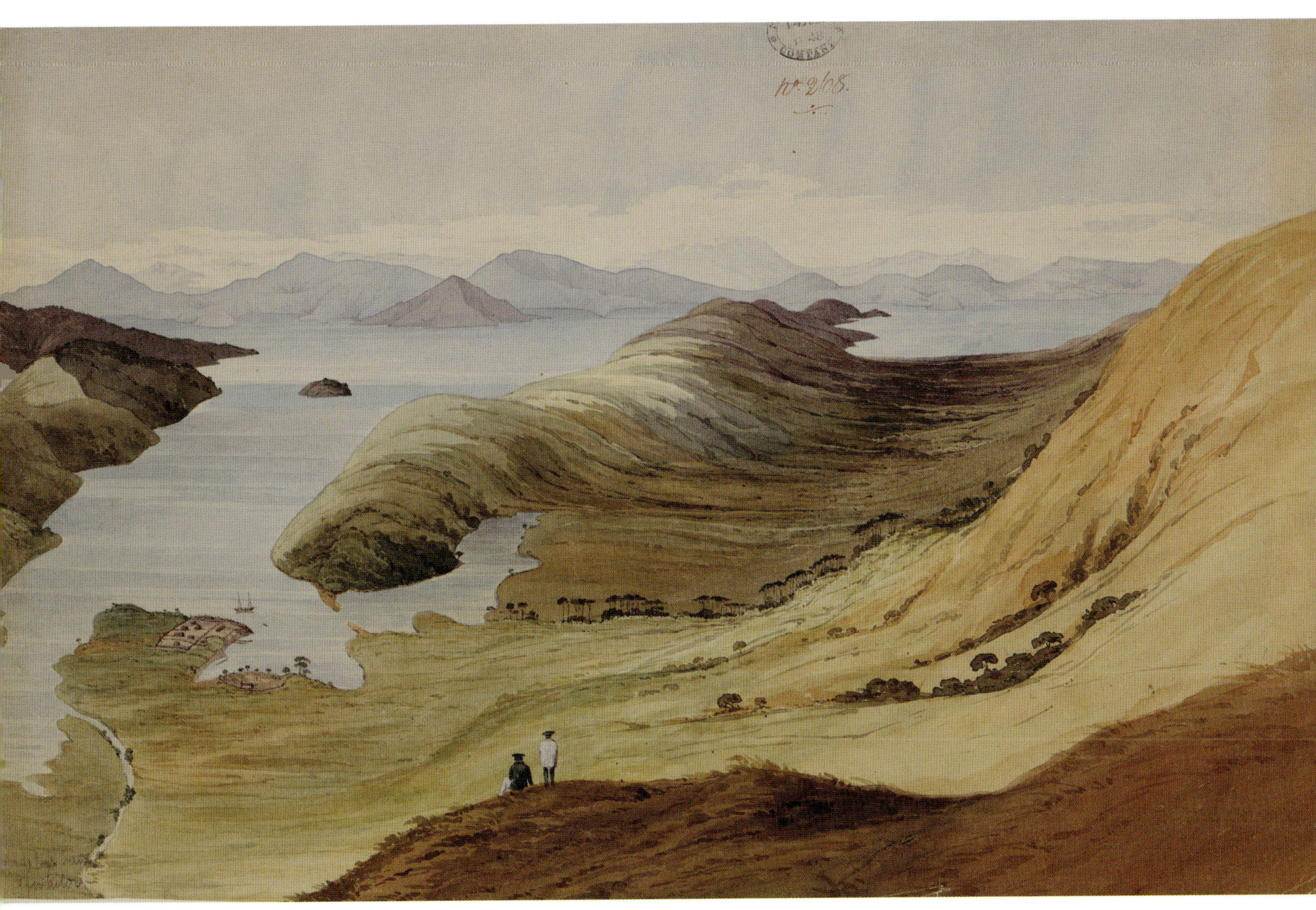

William Fox – Bird's eye view of Waitoi.

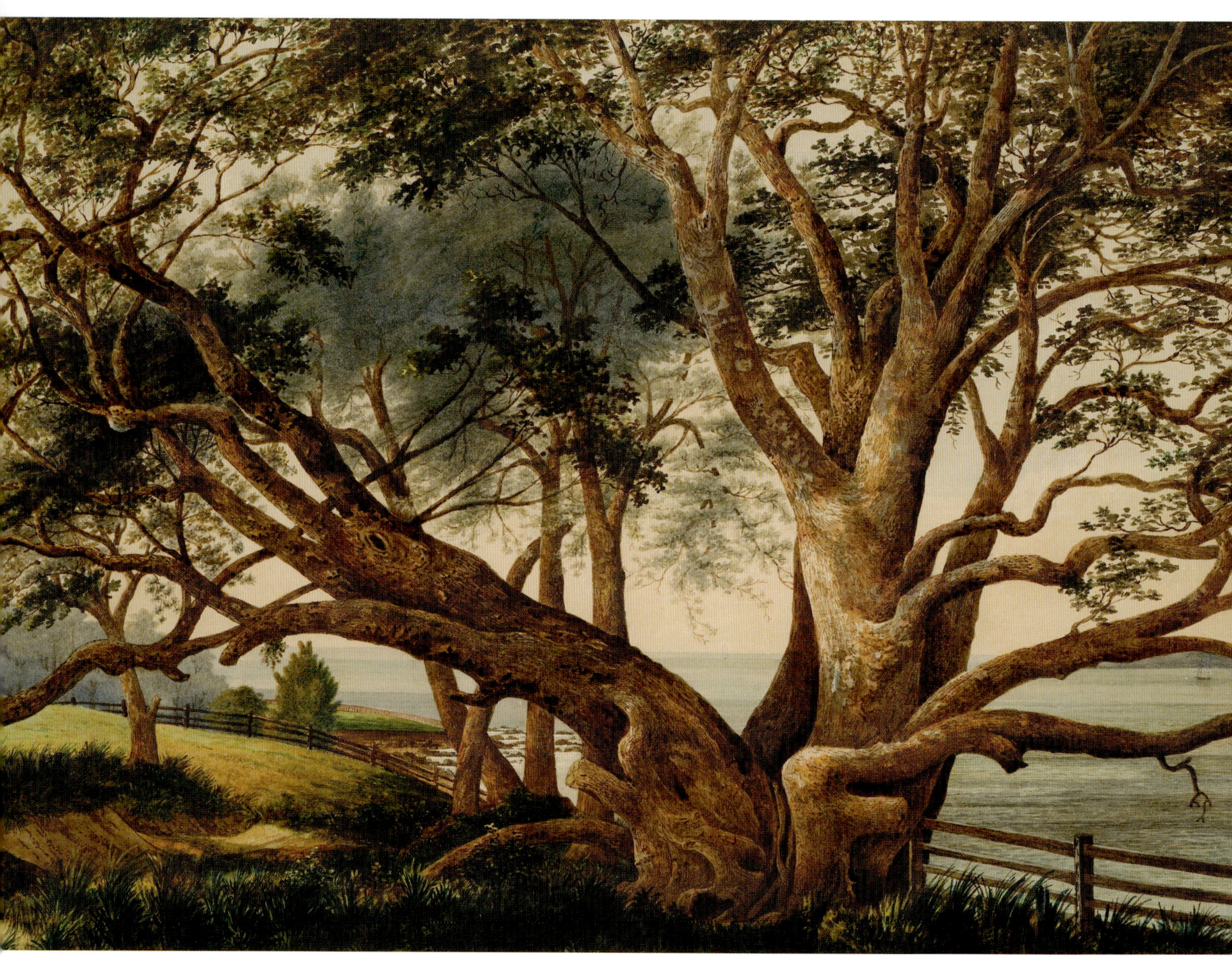

Alfred Sharp – Pohutukawa, near the landing place below Lake Pupuke, Takapuna.

Chapter 1

The Lost Colony

While the glint of gold was luring Spanish and Portuguese adventurers to seek to establish themselves on the coast of Central America, it was only in Elizabethan times that the first attempts were made by the English to establish settlements on the more northerly shores of the continent.

Sir Richard Grenville, encouraged by Walter Raleigh, set off in 1585 with the first group intent on finding a suitable place to establish a colony. With him he took, as artist and map-maker, John White. Though Grenville failed to found his colony, the paintings and drawings which White brought back of the Native Americans, their villages and their lifestyle, the first ever seen in England, were enough to excite Raleigh to appoint White as leader of a new venture to what is now the Carolinas, in 1587.

More than a hundred people, men women and children, took ship with him, including his own daughter and her husband. They reached what is now called Roanoke Island and disembarked with their ploughs, tools and seeds ready to start this unique undertaking.

Within only a few days White found himself with a baby granddaughter, named Virginia in honour of the Queen of England. She was the first English person to be born in America.

Although the natives on Roanoke were friendly, it soon became apparent that the new colony could not survive a winter without more supplies from home. White, by now entitled Governor of the colony, was reluctantly persuaded to return in their remaining pinnace. He even carried a signed letter from the new colonists declaring that it was their wish that he should go.

After a troubled crossing he arrived back in England to find that the looming threat of the Spanish Armada meant that the Queen had banned all shipping from leaving home waters.

It was not until 1590 that White was able to put together the necessary ships to return to Roanoke and his family and colony. When he got there, it was to find there was not a trace of the settlers at all except the word 'croatan', the name of a neighbouring island, carved in Roman letters on a tree. White found the relics of some notes he had buried. But nothing else. This was to become the Lost Colony, whose fate has remained a mystery ever since.

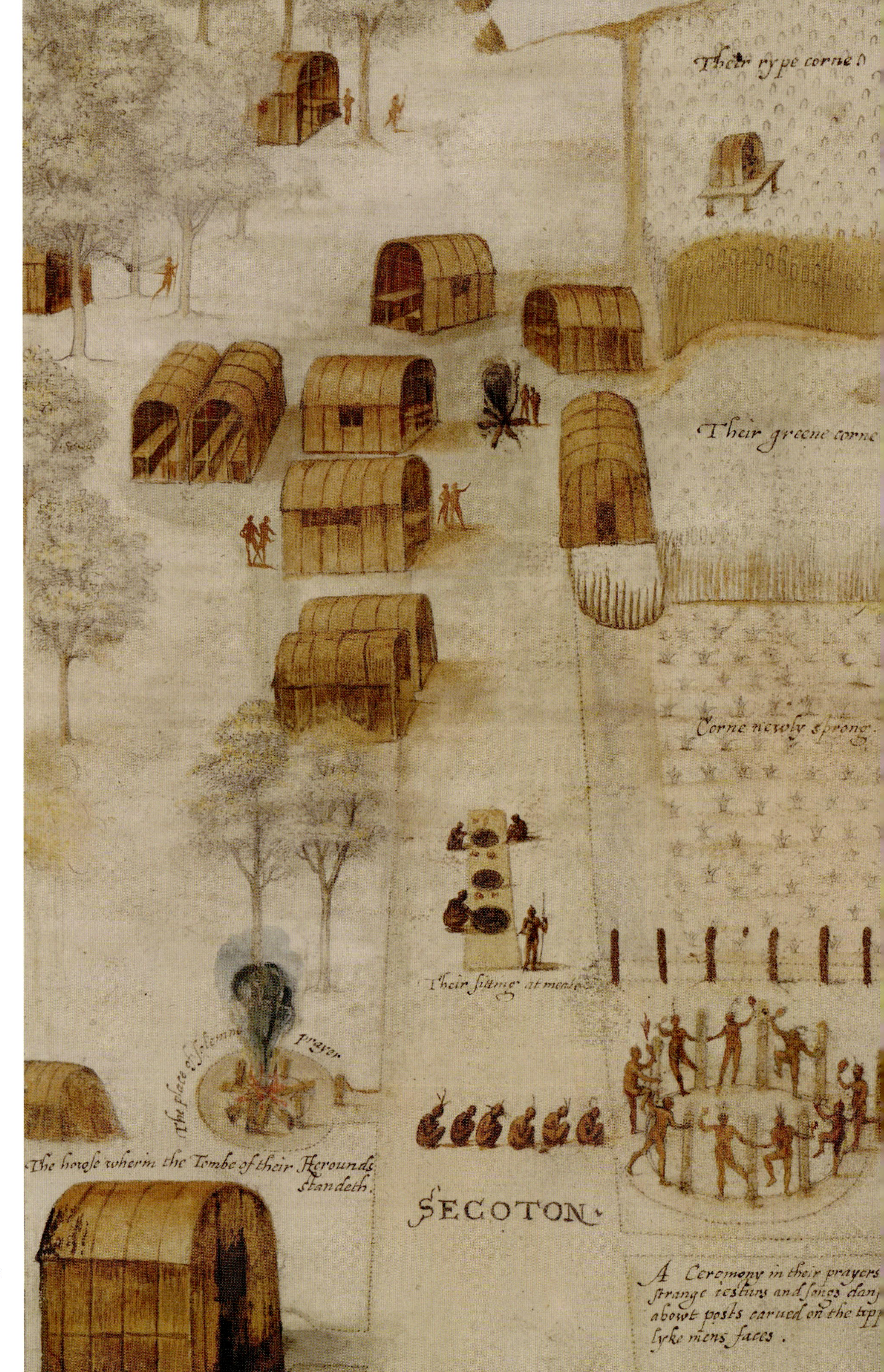

John White – The Indian village of Secoton.

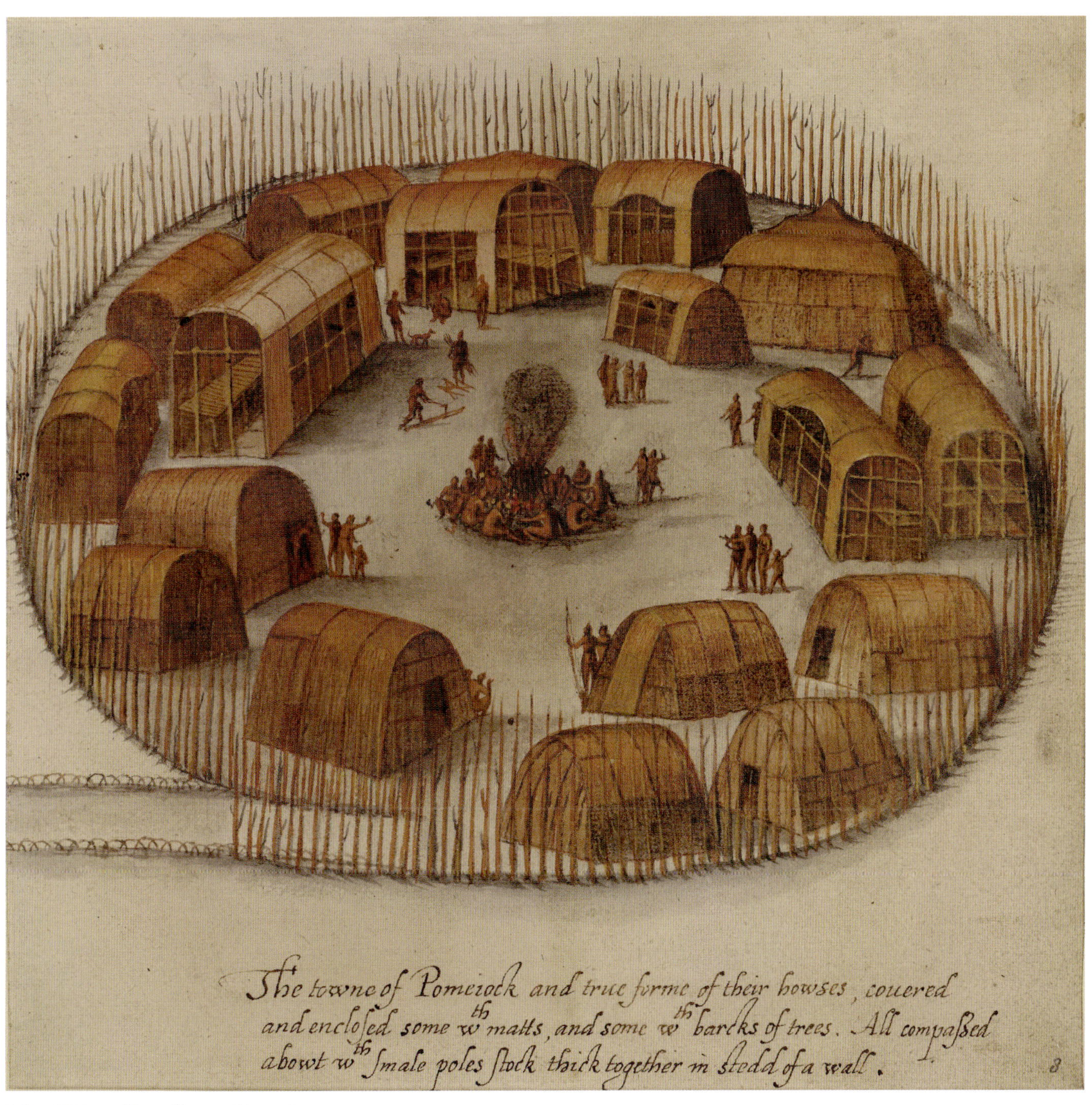

John White – The village of Pomeiooc.

Perhaps they became integrated with the natives. Perhaps White's young granddaughter really had become a Native American.

White returned to England a sad and bemused figure who always believed his family were alive somewhere. He never managed to get back to America. But his drawings and paintings remain as the first and fascinating evidence of life in Northern America before the white man came.

John White studied the Native Americans he met with great care, and his fellow colonist Thomas Harriot made extensive notes on what they were both seeing. Above all they were astonished at the level of social organization. White drew two of the villages they came across, called by the inhabitants Pomeiooc and Secotan. The two men were impressed deeply by the way these communities were run.

They contained a few dozen houses at most around a central open space with no rigid plan. The houses could be dismantled and moved elsewhere if required. The settlements were sited near the coast or inland waterways for fishing and transportation. The soil near water was also richer and thus better for growing corn; but summer rainfall in the area was not reliable enough to guarantee more than one harvest every year, and the people also hunted and gathered wild herbs and plants, carefully recorded for their medicinal, food and commercial properties

White and Harriot together argued in the most forceful and effective way that the American natives were social beings, possessing all the characteristics necessary to civility: community life and the family structure; a hierarchy and an orderliness that made it all possible; care for the morrow by cultivating and preserving foods; and all informed by a religious sensibility that honoured humanity's dependence on supernatural forces in the universe.

White's picture of Indians fishing reinforces that assessment of well directed work. Various techniques are shown here and described by Harriot in the text, including night fishing with a fire to attract the fish to the boat, spears barbed with fish bones or king crab tails, nets (which Harriot does not describe) and weirs or traps, which Harriot describes as of a more complicated form than the simple square seen here. The varieties of fish depicted include a catfish (far left), a burrfish (in front of the trap), a skate (in the trap), hammerhead shark, sturgeon and king crab.

White also drew individual full-length portraits of both men and women. The Indian priest wears what might be called a cassock, while the chief, with his bow, flaunts his tattoos, apparently about to attend a ceremony.

White wrote a final letter from his house in Ireland to Hakluyt in 1593, explaining sadly his resolve to voyage no more:

Thus may you plainely perceiue the successe of my fift & last voiage to Virginia, which was no lesse unfortunately ended then frowardly begun, and as lucklesse to many, as sinister to my selfe. But I would to God it had bene as prosperous to all, as noysome to the planters; & as ioyfull to me, as discomfortable to them. Yet seeing it is not my first crossed voyage, I remaine contented. And wanting my wishes, I leaue off from prosecuting that whereunto I would to God my wealth were answerable to my will. Thus committing the relief of my discomfortable company the planters in Virginia, to the merciful help of the Almighty, whom I most humbly beseech to helpe & comfort them, according to his most holy will & their good desire, I take my leaue from my house at Newtowne in Kylmore the 4 of February, 1593.

John White –
The manner of
their fishing.

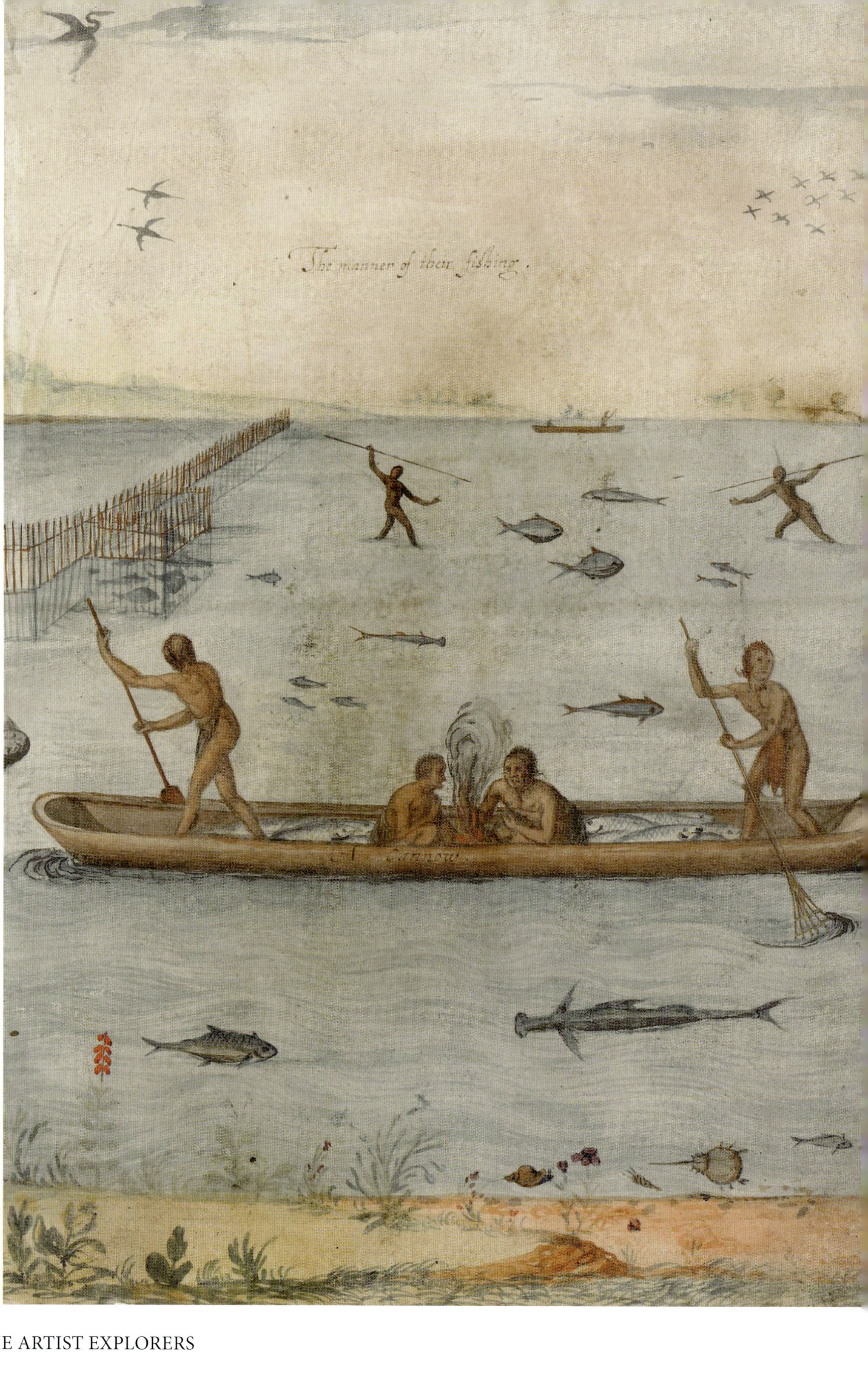

John White – The manner of their attire and painting themselves.

John White –
Indian conjuror.

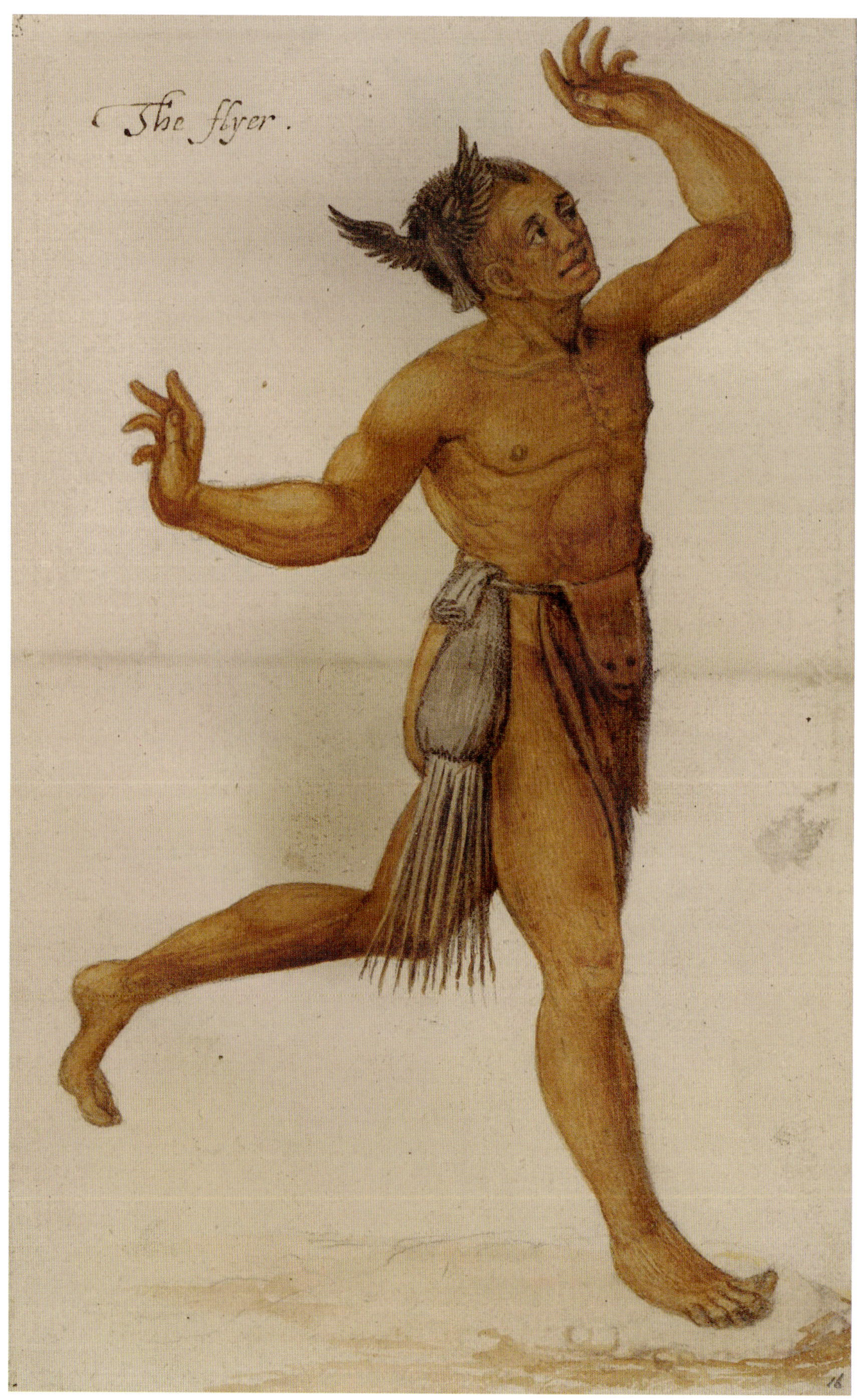

Chapter 2

Captain Cook

In the harbour at Whitby in Yorkshire, from which Captain Cook sailed for the South Seas, there is a full size replica of his ship the *Endeavour*. Gazing at this extraordinary vessel, the imagination is certainly taken back vividly the two and a half centuries to how the then residents of the town must have felt as they saw her set sail.

Virtually nothing was known of the southern seas at that time. There was known to be land, Van Diemen had found some. But there was speculation that there had to be a whole southern continent. If so, what humans lived there? Were there animals of which the northern world knew nothing? How long could it possibly be before Cook and the *Endeavour* might return to Whitby with answers?

Cook had been commissioned by the Admiralty and knew he had to bring back evidence. That meant words, of course, but particularly pictures. And so he insisted that the *Endeavour* should sail with artists on board. The Admiralty were quite precise in what they wanted for their money. The artists were instructed to 'make drawings and paintings of such places in the countries you may touch on in the course of the said voyage as may be proper to give a more perfect idea than can be formed from written descriptions only.'

The artist's job was, however, not only demanding but, as it turned out a real risk to health. Both the artists on *Endeavour* died at sea, probably as a result of conditions they were already suffering from. Sydney Parkinson left behind upwards of a thousand drawings and sketches executed as the ship made her way down to the southern seas. Little survives, though, of the work of his colleague Alexander Buchan.

With Cook meticulously charting and recording the channels and coastline of the places he encountered, including the east coast of what became New Zealand and Australia, it was the task of the artists to conjure up what these shores actually looked like, and indeed whether they might ultimately be suitable territory for colonists.

On Cook's second voyage, William Hodges was evidently transfixed by the native peoples they came across, and some of his most entrancing works are renderings of the people and particularly the warriors. In Tahiti Hodges painted the war galleys, elaborate large boats crowded with warriors and crew.

He had an eye for the dramatic. His picture of 'Cape Stephens in Cook's Strait', with two locals watching, shows the ship, apparently unscathed, emerging from the

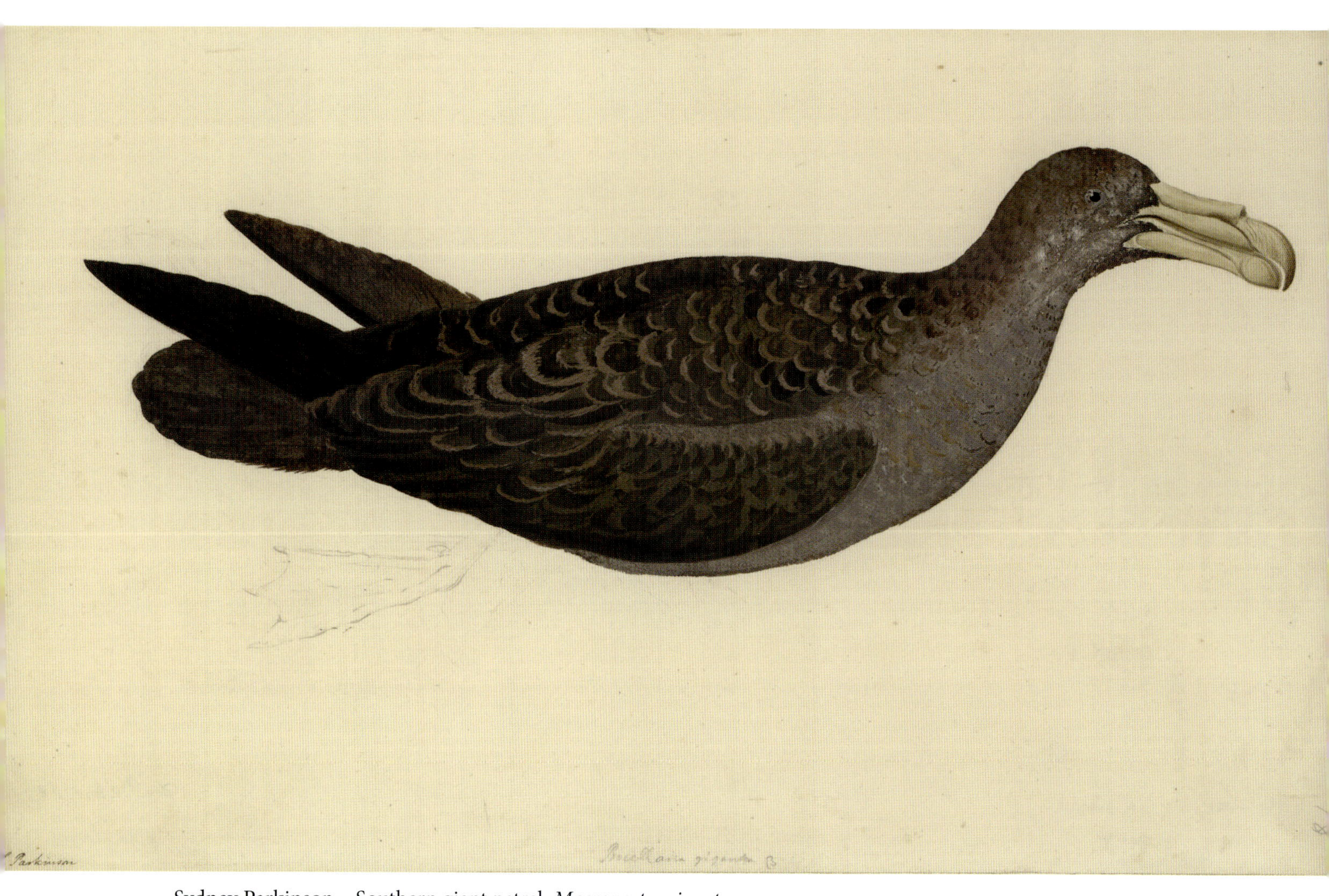

Sydney Parkinson – Southern giant petrel, *Macronectes giganteus.*

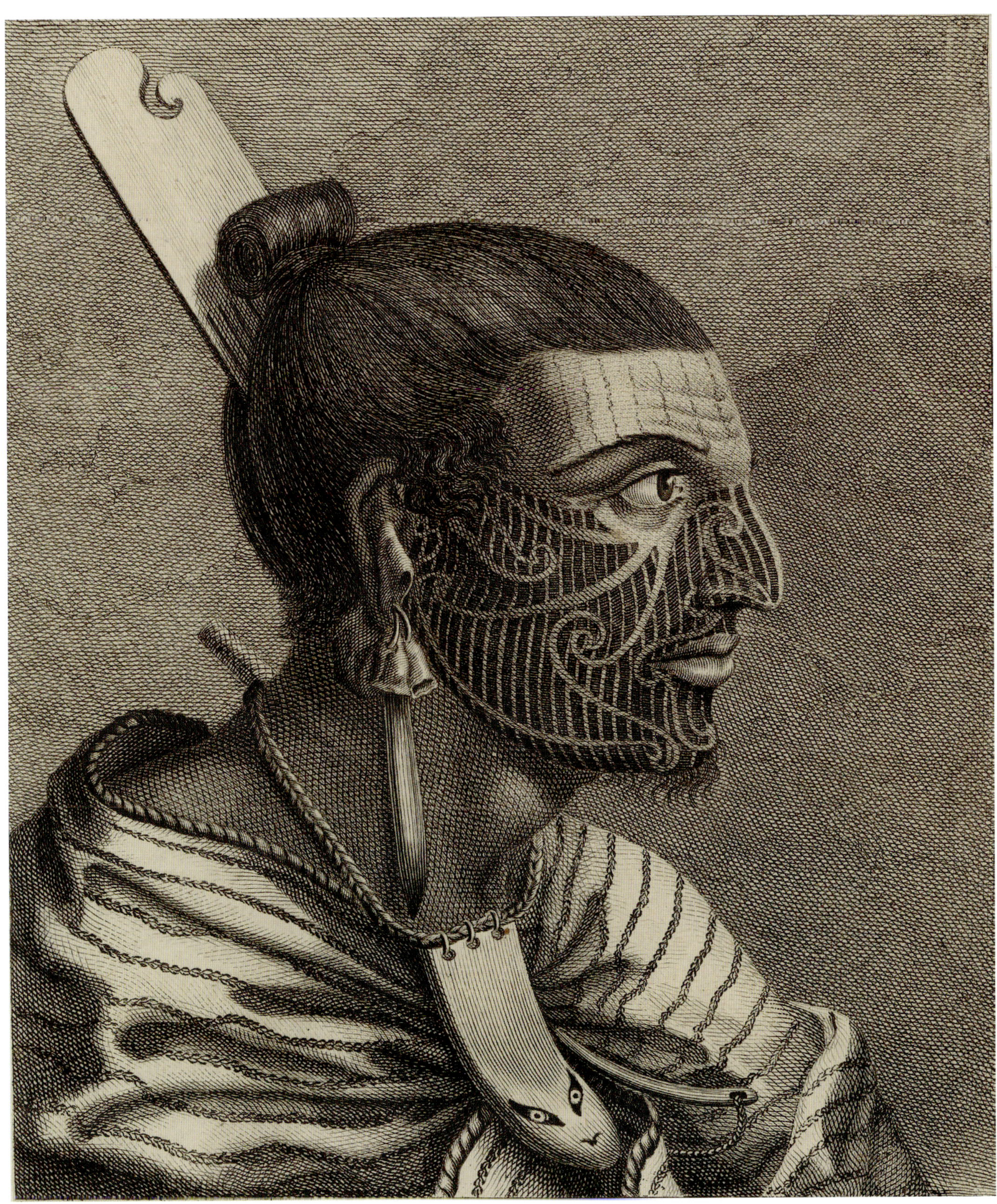

Sydney Parkinson – Head of a New Zealander, with a comb in his hair.

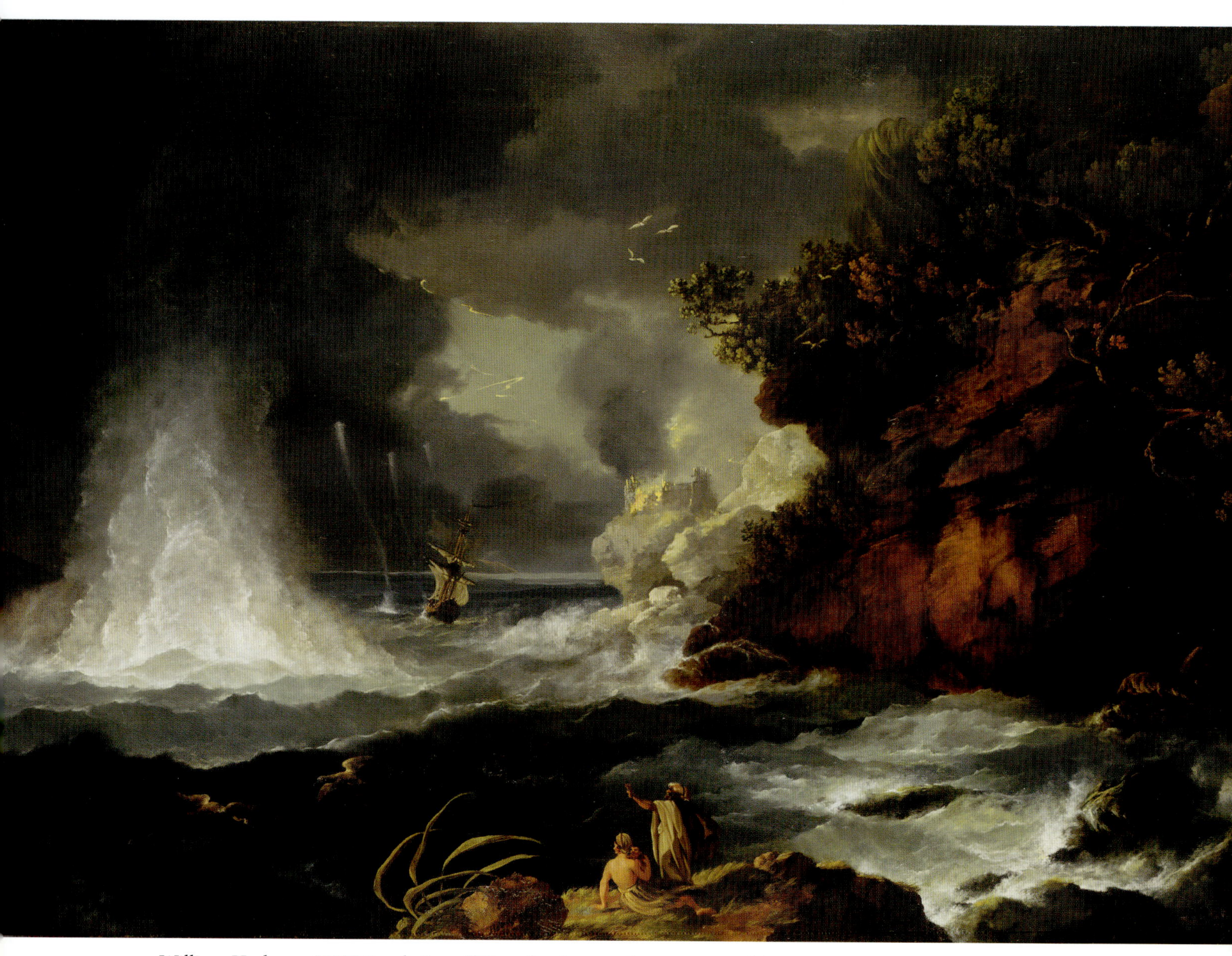

William Hodges – HMS *Resolution* off Cape Stephens with waterspout, May 1773.

William Hodges – A view of the Cape of Good Hope, taken on the spot, from on board the *Resolution*.

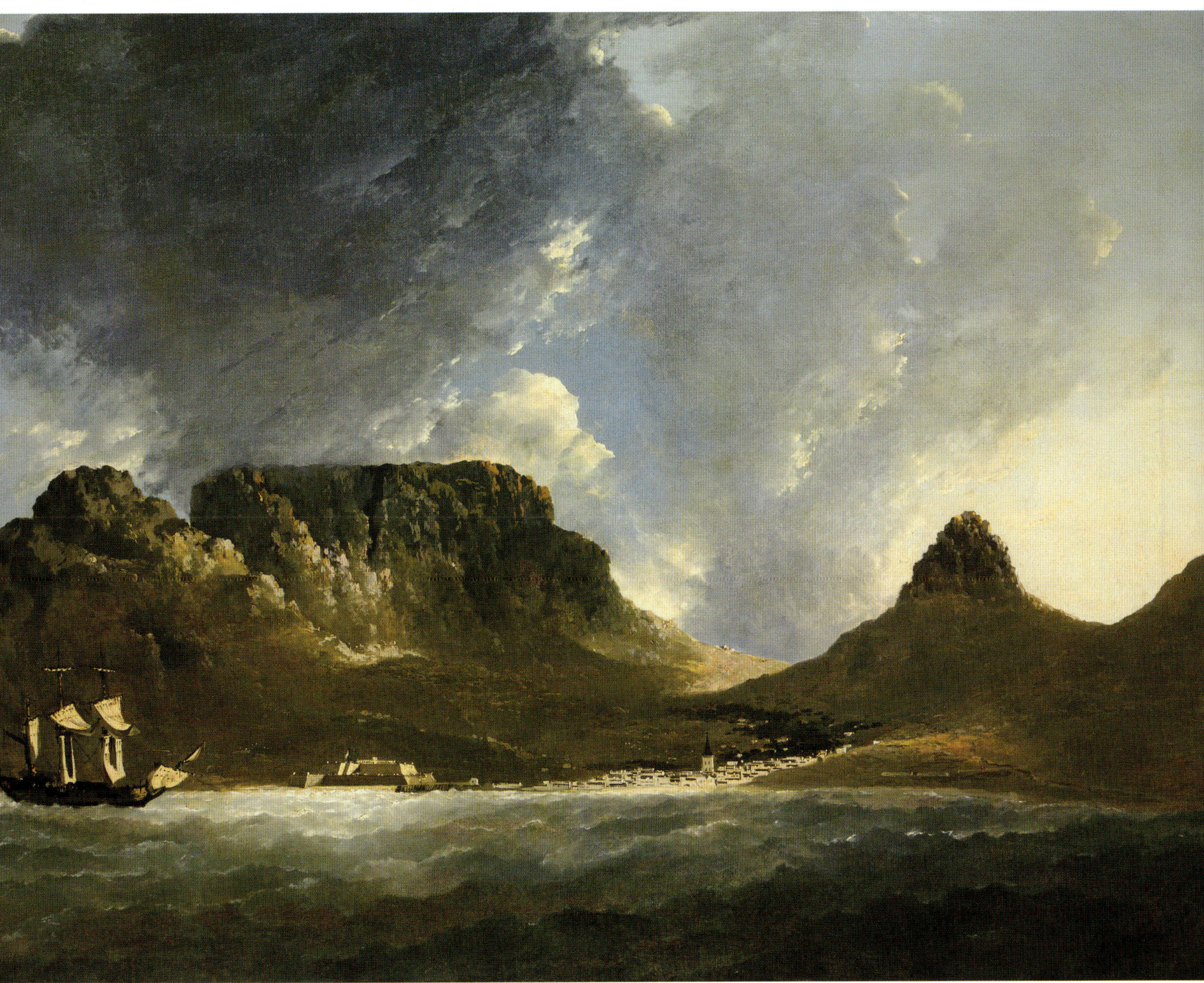

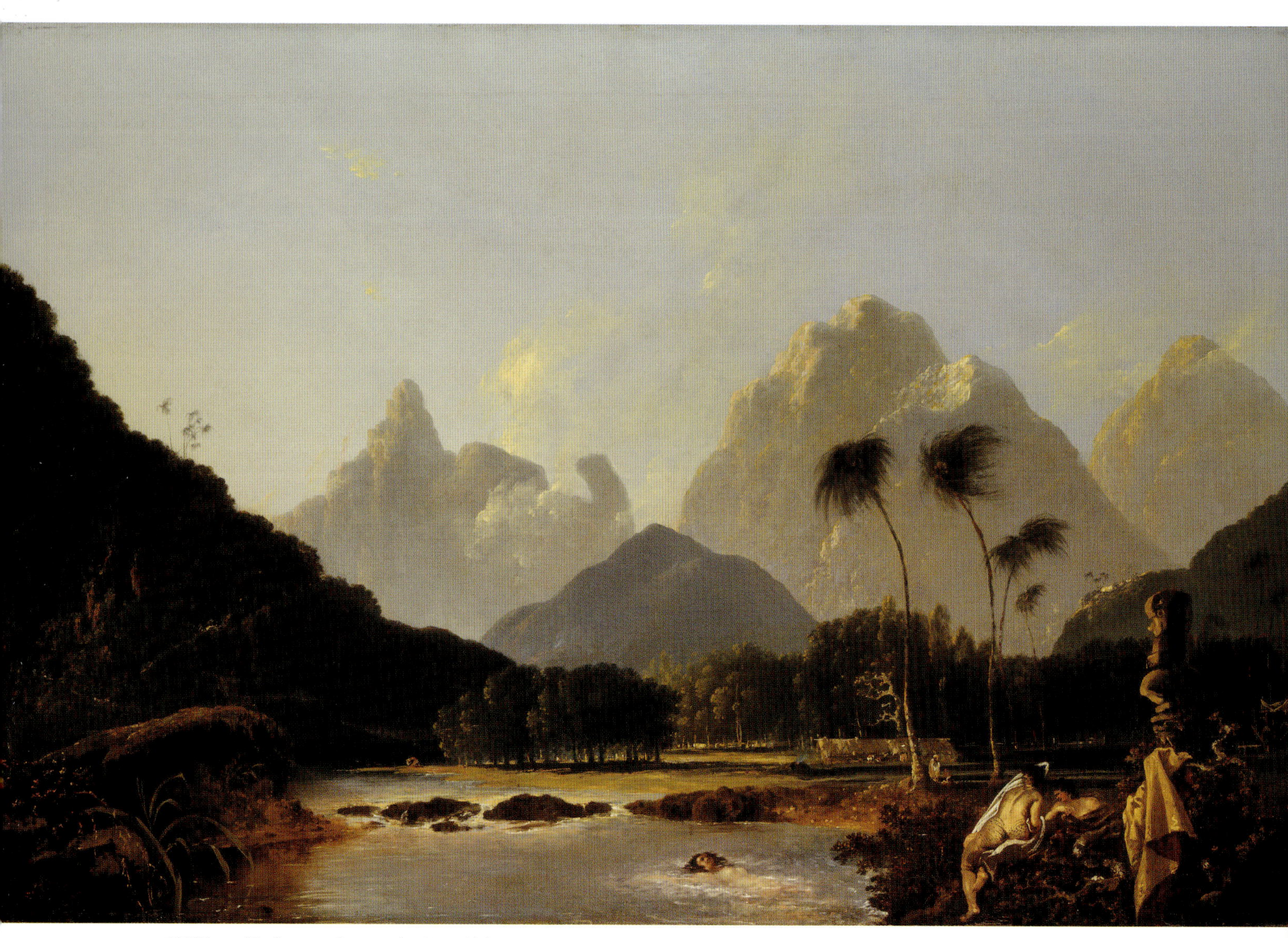

William Hodges – Oaitepeha Bay, Tahiti.

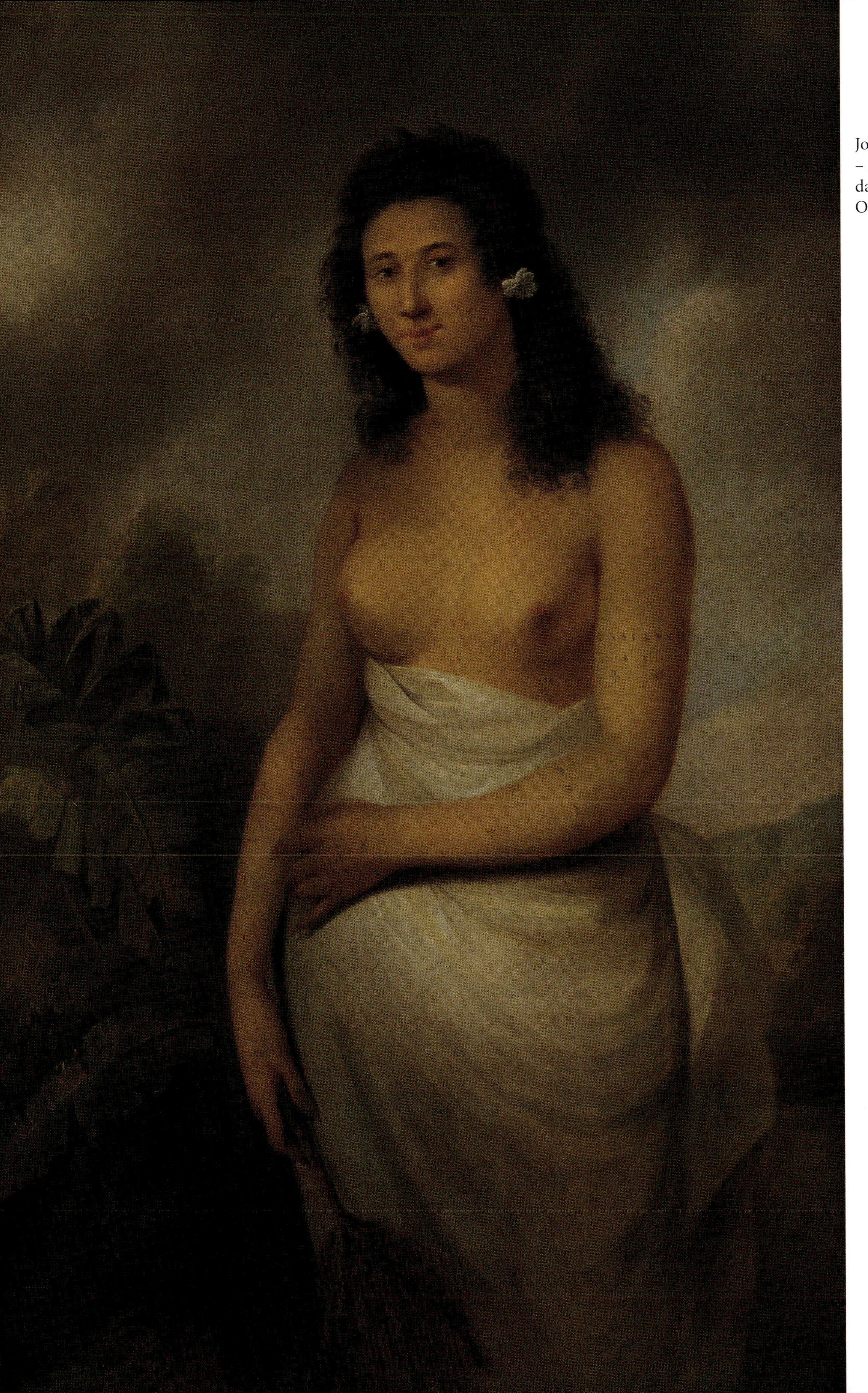

John Webber
– Poedua, the
daughter of
Orio.

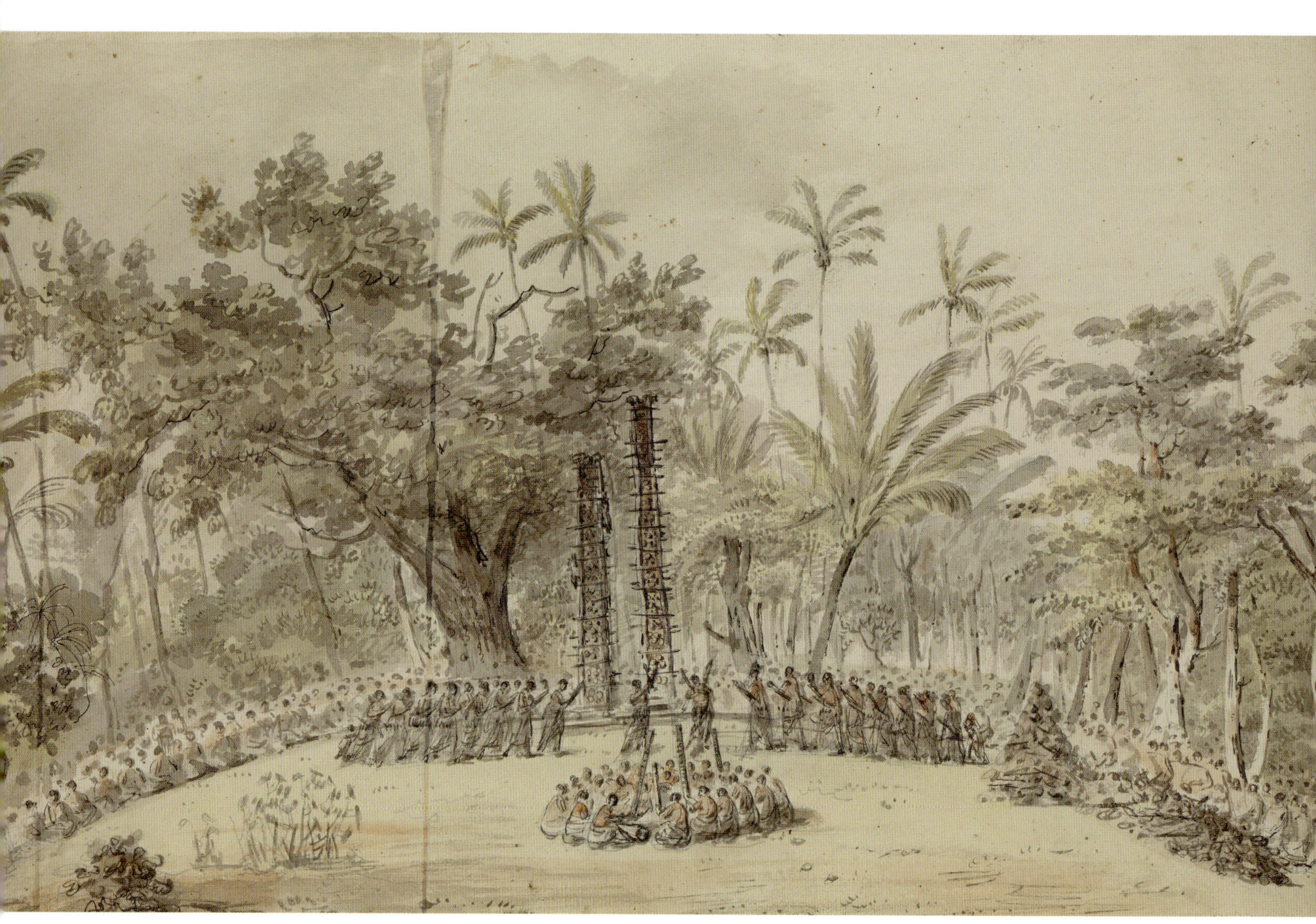

John Webber – A Tongan dance, probably on 21 June 1777.

waterspout and turbulent seas which had at first deterred the English mariners from attempting to make their way through the Strait.

Hodges returned with Cook to England, and his drawings and paintings were exhibited in Mayfair and used in Cook's own published account of that second voyage. But Hodges was apparently not deterred from travelling and soon left for India in the Warren Hastings era. He spent six years there, based mainly in Lucknow, supporting himself with commissions and portraits.

John Webber, the artist on Cook's last voyage, with the ships *Resolution* and *Discovery*, took immense trouble to record the elaborate and strange customs the crew encountered. In Tonga they saw the ceremonial procession in front of the royal burial ground, organized with compelling discipline. On the third voyage, when Cook touched the coast of Siberia, the Captain went ashore and was greeted by what Webber portrayed as formal ceremonial from the natives, complete with rigorous dancing to the beat of a drum.

Fundamentally, this was knowledge-gathering, and it was to be left to later artists to capture the magnificence of the New Zealand and Pacific landscapes. What became known as Pickersgill Harbour looks a woodland idyll, and Hodges' view of the mountains of Tahiti is romantic enough, along with the monuments of Easter Island, still unknowably strange to this day.

When the ship reached Hawaii, the fatal encounter occurred. John Webber was on board but did not accompany the party of marines which went ashore with Cook to try and force the recovery of the stolen ship's cutter. The only American member of Cook's crew, John Ledyard, later wrote a detailed account of what occurred.

Cook had made landfall at the islands and managed to engage in some trading with the locals, though it was often an acrimonious process, and *Resolution* and *Discovery*'s crews were happy enough to set sail again. Within days, however, a severe gale damaged *Resolution*'s mainmast and Cook decided it was best to return for repairs to a beach they already knew.

Ledyard wrote:

Our return to this bay was as disagreeable to us as it was to the inhabitants, for we were reciprocally tired of each other. They had been oppressed and were weary of our prostituted alliance … It was also equally evident from the looks of the natives as well as every other appearance that our friendship was now at an end, and that we had nothing to do but to hasten our departure to some different island where our vices were not known, and where our intrinsic virtues might gain us another short space of being wondered at.

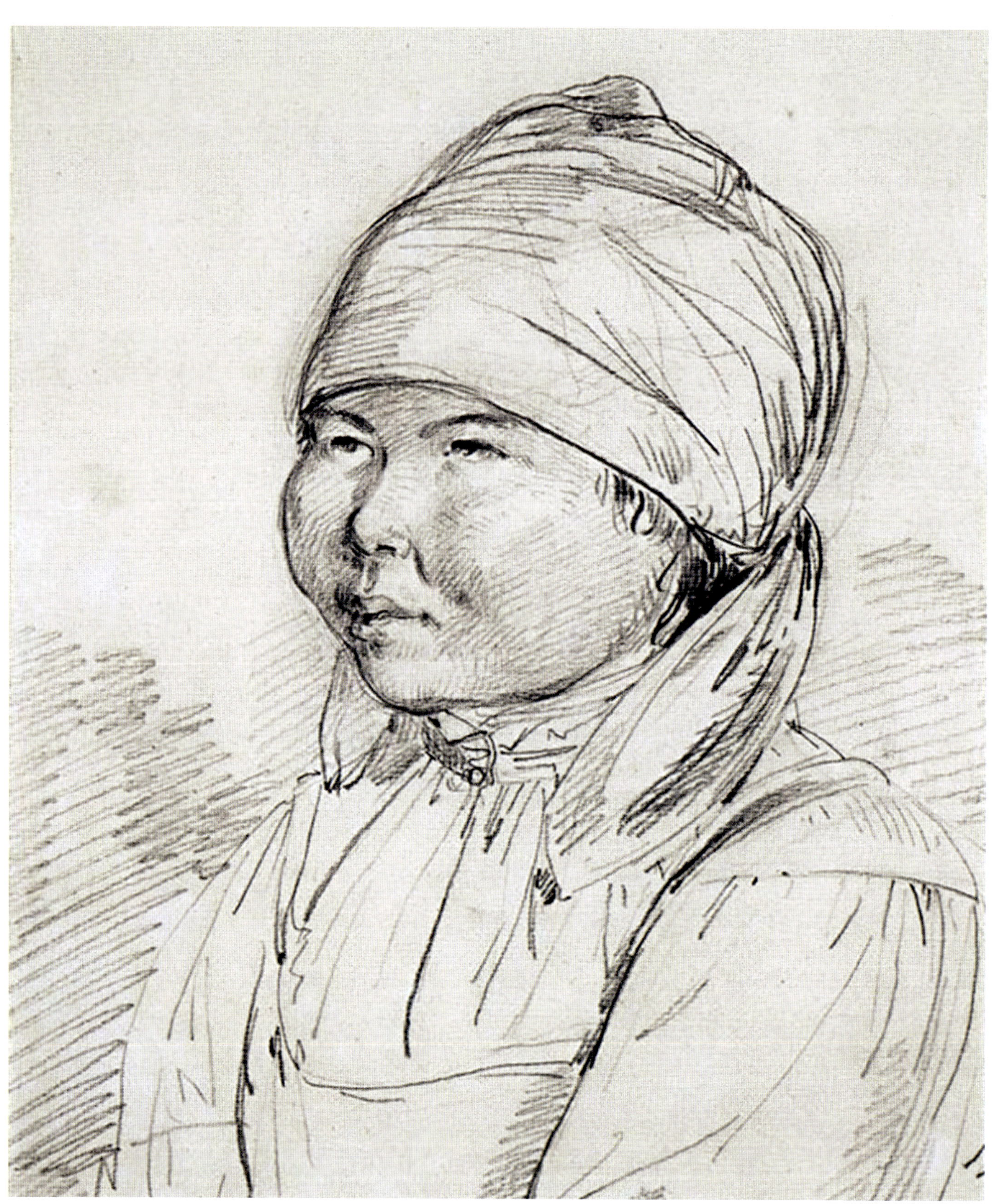

John Webber – Woman of Kamchatka.

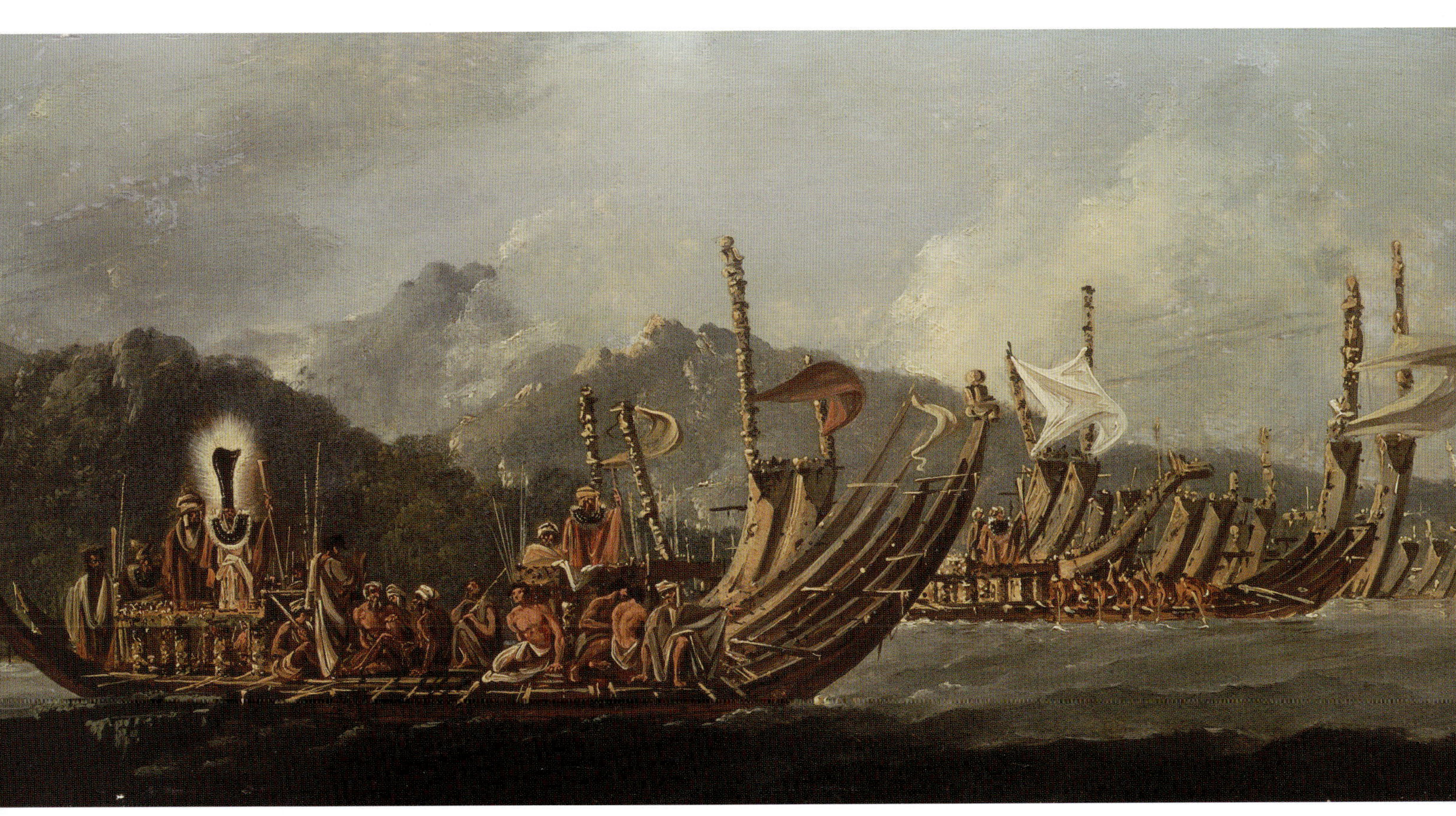

William Hodges – Review of the war galleys at Tahiti.

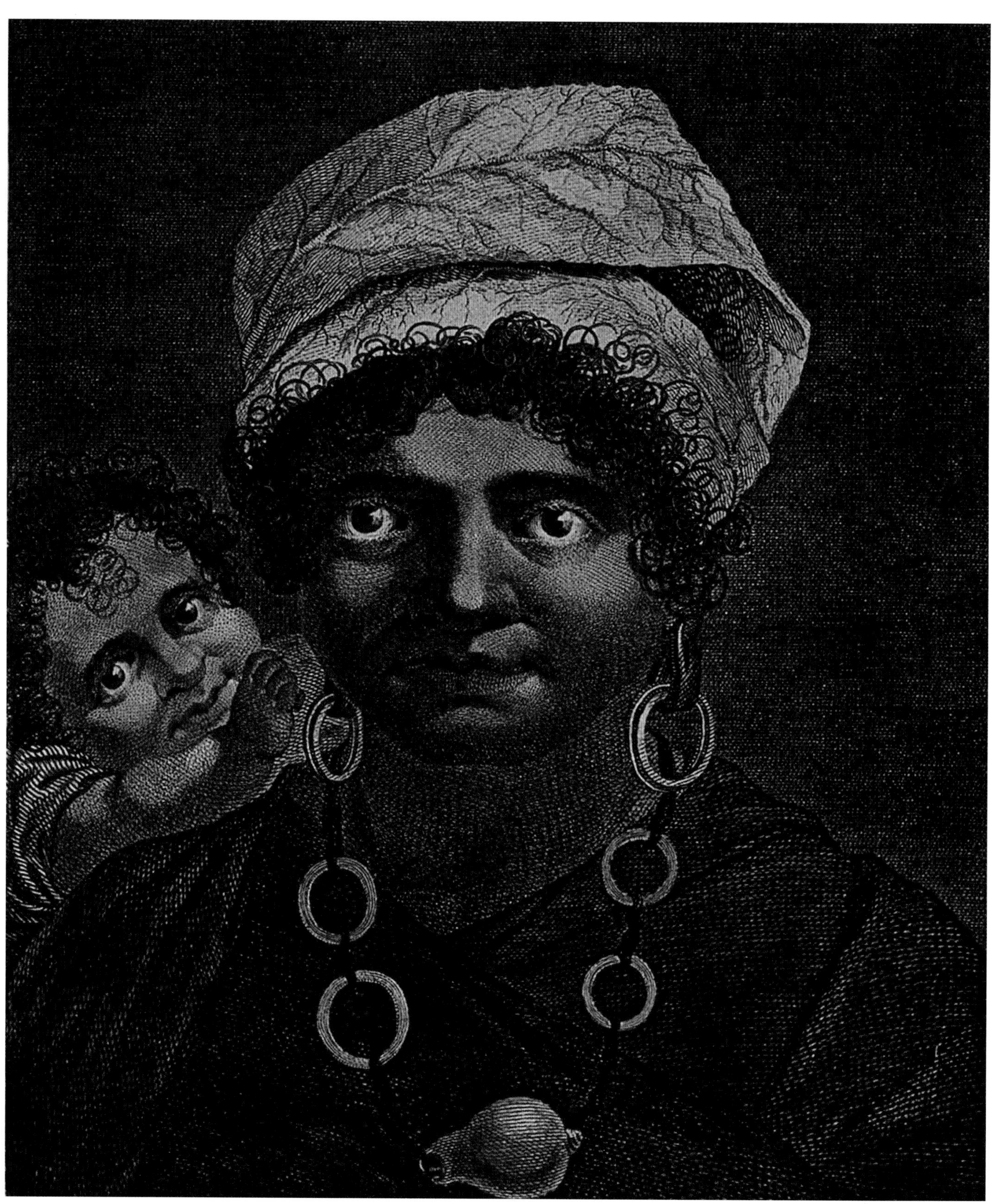

William Hodges – Woman of the Island of Tanna.

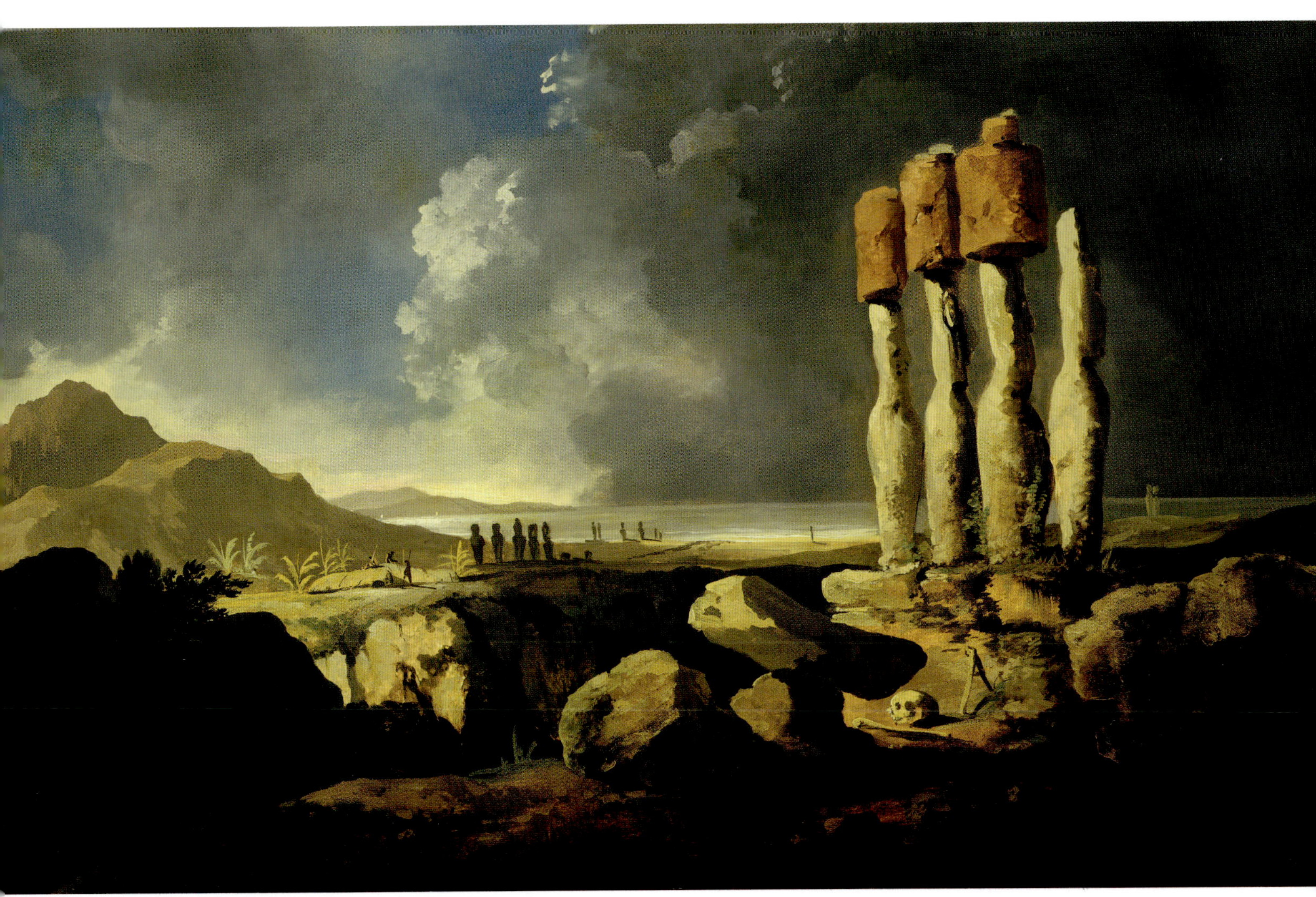

William Hodges – Monuments on Easter Island.

While the *Resolution* was anchored in Kealakekua Bay, one of her two longboats was stolen from the ship by the Hawaiians, perhaps testing the foreigners' reaction to see how far they could push this sort of activity. To try to obtain the return of the 'stolen' longboat from the Hawaiians, Cook attempted to kidnap the Ali'I nui (supreme ruler) of the island, Kalani'ōpu'u.

On the morning of 14 February 1779, Cook and his men left *Resolution* along with a company of armed marines. They went directly to the ruling chief's enclosure, where Kalani'ōpu'u was still sleeping. They woke him and directed him, urgently but without threats, to come with them. As Cook and his men marched the ruler out of the royal enclosure, Cook himself held the hands of the elderly chief as they walked away from the town toward the beach. Kalani'ōpu'u's favourite wife, Kānekapōlei, saw they were leaving and yelled after her husband, but he ignored her and did not stop. She called to the other chiefs and the townspeople to alert them to the departure of her husband. Two chiefs, Kana'ina (Kalaimanokaho'waha), the young son of the former ruler, Keawe'opala, and Nuaa, the king's personal attendant, followed the group to the beach with the king's wife behind them pleading along the way for the Ali'I nui to stop and come back.

By the time they got to the beach, Kalani'ōpu'u's two youngest sons, who had been following their father believing they were being invited to visit the ship again with him, began to climb into a boat waiting at the shore. Kānekapōlei shouted to them to get out of the boat and pleaded with her husband to stop. The ruler then realized that Cook and his men were not asking him to visit the ship, but were attempting to abduct him. At this point he stopped and sat down.

Cook's men were confronted on the beach by an elderly kahuna (shaman) who approached them holding a coconut and chanting. They yelled at the priest to go away, but he kept approaching them while continuing to chant. When Cook and his men looked away from the old kahuna they saw that the beach was now filled with thousands of Hawaiians. Cook told Kalani'ōpu'u to get up, but the ruler refused. As the townspeople began to gather around them, Cook and his men began to back away from the hostile crowd and raise their guns.

Kana'ina angrily approached Cook, who reacted by striking the chief with the flat of his sword. Kana'ina jumped at Cook, grabbed him and then pushed him to the sand. As Cook attempted to get up, Nuna lunged at him and stabbed him fatally in the chest with a metal dagger, obtained by trade from Cook's ship during the same visit. Cook fell face-down in the water, and a violent, close-quarters melee erupted between the Hawaiians and Cook's men.

Opposite: William Hodges – The Resolution in a stream of pack-ice.

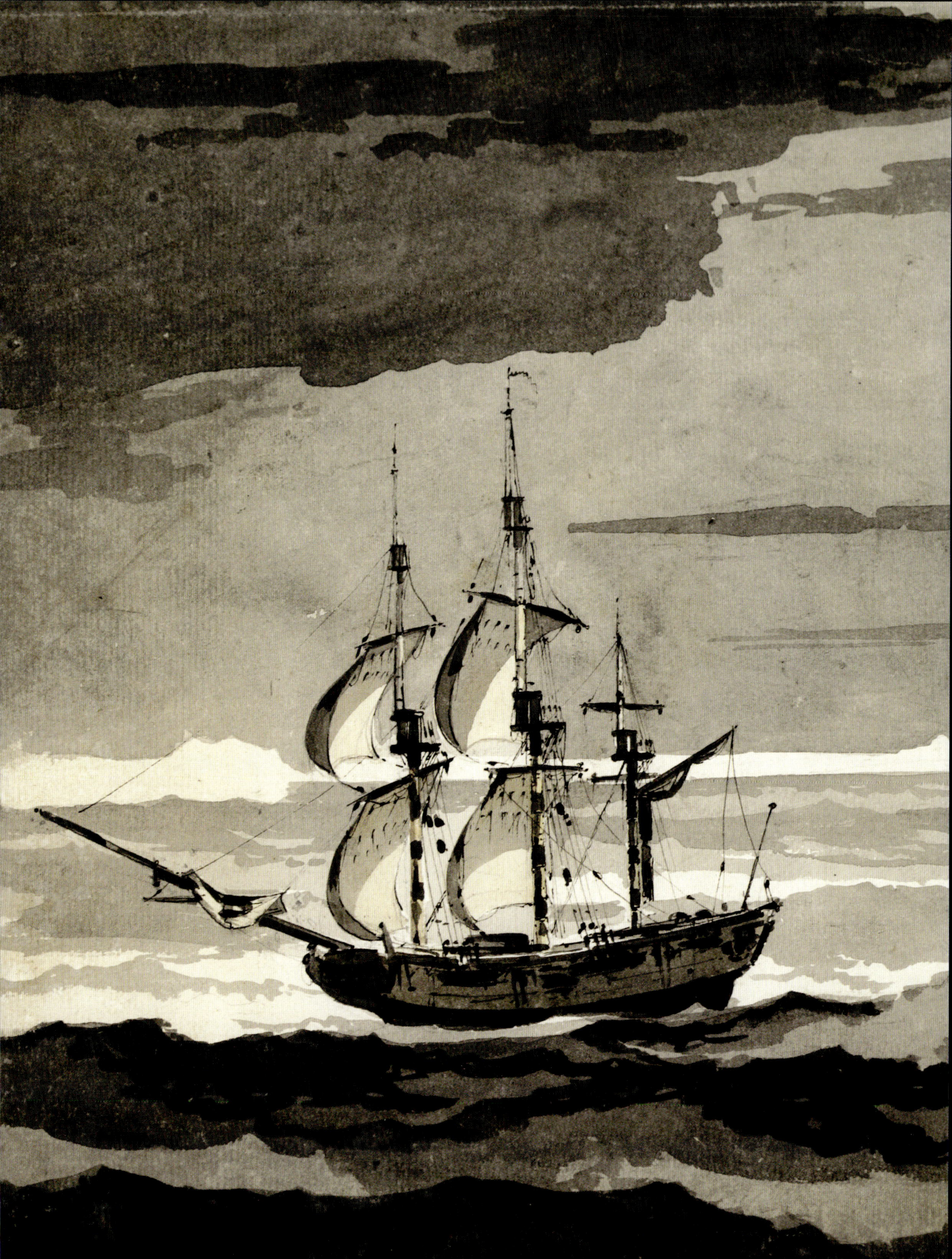

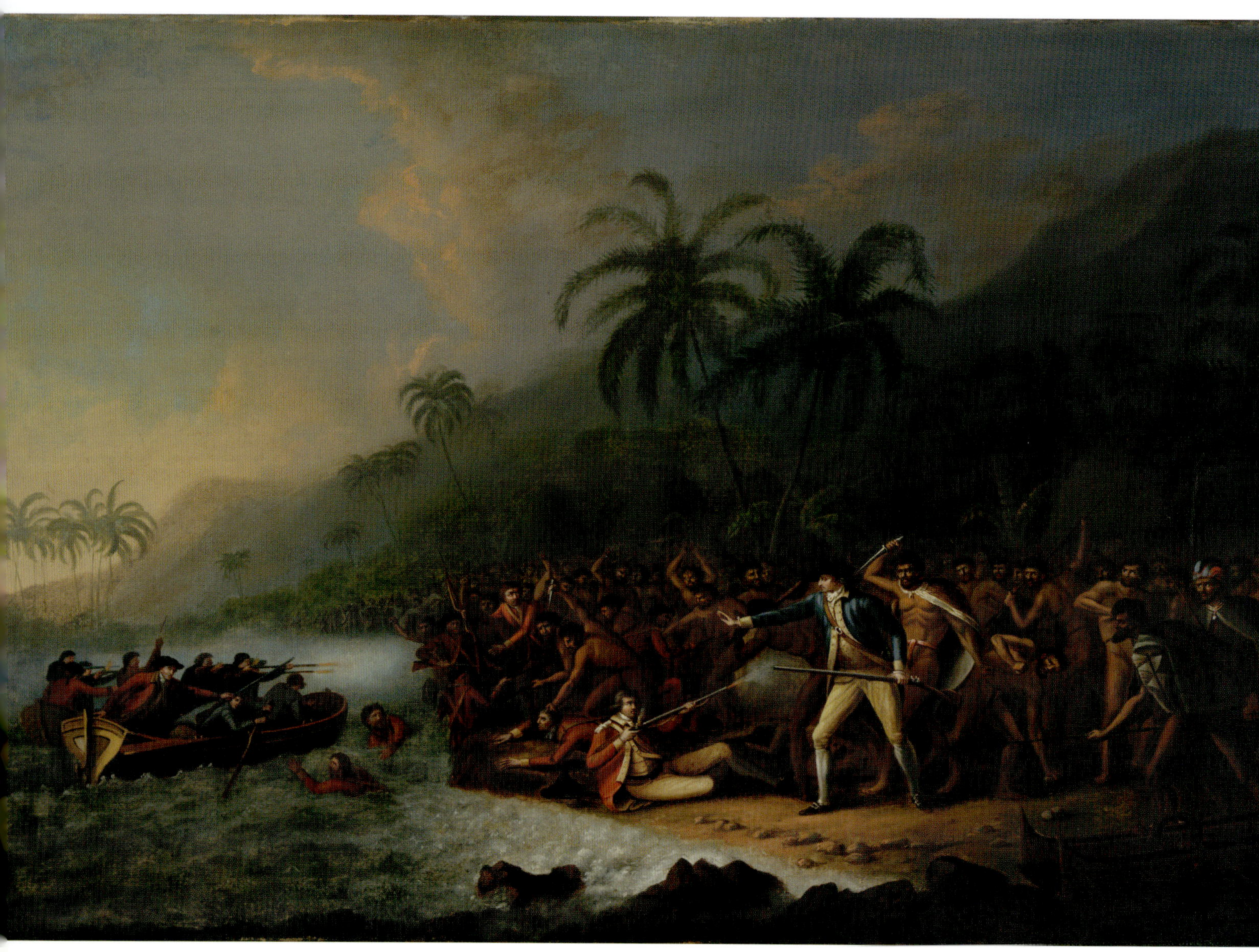

John Webber – Death of Cook.

Zoffany – Death of Captain Cook.

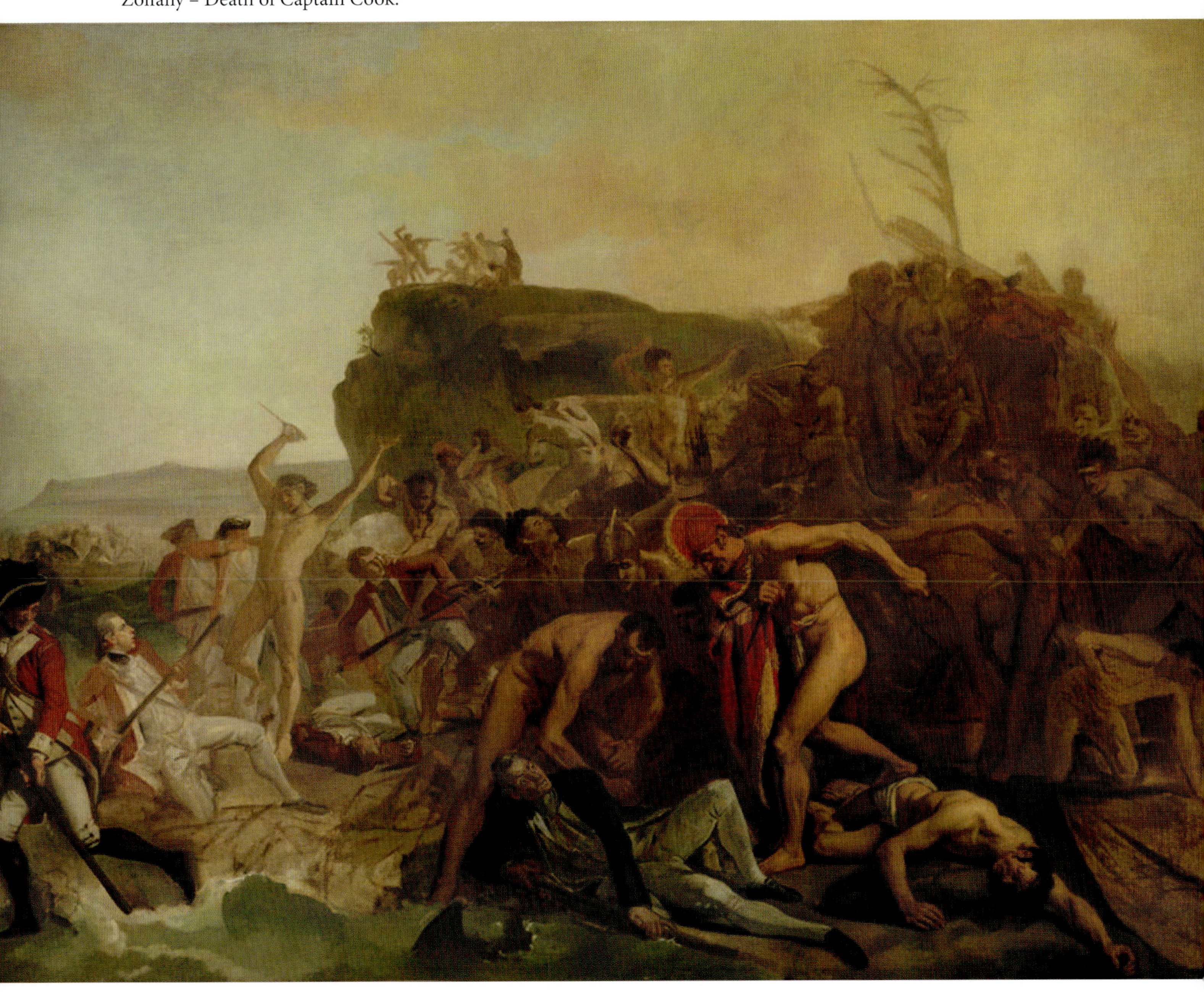

Four of the Royal Marines were killed. The remaining sailors and marines, heavily outnumbered, continued to fire as they retreated to their small boat and rowed back to their ship, killing several of the furious people on the beach, including possibly High Chief Kana'ina.

Cook's death, when he was already internationally famous, confirmed his place as one of the great figures of English history. There were paintings and drawings by many artists, of which the most celebrated was a heroic version by Zoffany.

*   *   *

Robert Dodd's picture of the *Bounty* has proved the most enduring image of the famous mutiny, which resulted in her Captain, William Bligh, being cast adrift with eighteen of her crew. Bligh had sailed with Cook on the *Resolution*.

Dodd had not been on the *Bounty*; indeed, she carried no official artist. But he was able to put the work together within three years of the mutiny, based on the descriptions and testimony of Bligh and some of the mutineers that Bligh had, incredibly, managed to bring back to England.

The mutiny erupted in 1790 when the *Bounty* had left Tahiti, after a four-month stay collecting, as instructed by the Admiralty, breadfruit plants to carry back to the West Indies as a much needed source of food for the plantation slaves. During that time a number of the crew, including, notably, one of Bligh's officers, Fletcher Christian, had spent a lot of time on shore and had fallen for the allure of the Tahitian women. The sailors were only with great reluctance persuaded back on board *Bounty* when Bligh decided it was time to leave.

Bligh's stern and unbending character seems to have added fire to this resentment, particularly in Fletcher Christian. On 28 April 1789, in the middle of the night, Christian, having purloined the key to the arms cupboard and recruited similarly-minded fellow sailors, seized Bligh in his cabin, then took him up and tied him to the foremast.

The rest of the crew were far from united behind the mutiny, and no one wanted to kill Bligh. Hence the solution depicted by Dodd: Bligh and eighteen loyal men were cast adrift in a ship's boat, it being assumed that the common fate of sailors in such circumstances would overtake them.

In fact, Bligh managed one of the greatest feats of navigation and endurance of any era, covering nearly 4,000 miles of the Pacific until reaching the Dutch settlement at Timor and thence making his way home.

Meanwhile, Christian and the *Bounty* returned to Tahiti, picked up a dozen of the women with whom they had formed attachments and set off to seek a refuge safe from the retribution which the Royal Navy would certainly seek to wreak on them.

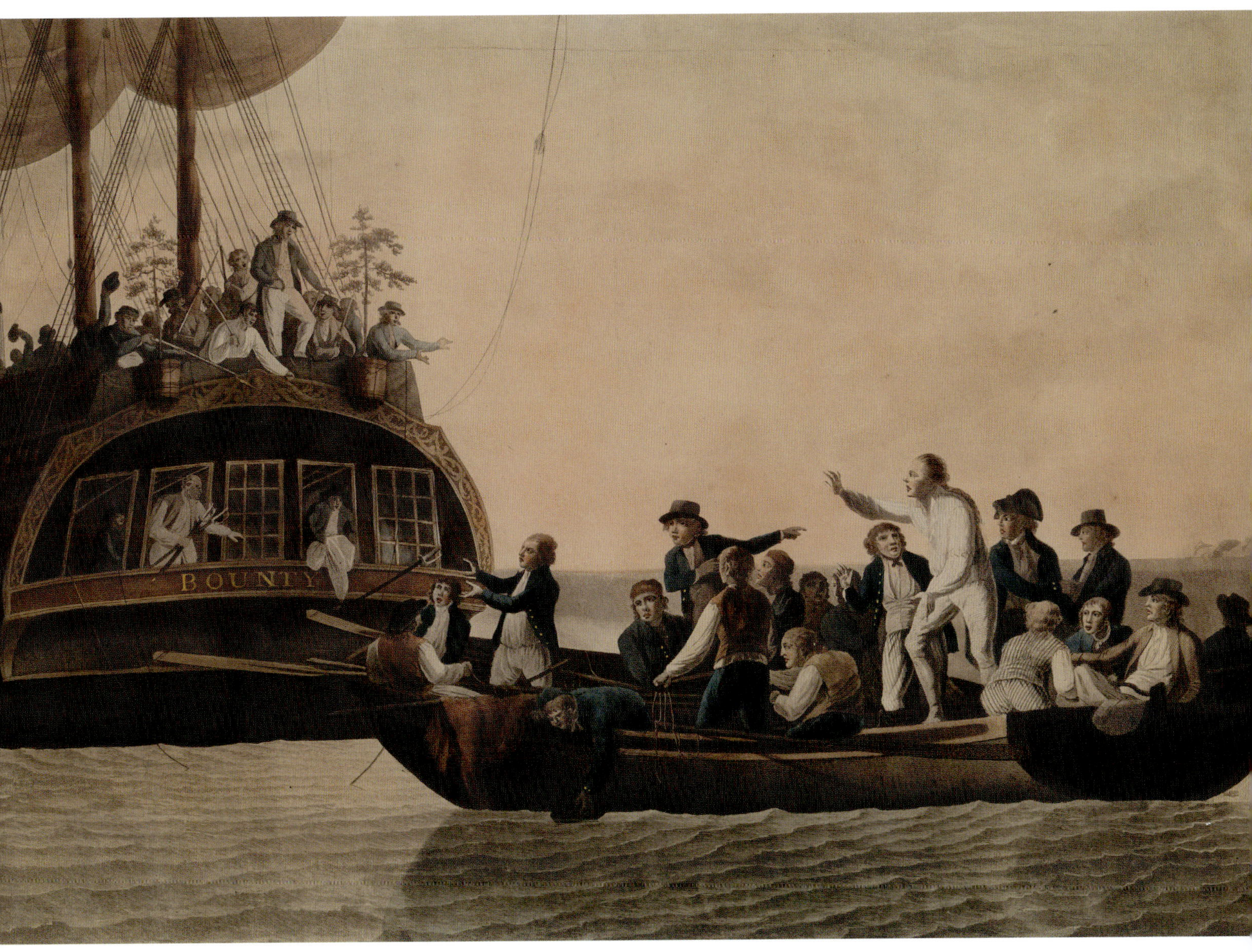

Richard Dodd – The mutineers turning Bligh and his crew from the *Bounty*, 29 April 1789.

By luck or good judgement, they were able to find the Pitcairn Islands, not marked correctly on any charts, and get ashore. Then, in an act designed to ensure there would be no dissent among them, they burned the *Bounty*.

It was to be many years before the British government discovered where they had ended up. But by then, with the Napoleonic Wars in full swing, it was evident that no ship could be spared to bring the mutineers home to justice. Christian started a family with his Tahitian wife, whom he called Isabella, and their descendants live on Pitcairn to this day.

Chapter 3

Baines and Southern Africa

The exquisite picture of the great cataract of Victoria Falls in Southern Africa was painted by the man who almost certainly was the first European to see them. As he made his way through the forest he heard, as he described in his notes, an extraordinary sound, like thunder. Then, as the trees thinned out, he was presented with the sight that is to this day one of the wonders of the natural world. The man was Thomas Baines. He had come down the Zambezi River with Dr Livingstone, but parted company with him and put together his own expedition to try to discover how the great river reached the sea. At the Falls, with their permanent rainbow and wall of water, the Zambezi forces its way over vertiginous cliffs and makes its way onwards. Baines immediately started to make the sketches which were to be the foundation of his superb picture. Finished, it would be sent back to Europe and the illustrated magazines of the day. For this was how the old world of Europe discovered new worlds. Thomas Baines was to give people at home in England an array of intriguing and appealing pictures of the African world – his herds of quagga zebra, soon to become extinct, a Matabele chief in the robes of tribal royalty, and the joy of discovering a much-needed water hole.

Baines, based in Cape Town, covered the Third Kaffir War as an official war artist for the British Army and captured the scene during the landing at Alcoa Bay. The Third Kaffir War in Cape Colony began in December 1850 when native chiefs reacted adversely to attempts by the Governor, Lieutenant General Sir Harry Smith, a Rifle Brigade veteran from the Peninsular War and Waterloo, to curb their powers. After a fresh outbreak of trouble in autumn 1851, Sir Harry called for reinforcements from UK, and on 17 December 1851, 1st Battalion, The Rifle Brigade (1 RB), stationed at Dover, was warned for service in Cape Colony. On 2 January 1852 the whole battalion of 700 officers and men, under the command of Colonel George Buller CB, with eighteen women and twenty-nine children, embarked on HM Steamship *Megaera*, an iron screw troop ship.

After a series of gales and fires on board, the *Megaera* eventually made it to Simon's Bay (Cape Town), via Madeira and Sierra Leone, on 24 March. This was the cause of great relief, as on 26 February 1852 HM Troopship *Birkenhead* had been wrecked off Danger Point and there was much concern for the fate of the *Megaera*.

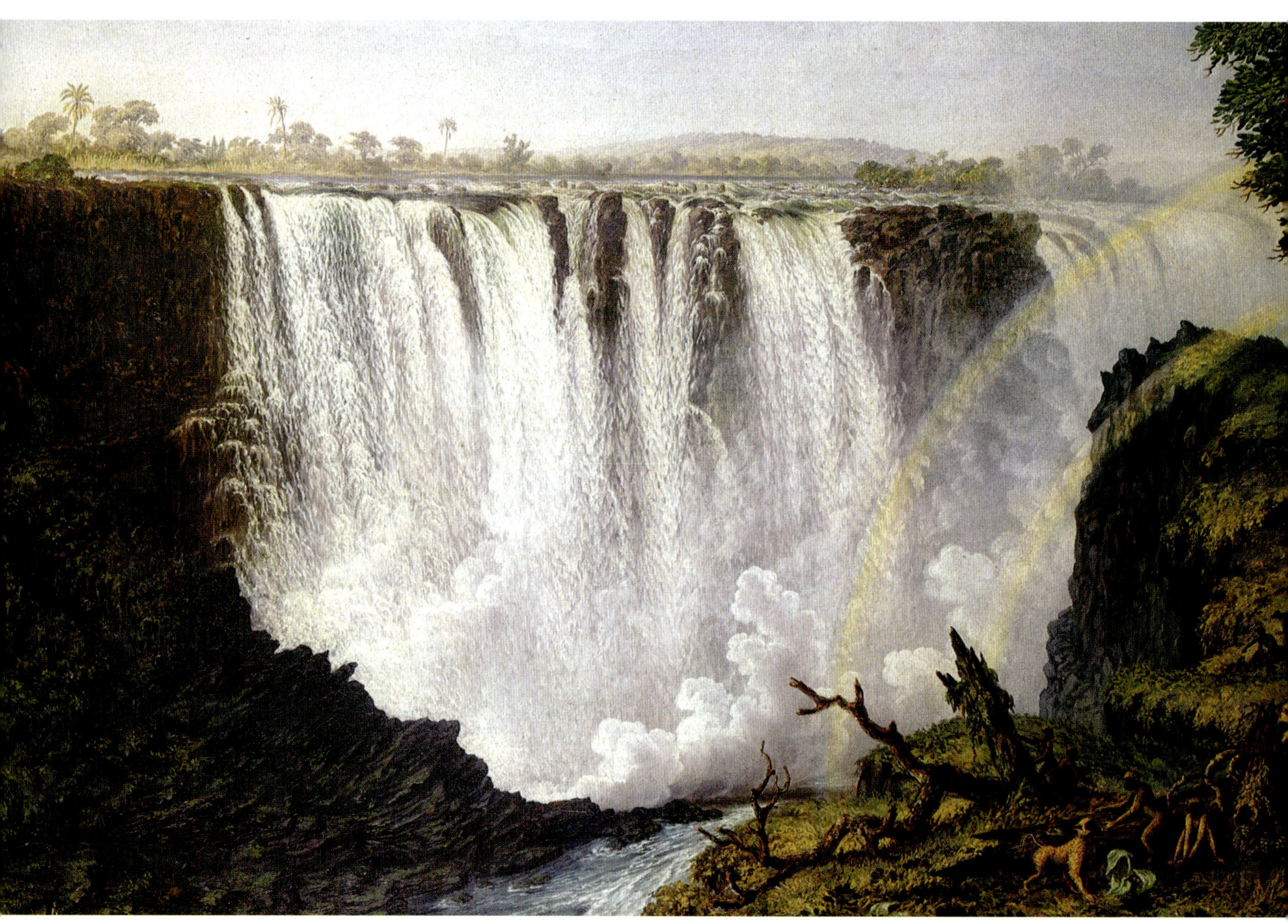

Thomas Baines – Victoria Falls.

Thomas Baines – *Equus quagga quagga.*

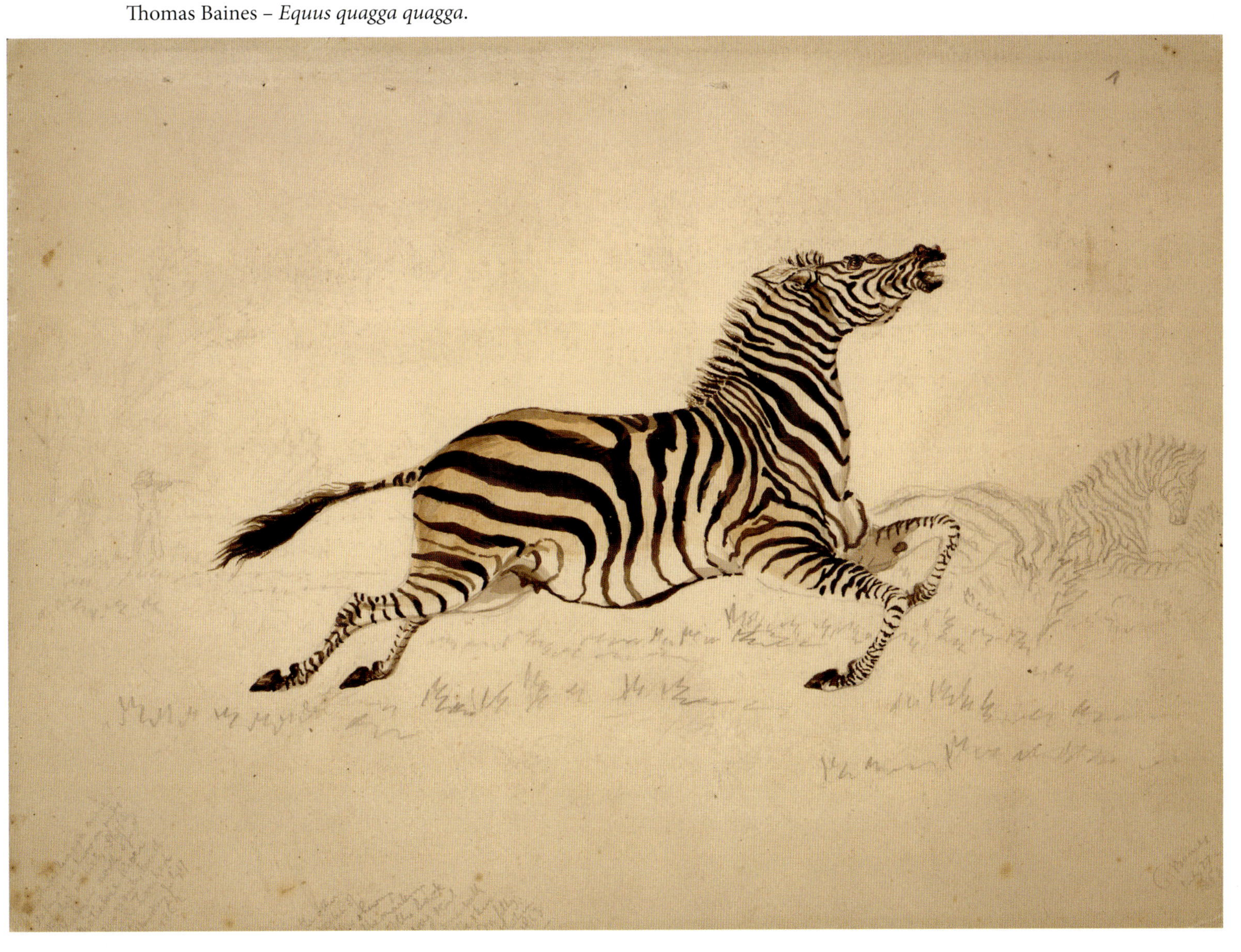

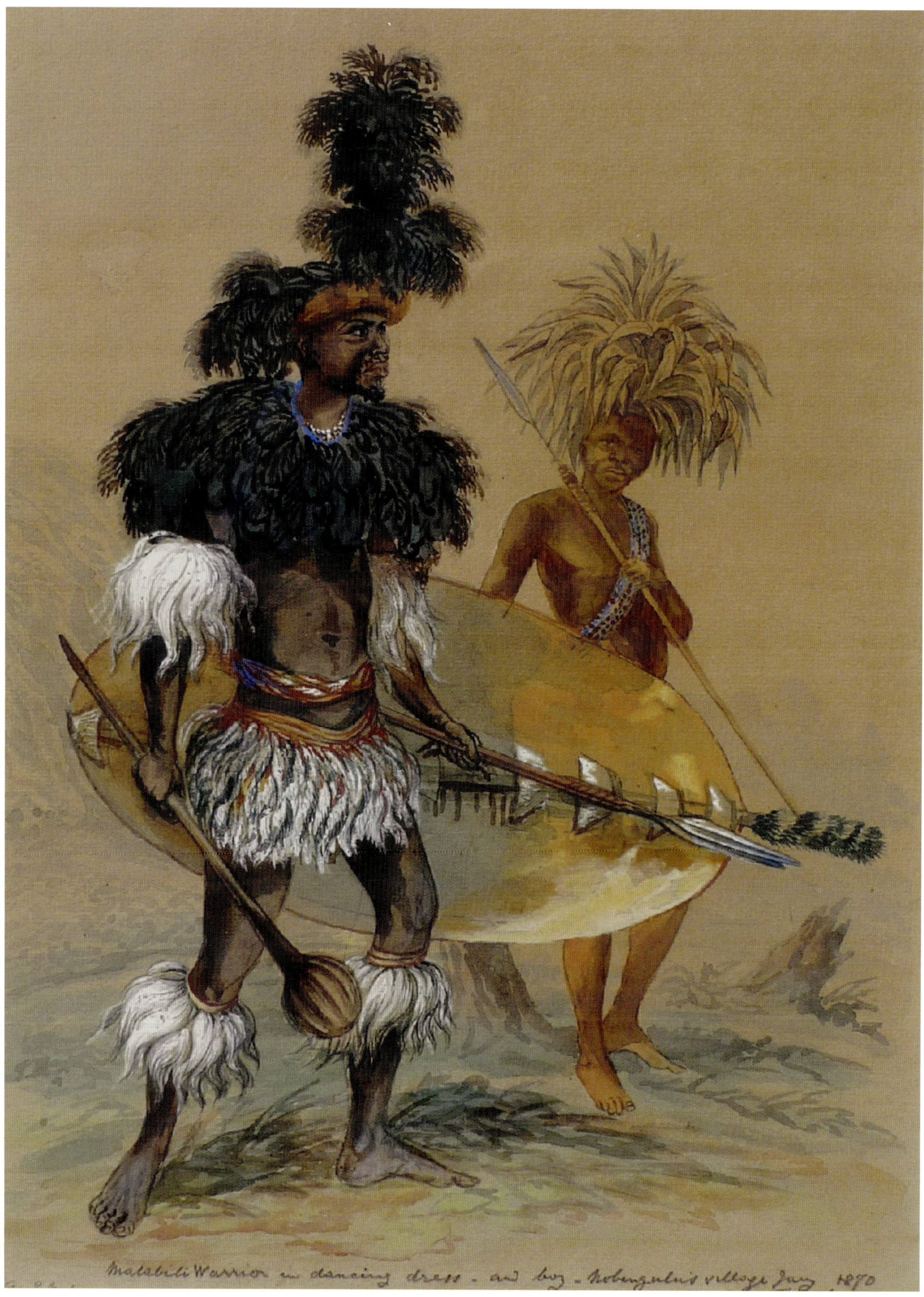

Matabili Warrior in dancing dress - and boy - Mobengula's village July 1870

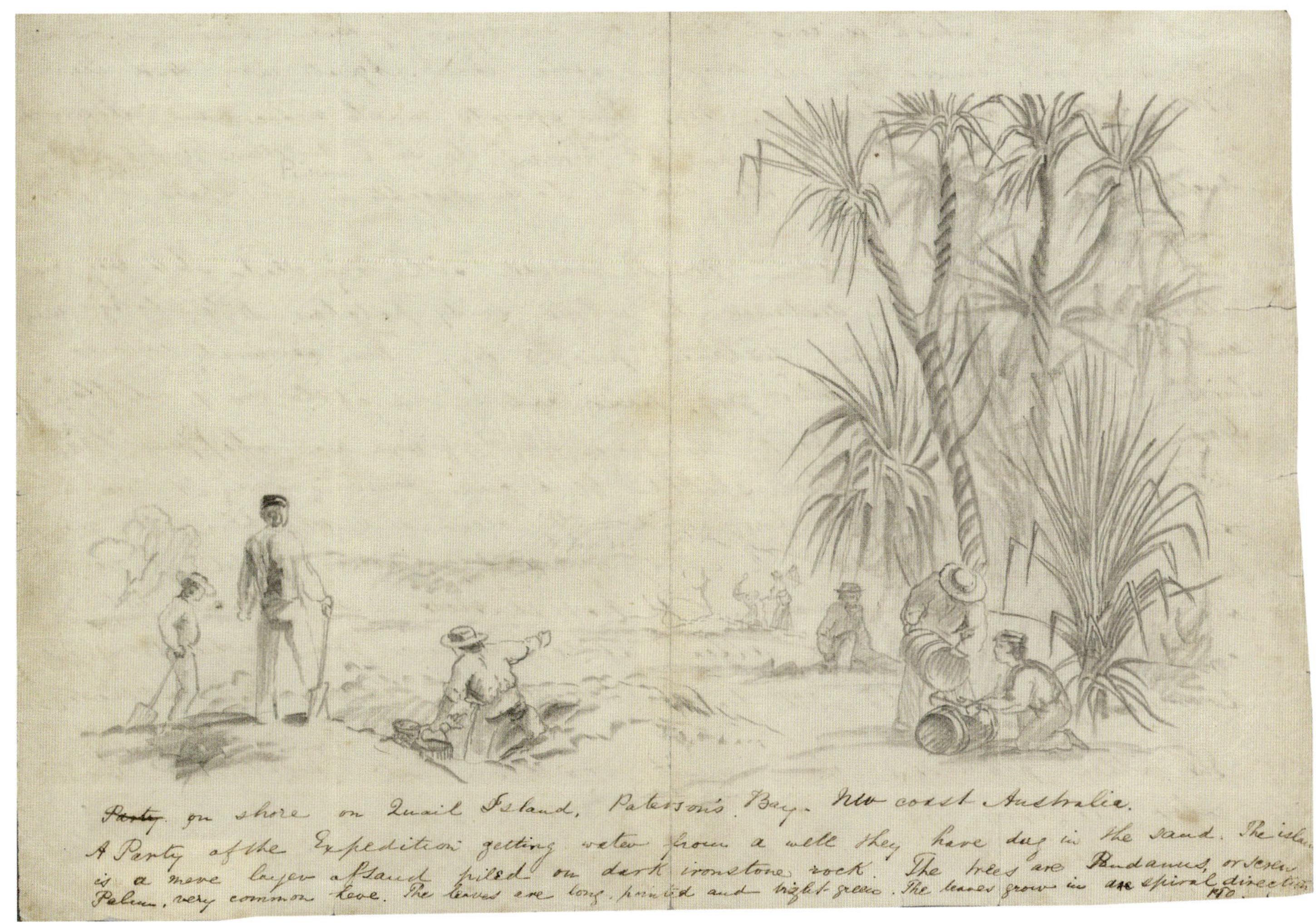

Thomas Baines – Party on shore on Quail Island, Paterson's Bay, NW coast, Australia.

Opposite: Thomas Baines – Matabele Warrior.

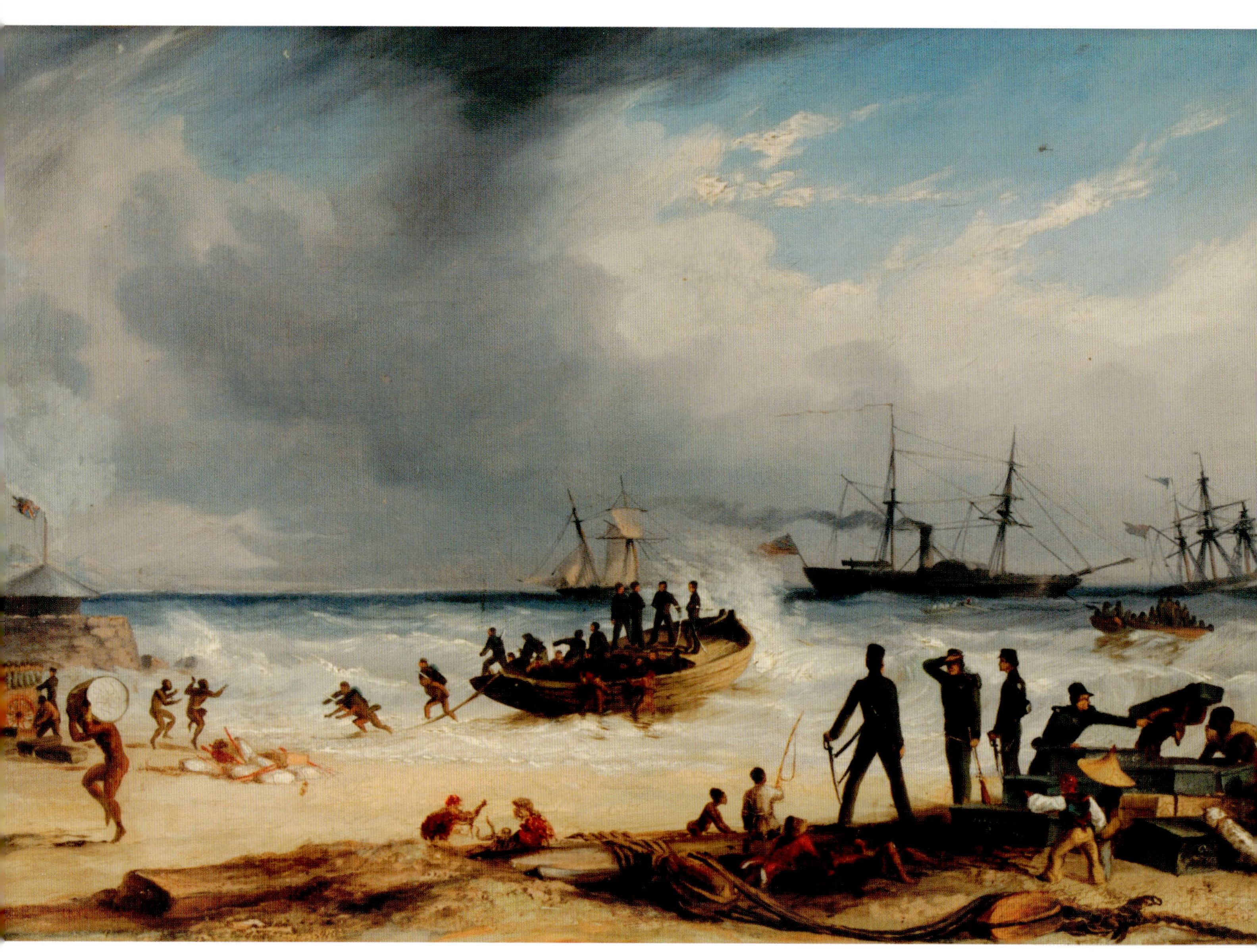

Thomas Baines – Landing in Surf at Algoa Bay, Cape of Good Hope.

Thomas Baines – Fish River Bush 8th Frontier War.

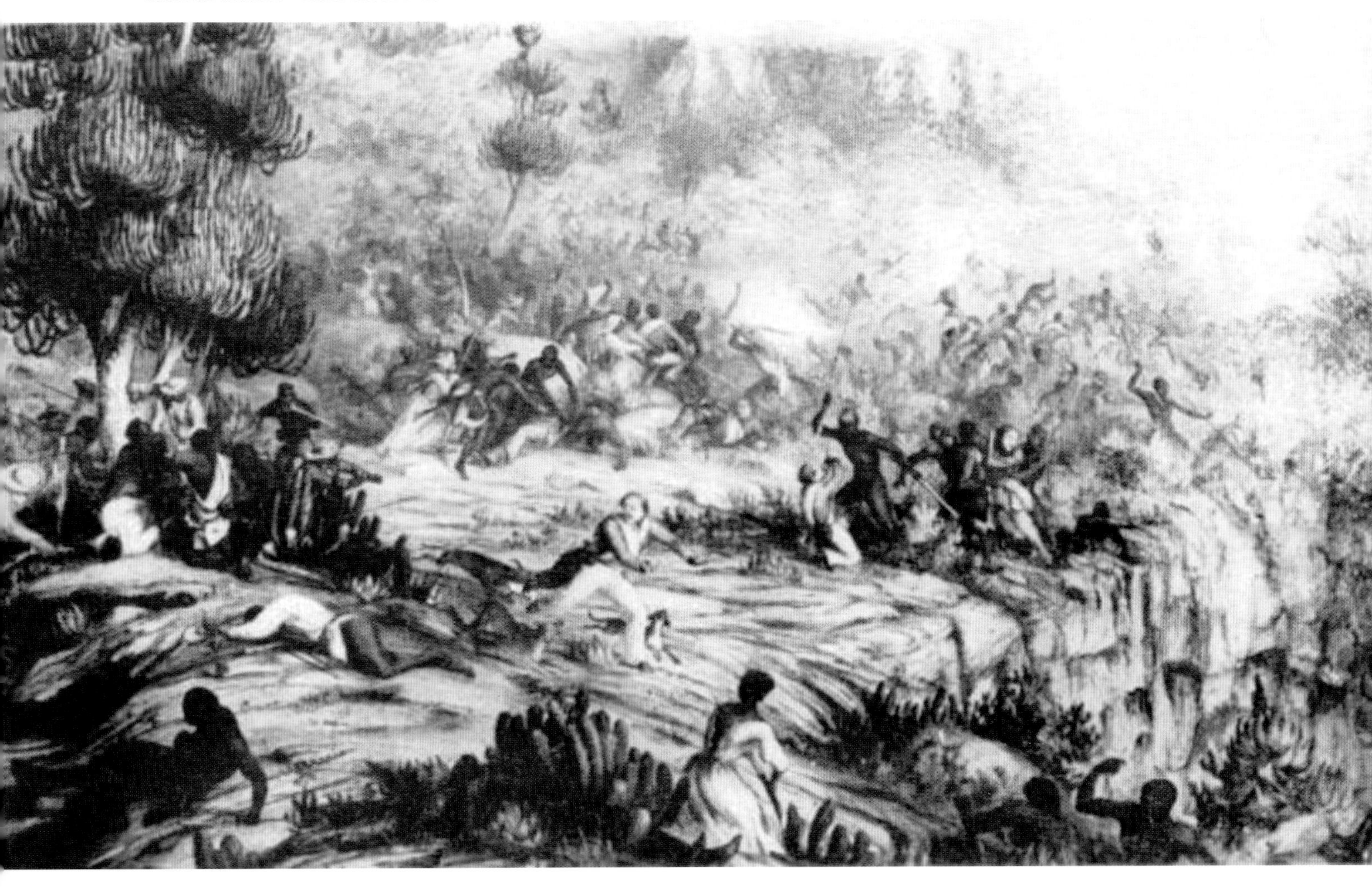

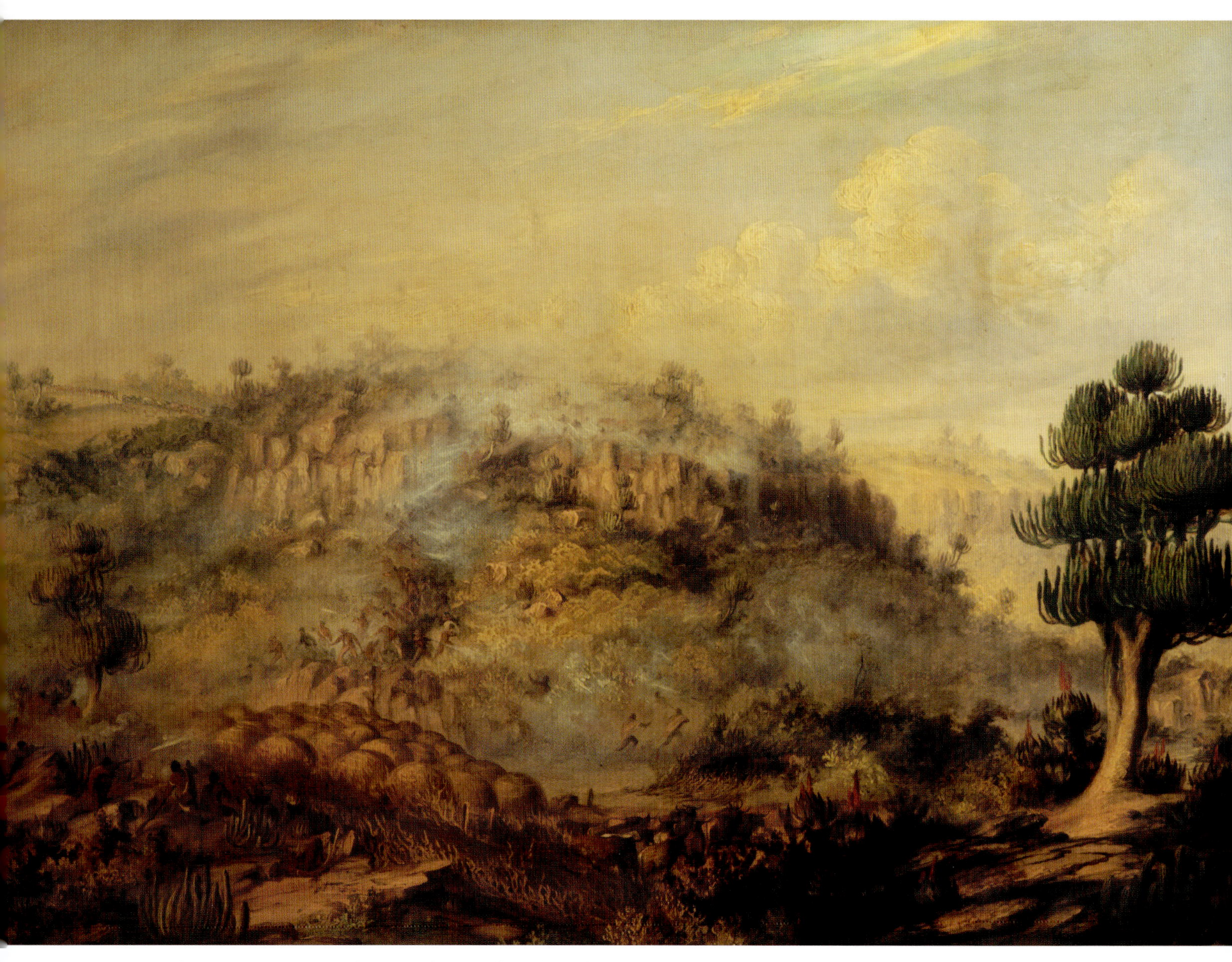

Thomas Baines – Attack on Stocks Kraall in the Fish River Bush.

On 27 March, the *Megaera*, having disembarked the women and children, sailed from Cape Town and on 30 March anchored in Algoa Bay (Port Elizabeth). As the Algoa Bay painting shows, the Rifle Brigade were landed ashore by means of surf boats with the help of the native population, who were referred to at the time as 'Fingoes'.

Baines had been in South Africa for almost a decade when in 1851 he was invited again to accompany British troops as an official artist in what became known as the Eighth Kaffir War (there were eventually nine), designed to stop cattle-raiding and depredations by local tribes against the British and Dutch colonists who were carving out stations in the bush.

Baines' painting shows one of the particularly tough encounters on the edge of the Fish River. Regular troops from the British Army were involved, including the Queen's Regiment. But they had little or no experience of bush fighting with its opportunities for surprise attacks, and the Fish River Battle turned out to be something of a rout, the British retreating having suffered nearly a hundred casualties. Baines gives a vivid picture of what was a brutal day, and he produced a large number of paintings of the war before returning to more peaceful subjects of portraits and landscape in Cape Town.

Baines' account of his trek back to the Zambezi accompanied his vast array of pictures which showed southern Africa to readers at home in Europe. It was in fact his father who introduced Thomas to the reading public, in his preface to Baines' book:

This work was written by my son during a journey from Walvisch Bay, on the west coast of Africa, to the Victoria Falls of the Zambezi River, in company with Mr. J. Chapman, a former friend of the author's, who had spent many years in travelling and was well acquainted with the country and the language of the natives. In 1858 Mr. Baines was appointed artist to the Zambezi expedition under Dr. Livingstone, and accompanied his party to Tete, the principal town in the Portuguese territory, on the eastern coast of Africa; but leaving that expedition in 1861, he returned to Cape Town.

On recovering from a severe illness, which was attended with fever and loss of sight for several weeks, he resolved to explore the interior himself, and if possible to cross the continent from the west coast to the Zambezi on the east. For this purpose he built two copper boats, so constructed as to be used singly, or, when the river admitted, side by side, with a platform on which he could form a house or cabin. This he accomplished with his own hands, with the exception of a smith for a few hours' work.

Having provided himself with the requisites for such an undertaking, he left Table Bay, March 21, 1861, and arriving on the 29th of that month at Walvisch Bay, there began his overland journey. The journal was written under many difficulties, till they arrived at the Victoria Falls, when fever, famine, and the murder of many of their attendants obliged them to return at a time when they had hoped in a few weeks to begin their voyage down the Zambezi.

With extraordinary confidence and enterprise he first, at his starting point on the coast, built two copper boats which could be broken down into six parts and carried by ox cart – as they were for many months – and when the Zambezi was reached reassembled and used to float down the river and discover its mysterious route to the sea.

Baines himself wrote:

The young oxen sent down the country for us were as yet untrained and stubborn, and one of them took a fearful amount of punishment unflinchingly.

The lash, however, was in the hands of a man of strength and judgment. Measuring his distance fairly, Bonnie stood upon a slight elevation, and deliberately laid on stripe after stripe, the long boor-slag marking its track with blood from shoulder to hip, till one well-aimed blow falling in line with a previous one, the obstinacy of the beast gave way, and smearing the tree with gore as he passed under it, he applied his strength to the yoke. Half a score of active young Namaquas came to our help, and with shouts and screams, twisting and biting of tails, every mode of inflicting pain (except the last resort of fire) that ingenuity could suggest, succeeded in forwarding us about half a mile before the little urchins, like boys in all countries, were making believe at the same time to help by straining their young muscles at the spokes of the after-wheel.

This 18-month journey across bush, waterless desert and forest Baines described and drew in dauntingly extensive detail. Water was a perennial problem, and he painted and described one incident of finding it:

At the first faint scent of distant moisture, the cattle had broken into a trot, and increasing their speed as they came on, would in a few minutes have rushed over the brink, where the foremost, urged on by those behind, must have plunged into the pit and choked it with their carcases. All hands were pressed into service now; athletic men, women and girls, old or young, stout or meagre, surrounded the well and formed front to resist the charge; stones, knob keeries [wooden clubs], and big sticks were ruthlessly applied, while the shouts and screams and savage yelling of the men and dogs, to say nothing of the shrill voices of the fair sex, rising above the lowing of the impatient herd, formed a perfect pandemonium let loose.

One man in the well and one or two up the sides passed up the water and poured it into a hole, where the few that were admitted to drink at a time jostled and thrust each other about in their eagerness. The supply gave out before half the cattle were satisfied, but two or three fine fellows among our people set to work with a will, and as they cleared out the earth, we soon heard the music of the clear liquid trickling over the sandstone rock, and taking care that they did not dig too deep, and (as sometimes is the case) pierce the clay beneath and let the water off, we had from this time an ample supply for all purposes.

Negotiations with Hottentots (a term now considered offensive), Bushmen and other tribes produced much to attract Baines' brush:

We passed a kraal and a few huts, a wagon full of Hottentots, followed by a young woman astride an ox and managing the reins very gracefully; and about three stuck again in the Elephant river. Tayinyoka made me a sleeping place, blocking up the narrow channel with bushes and spreading out my blankets diagonally under a small rock, where after supper I made and coloured a rather successful sketch of my lair, working on with it till it was too late for an altitude of any star now available.

But such business was always complicated:

Ukana's idea of the incessant begging of the Hottentots, is, that they hardly know or mean what they are saying, but that it is a kind of sickness!

I confess I never knew or heard before of so entirely universal an affliction. Among the Damaras was one to whom Ukana had given the name of Kotzebue (his real one being nearly similar in sound), the finest man I have seen in this part of Africa. He was as tall as most Europeans, and perfectly made; his eyes open enough to look another fairly in the face, his nose only moderately broad, and his lips, though still thick, shapely and not over large. The prominence of his cheek bones was slight; and though with a white skin his features would have been called far from perfect, yet as a Damara he seemed so superior to the generality of his race, that I took the first opportunity of sketching him, but not having any colours by me, I determined to leave my outline untouched as a guide to work from it at a future opportunity.

Returning to our wagon, Chapman bought an ox for two bags or ten pounds of powder, and a sheep for three beakers of coffee, and on Saturday morning I gave one stout cotton shirt for a goat.

One fellow was highly offended when I compared him to a Bushman and asked where he had been 'made great' (equivalent to the Yankee 'raised'), till he had the effrontery to demand coffee instead of waiting till it was offered him.

Another of the party, after Chapman's return, seeing him rise from his seat for a moment, coolly took possession of it himself, and when reminded of his error, just shifted so far as to leave a corner of the chest unoccupied, his object being, of course, to raise himself in the estimation of the Damaras by forcing a white man to sit beside him. To put one's self on a level with a Hottentot by quarrelling with him, would be in his estimation almost as good as submitting to his insolence, but in both senses he was disappointed; for my companion, after five or six times desiring him to move, and once appealing to an old man of more decent behaviour, quietly pushed him on one side and took the seat to himself; and Robin Red-breast finding that after this we gave him no more coffee, accepted in rather a crest-fallen style a pannikin at second-hand from Bonnie.

About nine in the evening the brothers Polson arrived with two wagons, and spanned out just beyond us, having been compelled to purchase the forbearance of old Jonker with, I believe, thirty bags of powder. They had resisted as long as possible, but the unmanly submission of Cator and Smutz (who had been the greatest boasters in Otjimbingue) had encouraged the old chief, and he now openly demanded tribute for permission and travel on 'his' road, the said road being the tracks made by white men's wagons, or cut by their axes through the bush.

The helpless condition to which travellers are reduced by being obliged to send back their own cattle on suspicion of lung sickness places them still more at the mercy of savage.

Baines had indeed created his own copper double canoe, which could be deconstructed to be hauled by wagon across desert, veld and mountain, so that he would have the means of going down the Zambezi when he got to it.

In the fifteen months of travel which it took him to reach the great river he managed to haul his boat almost all the way. But not quite. However, he did reach Victoria Falls, and his meticulous account of the trip – with precise details of astronomical readings and sextant bearings, and frequent desperate searches for water – erupts into a most lyrical account of the sight which confronted him and which he was to paint in such glorious detail.

Tell me if heart of man ever conceived anything more gorgeous than those two lovely rainbows, so brilliant that the eye shrinks from looking on them, segments of which, rising from the abyss, deep as the solar rays can penetrate it, overarching spray, rocks and forest, till rising to the highest point they fail to find refractory moisture to complete the arch. The imagination is bewildered and embarrassed by such magnificence. I approach the edge and look with awe into the troubled narrow stream beneath. The influence of the water downward, eternally downward, seems to meet a response within me, and kneeling down I rest on one hand to look further, but down comes my little bush boy to rescue me from the supposed danger, nor will he be satisfied till we have removed from the verge.

Baines had had audible warning the night before: 'In the stillness of the night there steals upon the ear a low murmuring like the sighing of the ocean before an impending storm, rising and swelling gradually into the deep-toned monotonous roar of a continuous surf forever breaking on some iron bound coast.'

Baines had planned to finance his journey, accompanied by the trader brothers James and Henry Chapman, by collecting skins and specimens of the Southern African animals, and by careful map-making of the route through the uncharted forest and veld, as well as producing pictures for the market at home. His journal describes the oils, the watercolours, the canvases which he took with him on the fifteen-month journey. Thus when he got to Victoria Falls, he was equipped to make remarkably exact measurements of their size. He recorded the height of the spray as 1,114ft and the breadth of the Falls as about 2,000 yards (2,700 strides in fact). His paintings of the Falls – the first depiction of them that anyone in Europe had seen – were exhibited all across the Continent and offered the first visual context for the romantic view of Southern Africa which David Livingstone had brought to the British public and which drove the impetus of imperial expansion in the inland vastnesses of that part of the continent.

Baines and his parties made their way through the country of the Hottentots, then the Bushmen and the Damaras. They relied for their safety on the fact that the chiefs and their peoples knew that they carried desirable items that could be traded – guns, ammunition, beads, sugar – and that white men would not venture into tribal territories with such treasures if they knew there was a risk of being attacked or killed. But there was always the risk of being robbed or duped in the protracted negotiations with the chiefs and their peoples, which Baines records as often lasting many days.

It was after one of these experiences, when a Hottentot chief tried to punish a white man, that Baines fumed in his diary and invoked the justification which was, perhaps, widely felt in the mid-nineteenth century for expanding the Empire:

There is evident necessity of some form of government being adopted by the white people for the better control of such persons as are not able to command themselves. I cannot but think that our own government is too tardy in extending its authority where its subjects spread themselves. Settlements of our countrymen, desirous and petitioning to be governed by their own laws are ignored until they either become involved in disputes with the native tribes, or as in the case of the first little community in Natal, the deserted people of our Sovereignty are obliged to incorporate themselves with any more powerful body of emigrants in the vicinity, even though, as with the Dutch, they should be at variance with the British Government.

In respect to justice to the native tribes, the sooner British authority is interposed the better for them, unless to be plundered and butchered by a horde of semi-barbarians like the Namaqas be considered better than to live in peace and security under the control of a powerful nation like our own.

Baines, an Englishman from Norfolk, had trained as a coach painter and had gone to South Africa at the age of twenty-two and established himself as a portrait artist. But his aspiration to travel and to paint unknown lands had been excited when he was invited to be the artist appointed to the Royal Geographical Society's expedition in the north-west of Australia, designed to see if that, then unknown, land might be suitable for colonial settlement. His paintings on that expedition made him sufficiently celebrated that a mountain in that part of the Northern Territory was named Mount Baines. Settlement did indeed follow.

Chapter 4

Australia and Cape Town

From the moment Captain Cook returned with Sydney Parkinson's hundreds of drawings and paintings of strange plants and animals and with John Webber's landscapes and natives, the fascination back in England with the southern lands grew ever more intense.

John Glover had enjoyed a long and successful career as a professional painter, before finally, at the age of sixty-three, he succumbed to the allure of Australia, set sail and actually landed there on his sixty-fourth birthday. He already had family there. He was to take up residence in what was still known as Van Diemen's Land (Tasmania) and become perhaps the best-known artist of his era, still painting until he was eighty and recording the bright scenes and unusual landscapes, like Constitution Hill, which took his eye around his new home.

He acquired land and painted the house he built there. The house looks like one that might be found in any English village.

But the profusion of new plants and trees bestows an idyllic lushness on the scene. He painted Hobart Town and Mount Wellington, and scenes with Aboriginals such as 'Natives on the Ouse River', as well as views from his own house.

Australian artists accompanied much of the exploration of the interior in the nineteenth century sparked by the discovery of gold, principally from 1851 onwards. One subsequent account told how these events were to bring nearly half a million new settlers to Australia in twenty years.

In February 1851, prospector Edward Hargraves claimed to find gold in a place he called Ophir, located near the city of Orange in New South Wales. By May 1851 the news had been reported in local papers, and 300 diggers arrived, eager to make their fortunes. The convict colonies of Australia were phased out, with towns and cities revolving around the gold rushes beginning to appear. Officials soon realized that giving convicts a free trip to Australia was no longer the punishment it once had been.

Australia had no shortage of gold and the discoveries soon spread to other states; July 1851 was the date of Victoria's first gold rush – at Clunes goldfield – and by the end of 1851, gold was being mined at Buninyong, Ballarat, Castlemaine and Bendigo.

When news of the discoveries reached England it was considered overstated – and was largely ignored – but when six ships arrived from Victoria in 1852 carrying eight

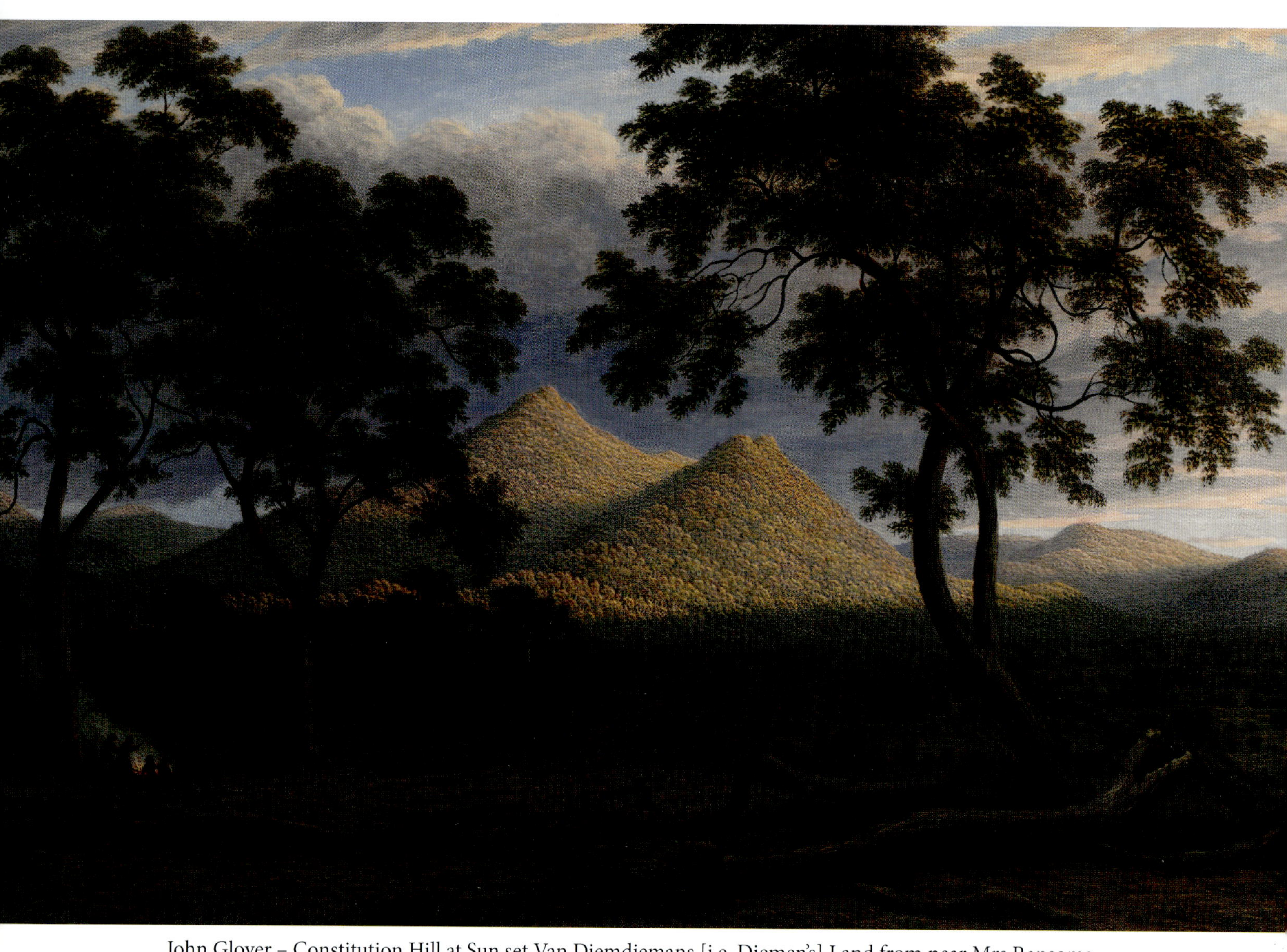

John Glover – Constitution Hill at Sun set Van Diemdiemans [i.e. Diemen's] Land from near Mrs Ransoms Publick House 29 Jane [January or June] 1840.

John Glover - A view of the artist's house and garden, in Mills Plains, Van Diemen's Land.

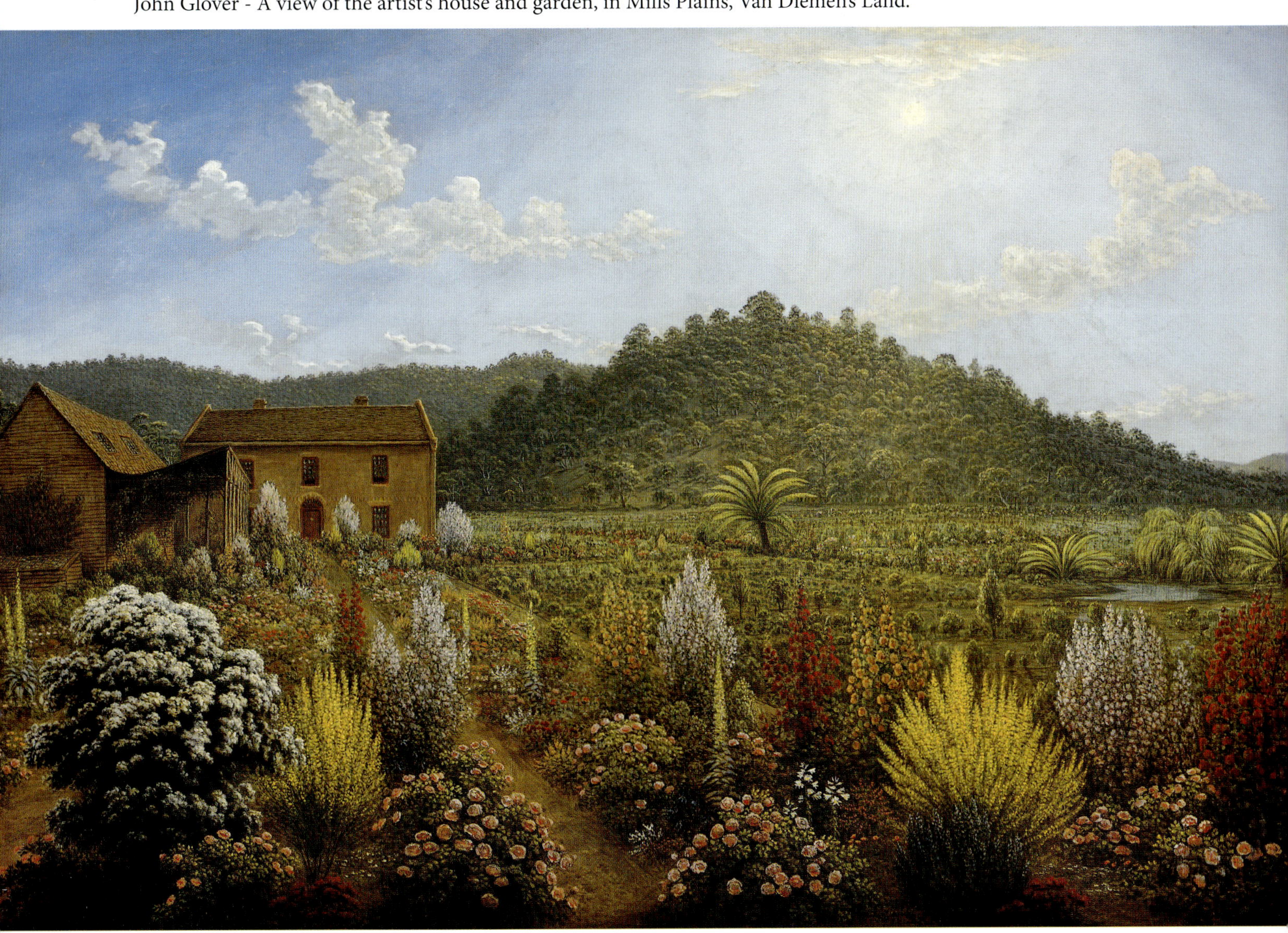

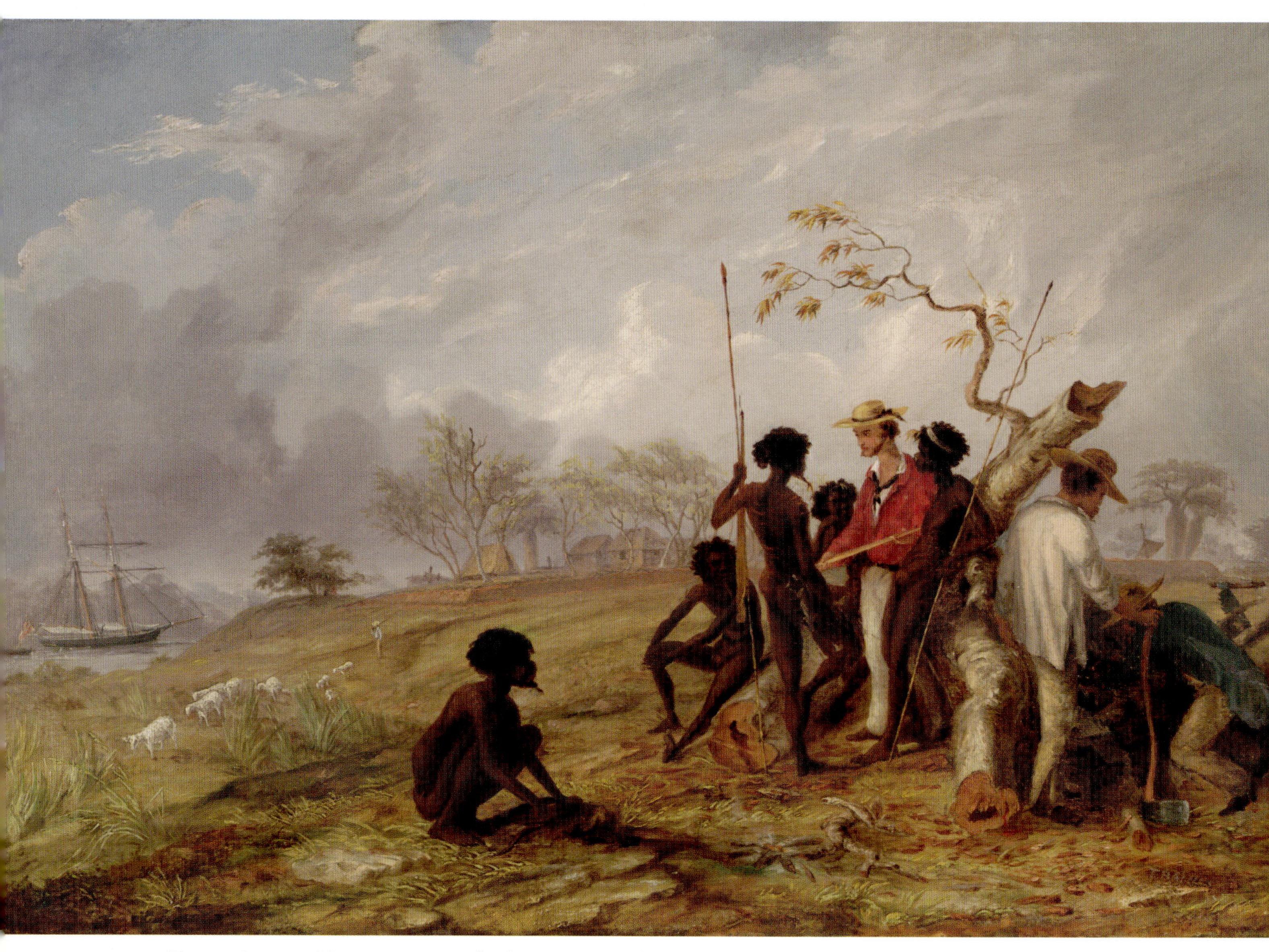

Thomas Baines – Thomas Baines with Aborigines near the mouth of the Victoria River, N.T.

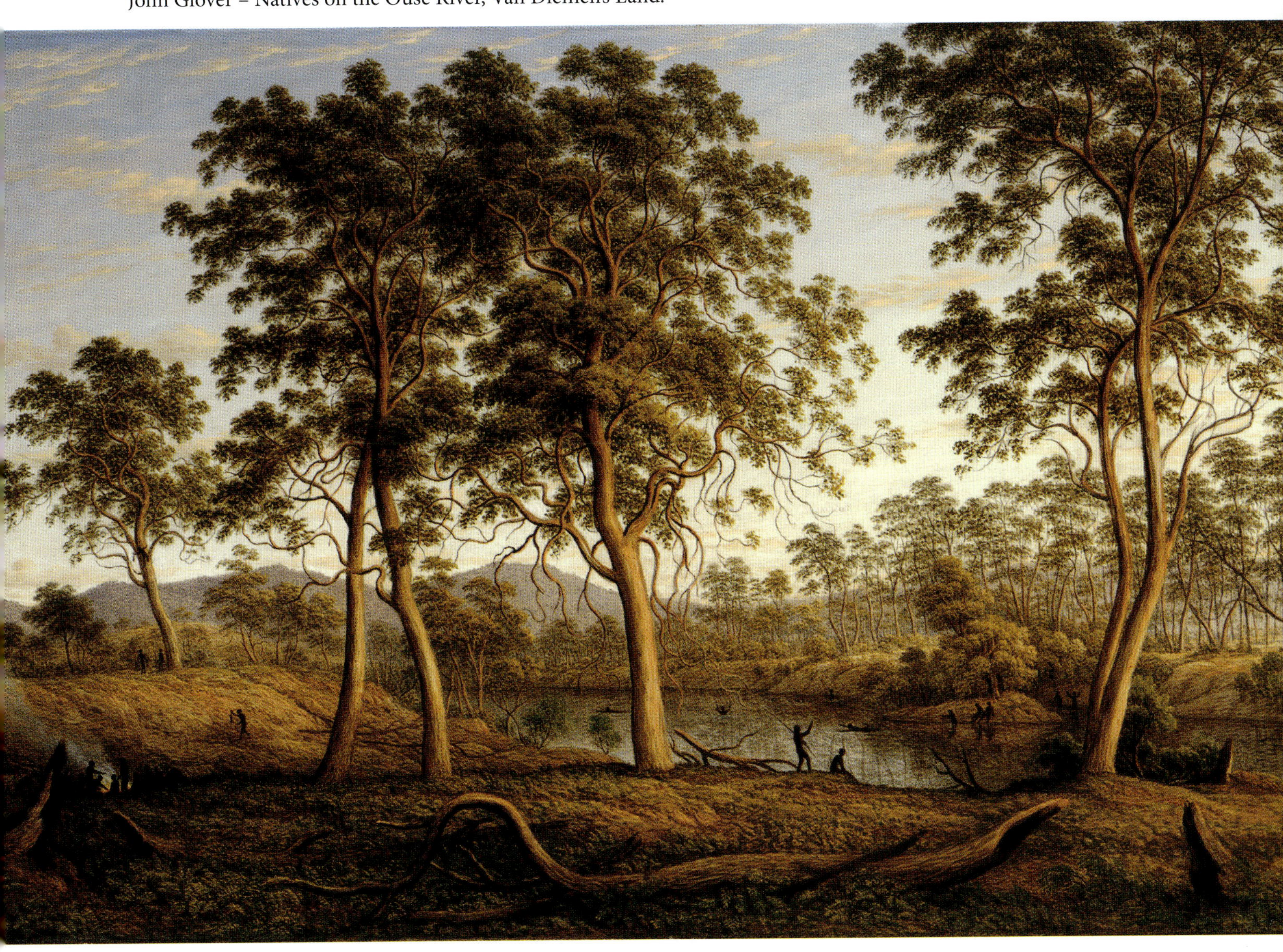

John Glover – Natives on the Ouse River, Van Diemen's Land.

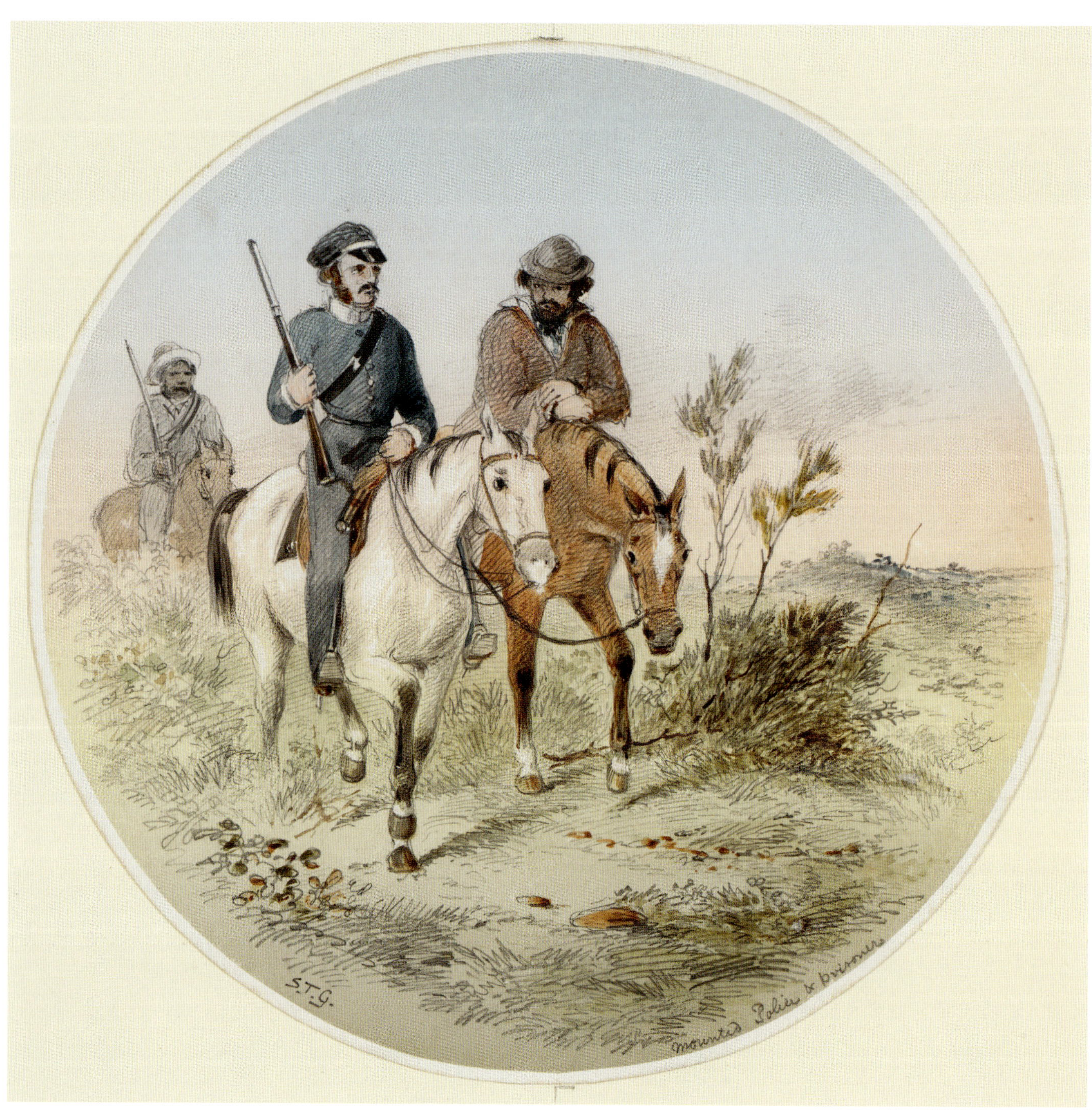

Samuel Thomas Gill – Mounted Police and Prisoner.

tonnes of gold, these doubts were erased. People migrated to Australia in droves, from the British Isles, Europe and America. Racial tensions with Chinese prospectors, as in the California gold rush, were once again an issue. Considered especially unwelcome, Chinese immigrants faced significant discrimination, and the state of Victoria even enacted the Chinese Immigration Act of 1855, restricting the number of people allowed to travel to the area. Undeterred, many Chinese migrants would land illegally in South-East Australia, and then travel 400km across rough country to the Victorian goldfields. The area was a prolific producer, and 174 tonnes of gold were extracted in 1852 alone.

In 1854 the Victorian Gold Discovery Committee, set up to help direct the efforts of prospectors and offer rewards for claims, said:

> The discovery of the Victorian Goldfields has converted a remote dependency into a country of worldwide fame; it has attracted a population, extraordinary in number, with unprecedented rapidity; it has enhanced the value of property to an enormous extent, it has made this the richest country in the world; and, in less than three years, it has done for this colony the work of an age, and made its impulses felt in the most distant regions of the earth.

Samuel Thomas Gill was one of the artists drawn to depict the gold rush. He particularly was attracted by the authorities' attempts to keep the peace with all the ex-convicts and to supply police to try and ensure law and order was maintained. Two mounted policemen are the centre of one of his best known pictures.

*   *   *

After Captain Phillip arrived at what would become Botany Bay with the first fleet bringing British convicts to provide a workforce for the colony, the new colonial presence remained confined to an area close to the coast. It was to be the best part of a century before much of the interior of Australia was explored.

To begin with, the Great Dividing Range, running parallel with the coast, proved a formidable barrier. Then after various expeditions managed to cross the hills, large tracts of country proved to be too marshy to contemplate farming. Then the rivers the explorers came across seemed all to flow west, and the speculation was that they must feed some enormous inland lake – sailors circumnavigating Australia saw no sign of rivers reaching the sea.

In the far west of Australia the first settlers – free men, not convicts – had arrived from England in 1829 and begun to develop the banks of the Swan River. This was to be the foundation of today's city of Perth. But there was no serious attempt to explore the huge area to the north. It was a man whose family had arrived on the Swan in the

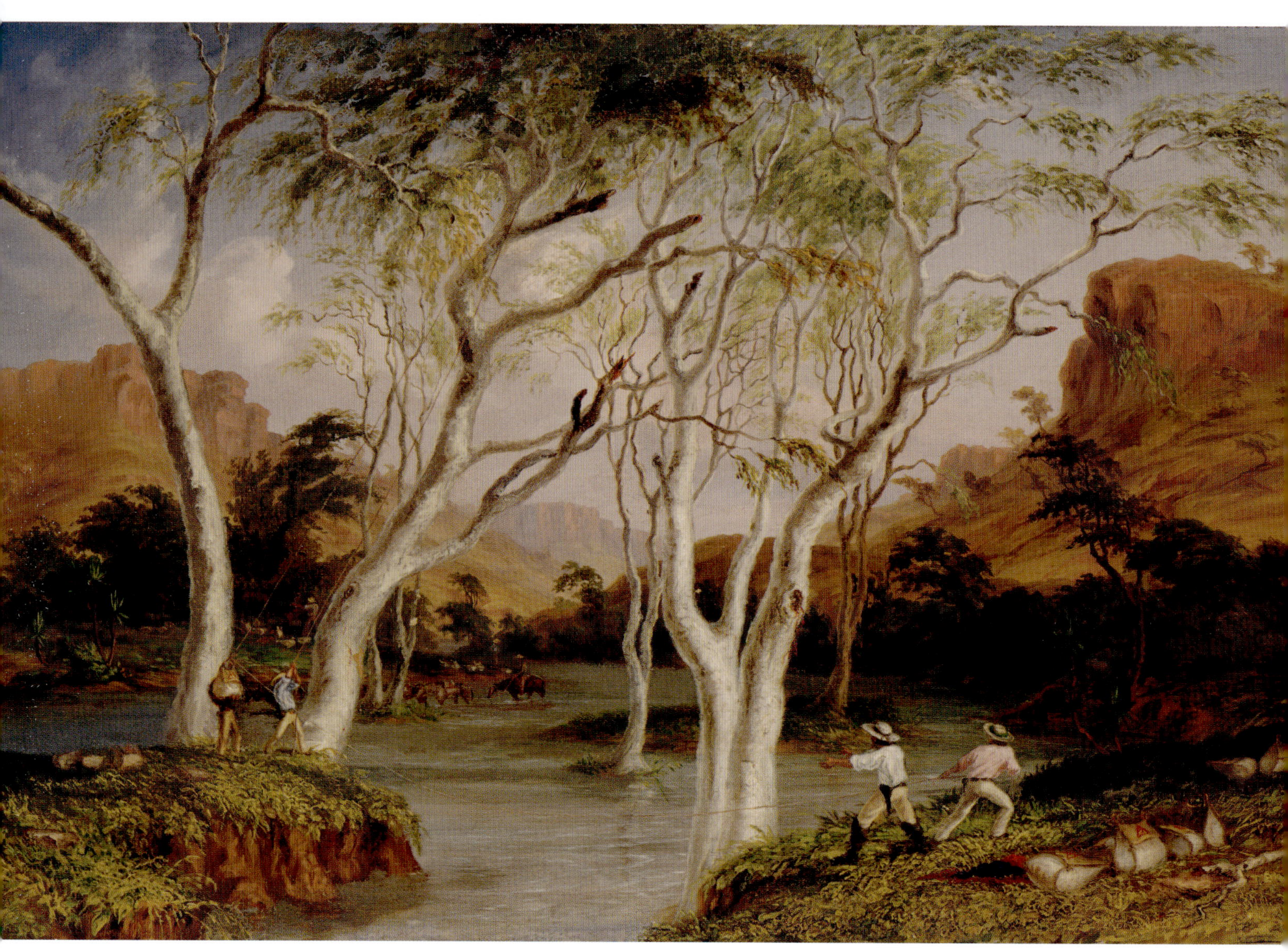

Thomas Baines – Incident in the North West Australian Expedition.

first 1829 ships who found himself commissioned in 1855 by the New South Wales authorities 3,000 miles away to put together the North Western Australia Expedition, in order to assess the potential of that vast area for colonization and agriculture.

Augustus Gregory, along with his brothers, had already undertaken a number of expeditions to Central Australia and was well aware that pictures as well as words were vital in telling the true story of these new lands. It is not clear how he heard tell of a young English painter who was making a name for himself across the Southern Ocean in South Africa. This was Thomas Baines, and after Augustus contrived to sign him up, Baines took ship from Cape Town in 1855. The painter was also paid as a storekeeper, but he succeeded in producing many of the most appealing pictures of the country, the people and the expedition, works which were to help encourage the first groups of people to come to work and farm the new territory. 'Incident on the North Western Expedition' shows the evidently quite hazardous crossing of a river against some undefined opposition.

The North Western Australia Expedition was deemed a success in opening up new territory, and Augustus Gregory emerged with a knighthood. Baines had the mountain named after him, and then went back to South Africa.

*　*　*

Wouter Schouten's 1658 painting of the fort that the Dutch built overlooking Africa's southernmost point and what became known as Table Bay shows the first European settlement on African soil, established to supply ships sailing to Holland's commercial bases in the Indian Ocean and beyond.

A century later, the British made their first attempt to supplant the Dutch, and fifty years later still, in the middle of the Napoleonic Wars, British troops forced an agreement on them.

The first British colonist arrived in 1820. Twelve years later, Thomas Bowler, a young artist of only twenty-two, landed at the Cape. He was to remain there for thirty years and produce paintings and drawings of how Cape Colony evolved in his time.

Bowler's painting of Table Bay gives the clearest impression of the land- and seascape in those earliest days. He was to show the first development of streets and buildings in Cape Town, the landing which became Port Elizabeth, and the array of shipping which passed through the Cape.

More than 500 of Bowler's paintings and watercolours survive, not only of the Cape, but from his extensive travels across Southern Africa in the turbulent years when the Dutch and the British often confronted each other, while determinedly pushing out into lands where the native population were trying to hold their own place. Bowler painted these encounters too.

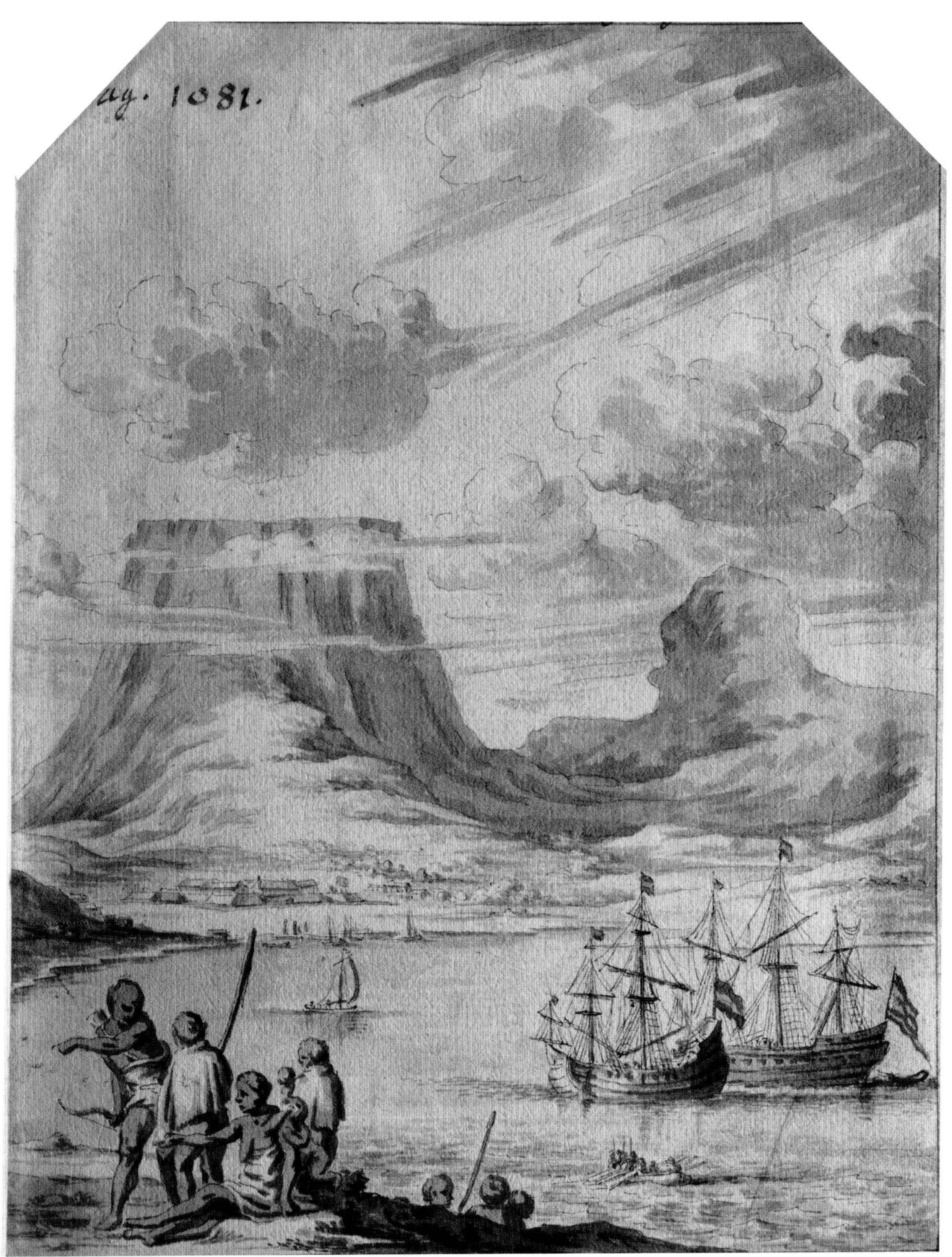

Wouter Schouten – Van Riebeeck's original fort on the shores of Table Bay.

Thomas Bowler – Table Bay.

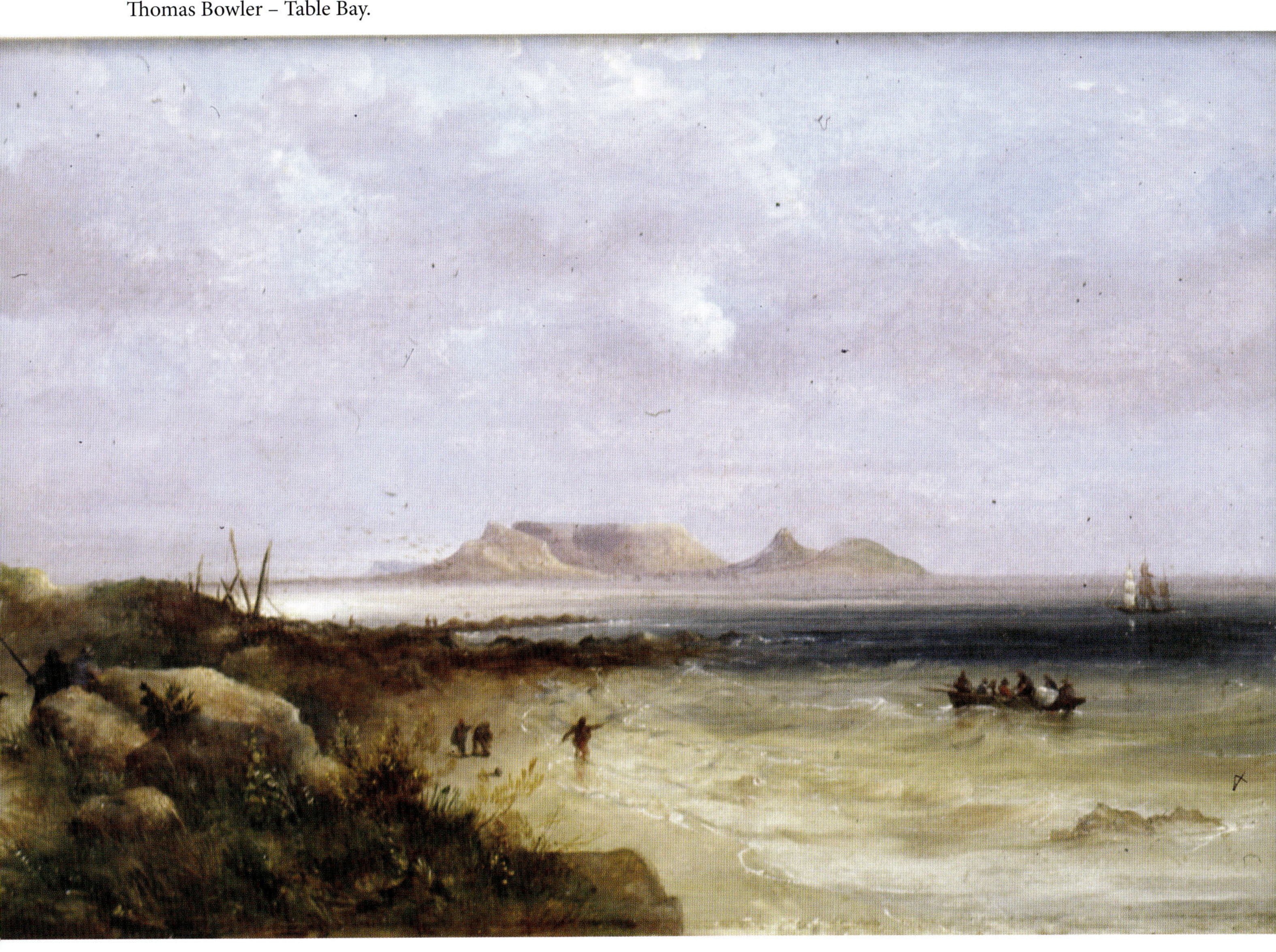

Chapter 5

Earle

The yearning back home in Europe to view far distant places and new worlds underpinned the success of illustrated magazines in the more peaceful years after the end of the Napoleonic Wars. And it produced a new breed of adventurous artists who took to the oceans and made not only a reputation but a livelihood from their travels.

Augustus Earle was perhaps the most prodigious – and precocious – of his time. He had already contrived, as a teenager, to have his work accepted by the annual Royal Academy exhibitions in London. In the next twenty years, before his early death at the age of forty-five, he took himself to North and South America, Australia, New Zealand and through the South Atlantic via Tristan da Cunha to Tierra del Fuego. He sailed with Charles Darwin, travelled to India and sailed around the world.

He was also one of the very earliest artists to visit New Zealand, having seen in Sydney some Māori men who had been brought to Australia and been impressed by their imposing physique.

Apart from traders gathering timber for Australian ship builders and some very early colonists, almost the only Europeans in New Zealand were missionaries; and although Earle was later scathing about them, when he heard a ship was taking a party of evangelists there, he managed to join them in 1827 aboard the *Governor Macquarie*. This was when he produced some of the first representations of Māori culture. The painting of a Māori council, for example, is a sympathetic depiction produced during a journey he made after the ship arrived at Hokianga on the coast of the North Island.

He found the Māori men incredibly strong and imposing, and though more than once he barely escaped from encounters with his life, he was nevertheless able to secure protection from their chiefs, even when the incessant bouts of war brought them into bloody conflict. He described one incident which threatened to cost him much of his property:

It was easily to be perceived that the Narpooes were determined on executing some atrocity or depredations before their return; they accordingly pretended to recollect some old offence committed by the English settlers at the other end of the beach. They proceeded thither; and first attacked and broke open the house of a blacksmith, and carried off every article it contained. They then marched to

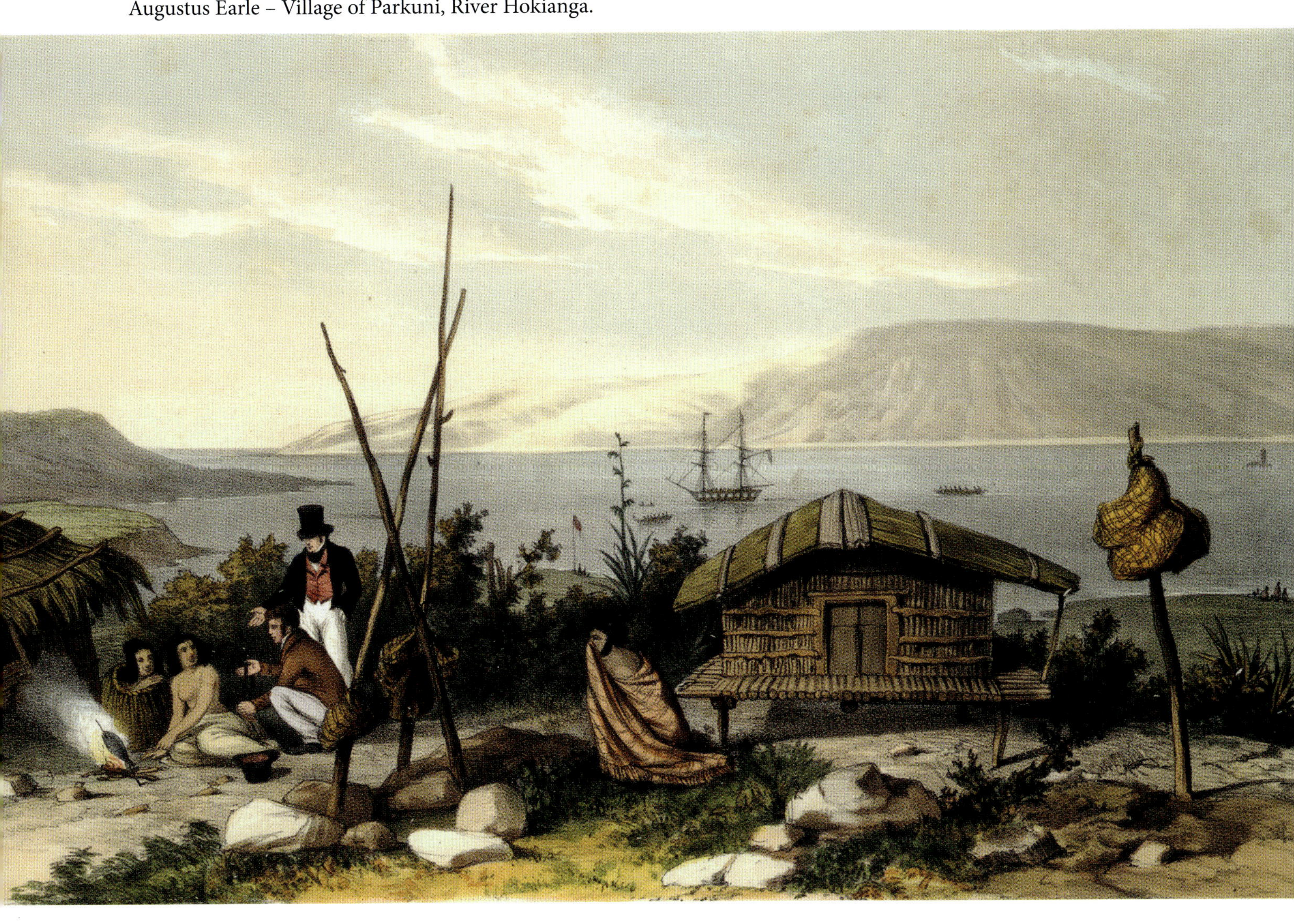

Augustus Earle – Village of Parkuni, River Hokianga.

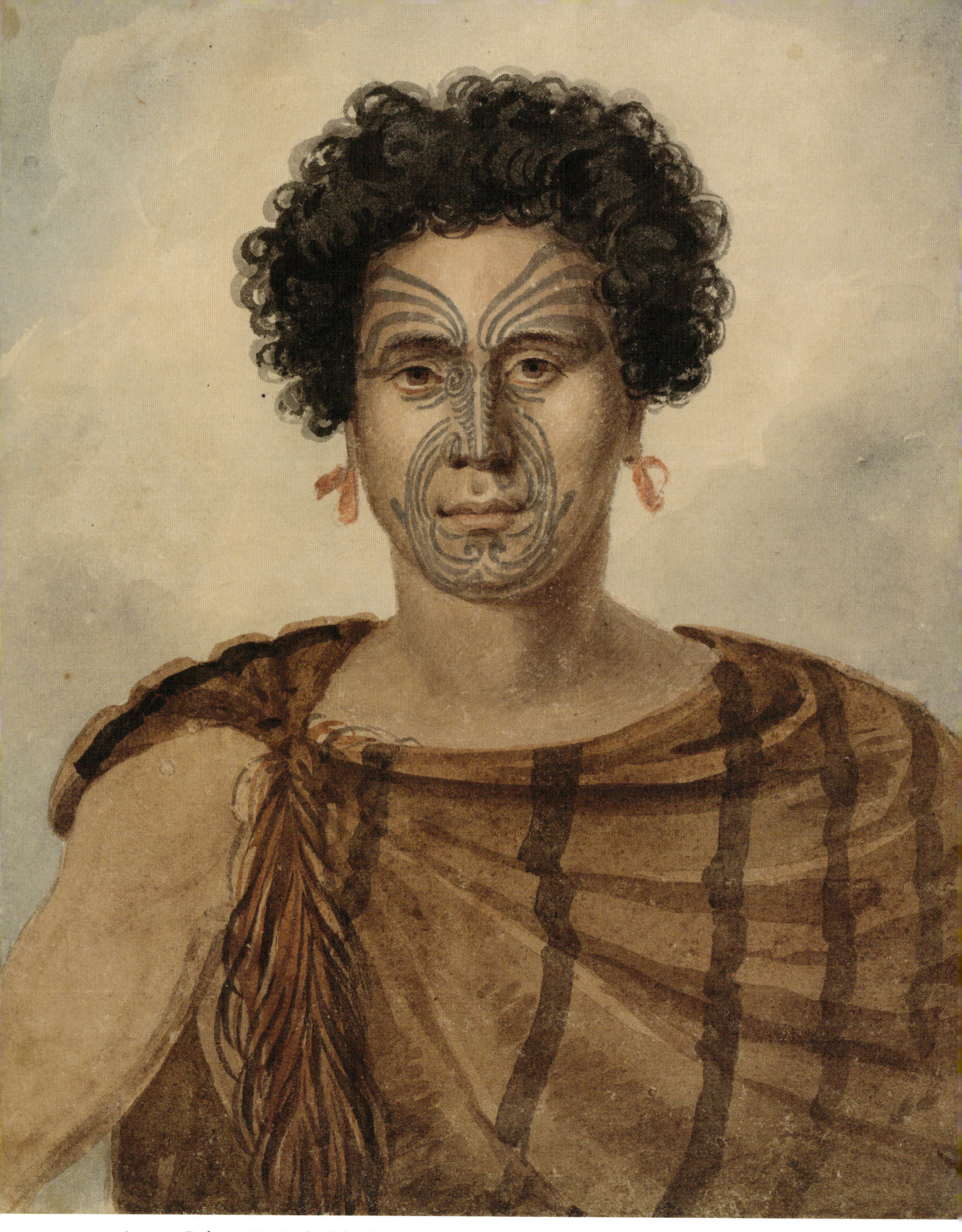

Augustus Earle – A New Zealand chief from Terra Naky [i.e. Taranaki].

the residence of an English captain (who was in England), and plundered it of
every thing that could be taken away; and afterwards sent us word they intended
to return to our end of the beach. Our fears were greatly increased by finding that
our friends were not sufficiently strong to protect us from the superior force of the
Narpooes; and our chief, George, being himself (we supposed) conscious of his
inability, had left us to depend upon our own resources.

We now called a council of war of all the Europeans settled here; and it was
unanimously resolved that we should protect and defend our houses and property,
and fortify our position in the best way we could. Captain Duke had in his
possession four twelve-pounders, and these we brought in front of the enclosure
in which our huts were situated; and were all entirely employed in loading them
with round and grape shot, and had made them all ready for action, when, to our
consternation and dismay, we found we had a new and totally unexpected enemy
to contend with. By some accident one of our houses was in flames. Our situation
was now perilous in the extreme. The buildings, the work of English carpenters,
were constructed of dry rushes and well-seasoned wood; and this was one of a very
respectable size, and we had hoped, in a very few days, would be finished fit for our
removing into.

For some seconds we stood in mute amazement, not knowing to which point to
direct our energies. As the cry of 'fire' was raised, groups of natives came rushing
from all directions upon our devoted settlement, stripping off their clothes, and
yelling in the most discordant pitch of voice. I entered the house, and brought
out one of my trunks; but on attempting to return a second time, I found it filled
with naked savages, tearing every thing to pieces, and carrying away whatever
they could lay their hands upon. The fierce raging of the flames, the heat from the
fire, the yells of the men, and the shrill cries of the women, formed, altogether,
a horrible combination: added to all this was the mortification of seeing all our
property carried off in different directions, without the least possibility of our
preventing it. The tribe of the Narpooes (who, when the fire began, were at the
other end of the beach) left their operations in that quarter, and poured down upon
us to share in the general plunder. Never shall I forget the countenance of the chief,
as he rushed forward at the head of his destroying crew! He was called 'The Giant';
and he was well worthy of the name, being the tallest and largest man I had ever
seen: he had an immense bushy black beard; and grinned exultingly when he saw
the work of destruction proceeding with such rapidity and kept shouting loudly to
his party to excite them to carry off all they could.

A cask containing seventy gallons of rum now caught fire and blew up with a
terrible explosion; and the wind freshening considerably, huge volumes of smoke

and flame burst out in every direction. Two of our houses were so completely
enveloped, that we had given up all hopes of saving them. The third, which was
a beautifully carved taboo'd one, some little distance from the others, and which
we had converted into a store and magazine, was now the only object of our
solicitude and terror. For, besides the valuable property of various kinds which
were deposited within it, it contained several barrels of gunpowder! It was in vain
we attempted to warn the frantic natives to retire from the vicinity of this danger.
At length we persuaded about a dozen of the most rational to listen while we
explained to them the cause of our alarm; and they immediately ascended to the
roof, where, with the utmost intrepidity and coolness, they kept pouring water over
the thatch, thus lessening the probability of an immediate explosion. About this
time we noticed the re-appearance of King George; which circumstance rekindled
our hopes. He was armed with a thick stick, which he laid heavily on the backs of
such of his subjects as were running away with our property; thus forcing them
to relinquish their prizes, and to lay them down before his own mansion, where
all was safe. By this means a great deal was re-collected. The fire was now nearly
extinguished; but our two really tolerably good houses were reduced to a heap of
smoking ruins, and the greater part of what belonged to us was taken away by the
Narpooes.

Despite these experiences, Earle was impressed by the Māoris:

I had heard a great deal respecting the splendid race of men I was going to visit,
and the few specimens I had occasionally met with at Sydney so much pleased me,
that I was extremely anxious to see a number of them together, to judge whether
(as a nation) they were finer in their proportions than the English, or whether it
was mere accident that brought some of their tallest and finest proportioned men
before me.

I examined these savages, as they crowded round our decks, with the critical
eye of an artist; they were generally taller and larger men than ourselves; those
of middle height were broad-chested and muscular, and their limbs as sinewy as
though they had been occupied all their lives in laborious employments. Their
colour is lighter than that of the American Indian, their features small and regular,
their hair is in a profusion of beautiful curls: whereas that of the Indian is strait
and lank. The disposition of the New Zealander appears to be full of fun and gaiety,
while the Indian is dull, shy, and suspicious.

In their combats with each other, fire-arms are used with dreadful effect. The
whole soul of a New Zealander seems absorbed in the thoughts of war; every

Augustus Earle – Solitude, watching the horizon at sunset, in the hopes of seeing a vessel, Tristan de Acunha [i.e. da Cunha] in the South Atlantic.

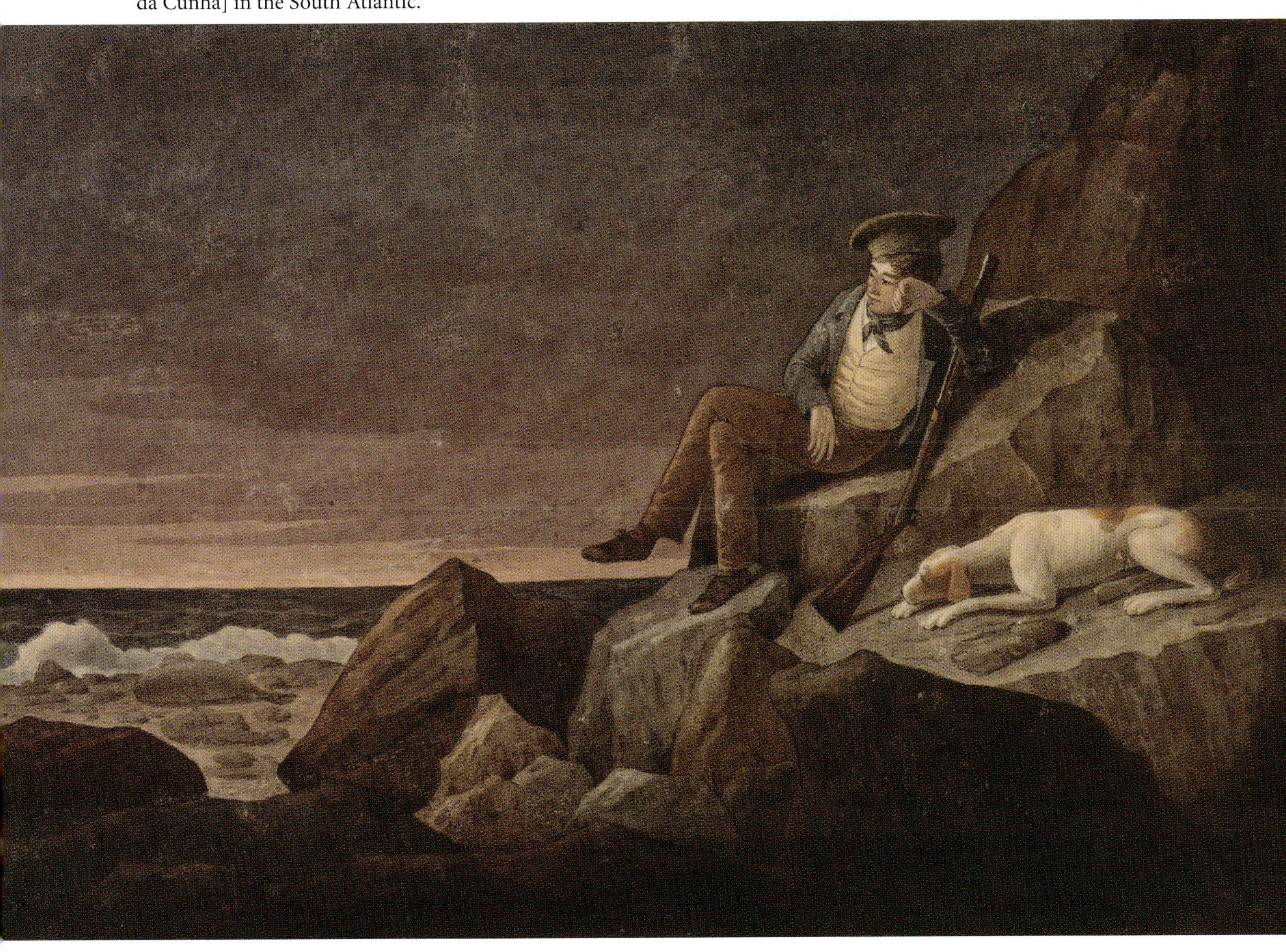

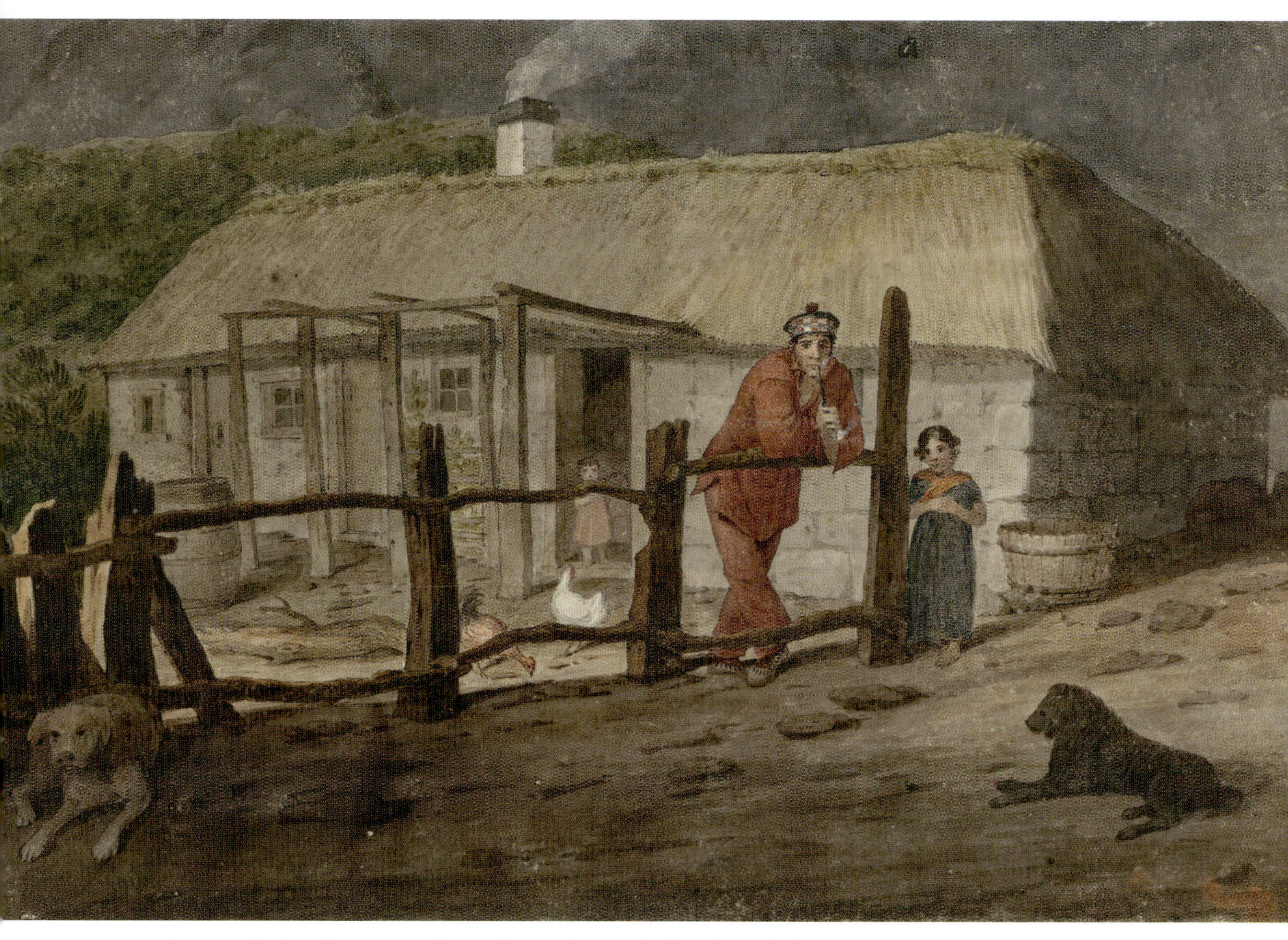

Augustus Earle – Government House, Tristan De Acunha [i.e. da Cunha].

action of his life is influenced by it; and to possess weapons which give him such a decided superiority over those who have only their native implements of offence, he will sacrifice every thing. The value attached by them to muskets, and their ceaseless desire to possess them, will prove a sufficient security to foreigners who enter their harbours, or remain on their coasts; as I know, from experience, that the New Zealanders will rather put up with injuries, than run the risk of offending those who manufacture and barter with them such inestimable commodities.

Earle left the ship and embarked on months of walking through the country, determined to draw and paint its landscapes and people. After weeks, or even months, in the interior, he still made optimistic arrangements for meeting up with ships.

*   *   *

Augustus Earle's 'Solitude', if not a self portrait, is at least a self contemplation. Already a much travelled artist, he had in early 1824 taken ship in Rio aboard the sloop *Duke of Gloucester*, bound, he hoped, to make his mark in the new communities of the Southern Ocean. The ship had stopped in the remote harbour of Tristan da Cunha, the rocky island claimed by the British but scarcely colonized.

Fascinated, it would appear, by this strange island, Earle went ashore delighted to paint a landscape which no one in Europe had ever seen. Then one morning, aghast, he was to see the ship set sail, abandoning him … He never came to know what emergency of supply or weather had driven the ship to leave. But for eight months, so he tells us, he spent much of his time, accompanied by his dog, it would seem, staring out to sea for a glimpse of a sail. He was sheltered by the little British community there who lived off growing potatoes and hoped to sell whale and fish oil to passing ships.

The custom was to light fires to attract such vessels to send a boat ashore. But they were few and far between. More than one such ship, even in calm weather, declined to make contact.

Earle recorded his fury: 'Their commanders must have known full well that there were some poor creatures in distress on this desolate spot. The captains must have known that by the smallest alteration of course they could have rescued persons probably perishing of want.'

He wrote: 'My time drags heavily on. As long as my paper and pencils lasted, they were a source of infinite amusement. But now, alas all are entirely used.'

By October he was writing: 'I complete six months miserable imprisonment on this wretched island. I sit for hours watching the horizon with the faint hope of catching sight of a vessel and thinking of my friends in England.'

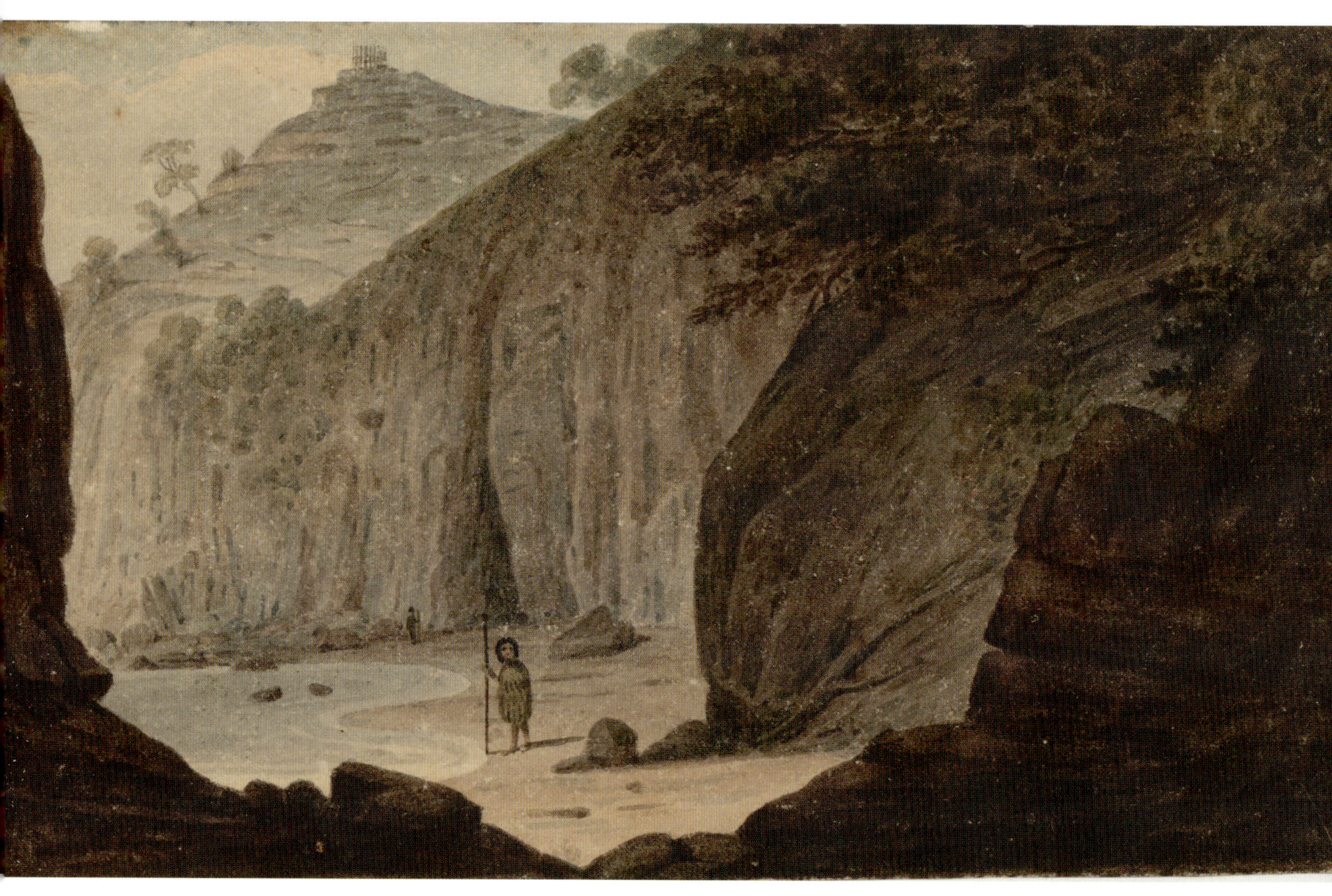

Augustus Earle – Ranghe-hue [i.e. Rangihoua] Bay of Islands, New Zealand.

It was early November when a brig was seen on the horizon. When she came closer, Earle got help from the islanders to launch a small boat through the surf and succeeded in getting on board what turned out to be the *Admiral Cockburn*.

Eight months had passed. But Earle was at last on his way to Australasia. 'Though my personal appearance must have been deplorable', he wrote, 'every one opened his chest to accommodate me with clothes of every description. I was soon completely new rigged.'

∗   ∗   ∗

He soon arrived in New Zealand.

We proceeded to Tipoona in two whale-boats: it was a most delightful trip, the scenery being strikingly beautiful. The village of Ranghe Hue, belonging to Warri Pork, is situated on the summit of an immense and abrupt hill: the huts belonging to the savages appeared, in many places, as though they were overhanging the sea, the height being crowned with a mighty par. At the bottom of this hill, and in a beautiful valley, the cottages of the missionaries are situated, complete pictures of English comfort, content, and prosperity; they are close to a bright sandy-beach: a beautiful green slope lies in their rear, and a clear and never-failing stream of water runs by the side of their enclosures. As the boats approached this lovely spot, I was in an ecstasy of delight: such a happy mixture of savage and civilised life I had never seen before; and, when I observed the white smoke curling out of the chimneys of my countrymen, I anticipated the joyful surprise, the hearty welcome, the smiling faces, and old Christmas compliments that were going to take place, and the great pleasure it would give our secluded countrymen to meet us, in these distant regions, at this happy season, and talk of our relatives and friends in England.

My romantic notions were soon crushed; our landing gave no pleasure to these secluded Englishmen: they gave us no welcome; but, as our boats approached the shore, they walked away to their own dwellings, closed their gates and doors after them, and gazed at us through their windows; and during three days that we passed in a hut quite near them, they never exchanged one word with any of the party.

However, he rapidly got on good terms with the natives, including a chief name Atoi.

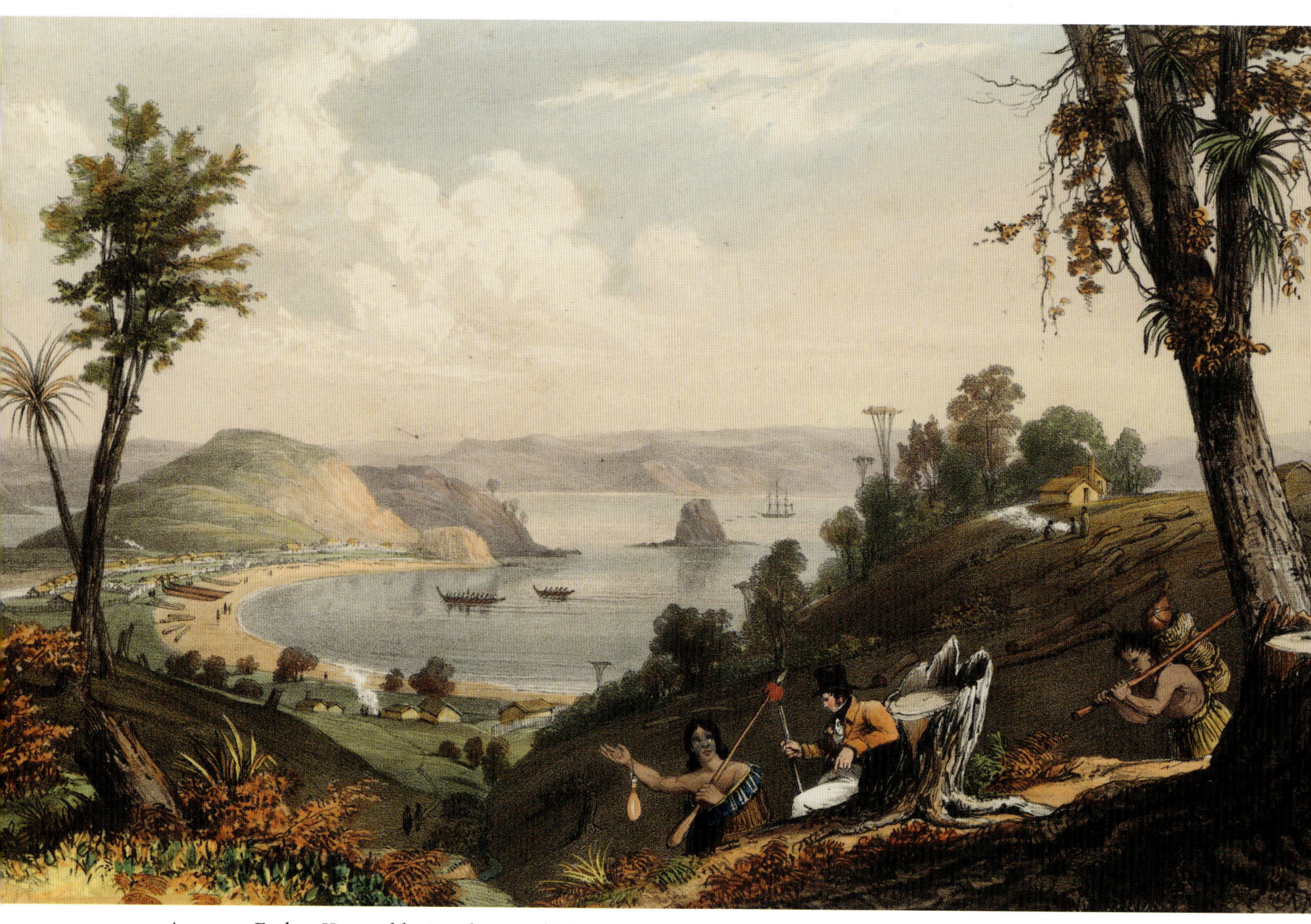

Augustus Earle – Kororadika Beach, Bay of Islands.

One morning, about eleven o'clock, after I had just returned from a long walk, Captain Duke informed me he had heard, from very good authority, (though the natives wished it to be kept a profound secret), that in the adjoining village a female slave, named Matowe, had been put to death, and that the people were at that very time preparing her flesh for cooking. At the same time he reminded me of a circumstance which had taken place the evening before. Atoi had been paying us a visit, and, when going away, he recognised a girl whom he said was a slave that had run away from him; he immediately seized hold of her, and gave her in charge to some of his people. The girl had been employed in carrying wood for us; Atoi's laying claim to her had caused us no alarm for her life, and we had thought no more on the subject; but now, to my surprise and horror, I heard this poor girl was the victim they were preparing for the oven! Captain Duke and myself were resolved to witness this dreadful scene.

We therefore kept our information as secret as possible, well knowing that if we had manifested our wishes they would have denied the whole affair. We set out, taking a circuitous route towards the village; and, being well acquainted with the road, we came upon them suddenly, and found them in the midst of their abominable ceremonies.

On a spot of rising ground, just outside the village, we saw a man preparing a native oven, which is done in the following simple manner: a hole is made in the ground, and hot stones are put within it, and then all is covered up close. As we approached, we saw evident signs of the murder which had been perpetrated; bloody mats were strewed around, and a boy was standing by them actually laughing: he put his finger to his head, and then pointed towards a bush. I approached the bush, and there discovered a human head. My feelings of horror may be imagined as I recognised the features of the unfortunate girl I had seen forced from our village the preceding evening!

We ran towards the fire, and there stood a man occupied in a way few would wish to see. He was preparing the four quarters of a human body for a feast; the large bones, having been taken out, were thrown aside, and the flesh being compressed, he was in the act of forcing it into the oven. While we stood transfixed by this terrible sight, a large dog, which lay before the fire, rose up, seized the bloody head, and walked off with it into the bushes; no doubt to hide it there for another meal! The man completed his task with the most perfect composure, telling us, at the same time, that the repast would not be ready for some hours!

Here stood Captain Duke and myself, both witnesses of a scene, which many travellers have related, and their relations have invariably been treated with contempt; indeed, the veracity of those who had the temerity to relate such incredible events has been everywhere questioned. In this instance it was no warrior's flesh to be eaten; there was no enemy's blood to drink, in order to infuriate them. They had no revenge to gratify; no plea they could make of their passions having been roused by battle, nor the excuse that they eat their enemies to perfect their triumph.

This was an action of unjustifiable cannibalism. Atoi, the chief, who had given orders for this cruel feast, had only the night before sold us four pigs for a few pounds of powder; so he had not even the excuse of want of food. After Captain Duke and myself had consulted with each other, we walked into the village, determined to charge Atoi with his brutality.

Atoi received us in his usual manner; and his handsome open countenance could not be imagined to belong to so savage a monster as he had proved himself to be. I shuddered at beholding the unusual quantity of potatoes his slaves were preparing to eat with this infernal banquet. We talked coolly with him on the subject; for as we could not prevent what had taken place, we were resolved to learn (if possible) the whole particulars. Atoi at first tried to make us believe he knew nothing about it, and that it was only a meal for his slaves; but we had ascertained it was for himself and his favourite companions. After various endeavours to conceal the fact, Atoi frankly owned that he was only waiting till the cooking was completed to partake of it. He added, that knowing the horror we Europeans held these feasts in, the natives were always most anxious to conceal them from us, and he was very angry that it had come to our knowledge; but, as he had acknowledged the fact, he had no objection to talk about it. He told us that human flesh required a greater number of hours to cook than any other; that if not done enough, it was very tough, but when sufficiently cooked it was as tender as paper. He held in his hand a piece of paper, which he tore in illustration of his remark. He said the flesh then preparing would not be ready till next morning; but one of his sisters whispered in my ear that her brother was deceiving us, as they intended feasting at sun-set.

We enquired why and how he had murdered the poor girl.

He replied, that running away from him to her own relations was her only crime. He then took us outside his village, and showed us the post to which she had been tied, and laughed to think how he had cheated her.

'For,' said he, 'I told her I only intended to give her a flogging; but I fired, and shot her through the heart!'

My blood ran cold at this relation, and I looked with feelings of horror at the savage while he related it. Shall I be credited when I again affirm, that he was not only a handsome young man, but mild and genteel in his demeanour? He was a man we had admitted to our table, and was a general favourite with us all; and the poor victim to his bloody cruelty was a pretty girl of about sixteen years of age!

While listening to this frightful detail, we felt sick almost to fainting. We left Atoi, and again strolled towards the spot where this disgusting mess was cooking. Not a native was now near it: a hot fetid steam kept occasionally bursting from the smothered mass; and the same dog we had seen with the head, now crept from beneath the bushes, and sneaked towards the village: to add to the gloominess of the whole, a large hawk rose heavily from the very spot where the poor victim had been cut in pieces. My friend and I sat gazing on this melancholy place; it was a lowering gusty day, and the moaning of the wind through the bushes, as it swept round the hill on which we were, seemed in unison with our feelings.

After some time spent in contemplating the miserable scene before us, during which we gave full vent to the most passionate exclamations of disgust, we determined to spoil this intended feast: this resolution formed, we rose to execute it. I ran off to our beach, leaving Duke on guard, and, collecting all the white men I could, I informed them of what had happened, and asked them if they would assist in destroying the oven, and burying the remains of the girl: they consented, and each having provided himself with a shovel or a pickaxe, we repaired in a body to the spot. Atoi and his friends had by some means been informed of our intention, and they came out to prevent it. He used various threats to deter us, and seemed highly indignant; but as none of his followers appeared willing to come to blows, and seemed ashamed that such a transaction should have been discovered by us, we were permitted by them to do as we chose. We accordingly dug a tolerably deep grave; then we resolutely attacked the oven.

On removing the earth and leaves, the shocking spectacle was presented to our view, the four quarters of a human body half roasted. During our work clouds of steam enveloped us, and the disgust created by our task was almost overpowering. We collected all the parts we could recognise; the heart was placed separately, we supposed, as a savoury morsel for the chief himself.

We placed the whole in the grave, which we filled up as well as we could, and then broke and scattered the oven.

A keen observer of everything he saw, Earle described a Māori celebration:

I was much amused with the punctilios used in the visit of ceremony paid to King George. Shunghie, accompanied by about a dozen of his chiefs, advanced towards our settlement, leaving their guns and hatchets behind them: as they approached, all our tribe discharged their pieces in the air. When they met, all rubbed noses (a ceremony never to be dispensed with on formal occasions). They were then conducted by King George to his huts on the beach; and in the enclosure in front of them the warriors squatted on the ground. Shunghie, being tabooed, or under the immediate protection of their Atua or God, still sat apart. Then the mother of George, called Tururo, or the Queen, and who is regarded quite as a Sybil [prophet] by the whole tribe, approached Shunghie with the greatest respect and caution, and seated herself some paces from his feet. She then began, with a most melancholy cadence (her eyes streaming with tears and fixed upon the ground) the song of welcome. All their meetings of ceremony or friendship begin with the shedding of copious floods of tears; and as Shunghie's visit was such an unhoped for and unexpected honour, so much greater in proportion was the necessity for their lamentations. This woeful song lasted half an hour, and all the assembly were soon in tears; and though at first I was inclined to turn it into ridicule, I was soon in the same state myself. The pathetic strain, and the scene altogether, was most impressive. As the song proceeded, I was informed of the nature of the subject, which was a theme highly calculated to affect all present. She began by complimenting the wounded warrior, deploring the incurable state of his wound, and regretting that God was wanting him, and was about so soon to take him from his friends! Then she recounted some of his most celebrated deeds of valour; naming and deploring the number of his friends who had fallen bravely in the wars, and lamenting that the enemies who had killed them were still living! This part seemed to affect them powerfully; and when Tururo ceased her song (being quite exhausted) they all rose, thus demonstrating their respect and approbation.

This was followed by a general attack upon the good things king George had prepared for them. The slaves came flocking in, bearing baskets of hot cameras [sweet potatoes], potatoes, and fish. I observed their tears had not spoiled their appetites: they ate voraciously.

After having done great honour to the feast, they all stayed on their feet for a dance, which lasted a long while, and with which they concluded the evening.

The dances of all savage nations are beautiful, but those of the New Zealanders partake also of the horrible. The regularity of their movements is truly astonishing; and the song, which always accompanies a dance, is most harmonious. They soon work themselves up to a pitch of phrensy; the distortions of woe and body are truly dreadful, and fill the mind with horror. Love and war are the subjects of their songs and dances; but the details of the latter passion are by far the most popular among them. I was astonished to find that their women mixed in the dance indiscriminately with the men, and went through all those horrid gestures with seemingly as much pleasure as the warriors themselves.

Augustus Earle – Amoko, Eana, Hepee.

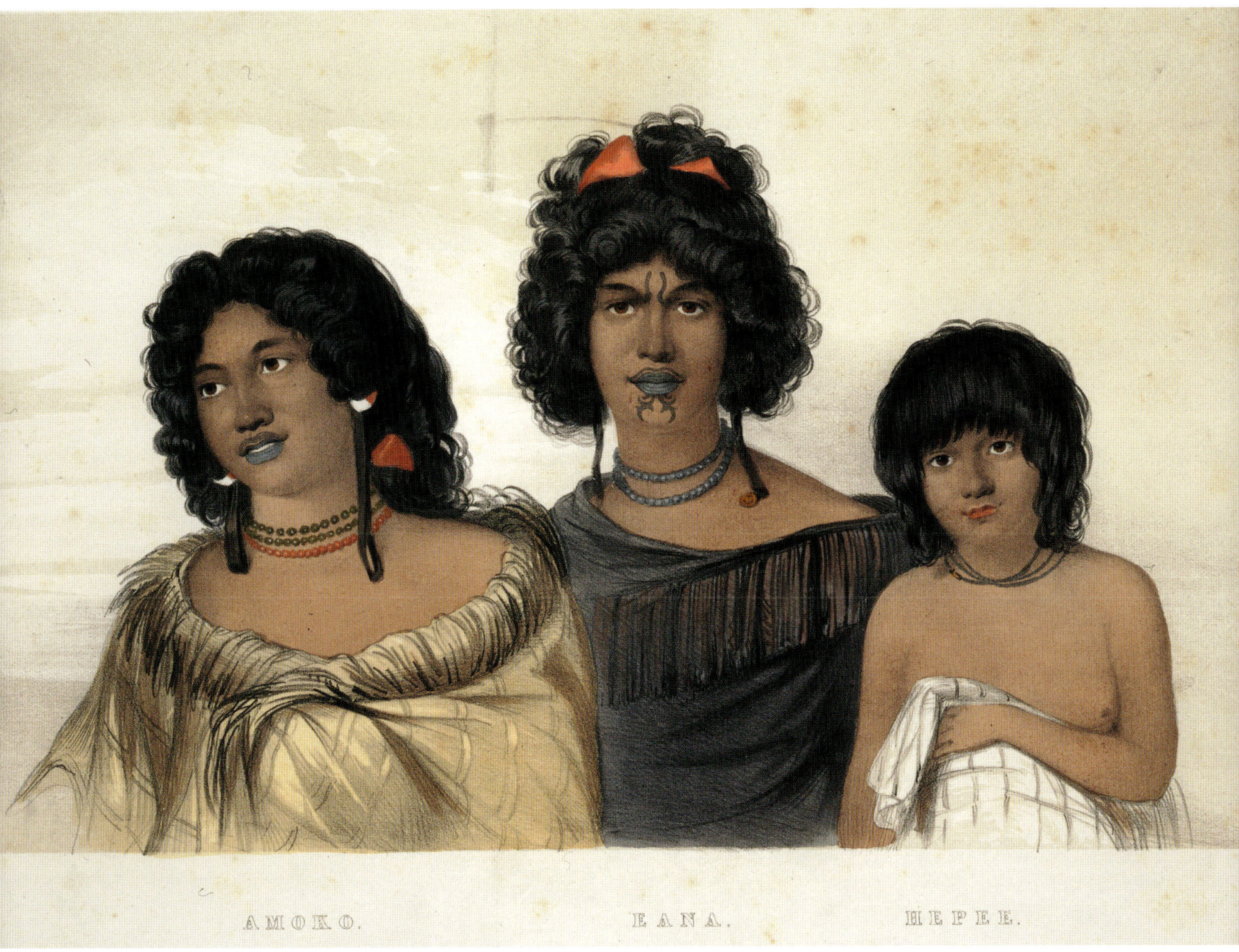

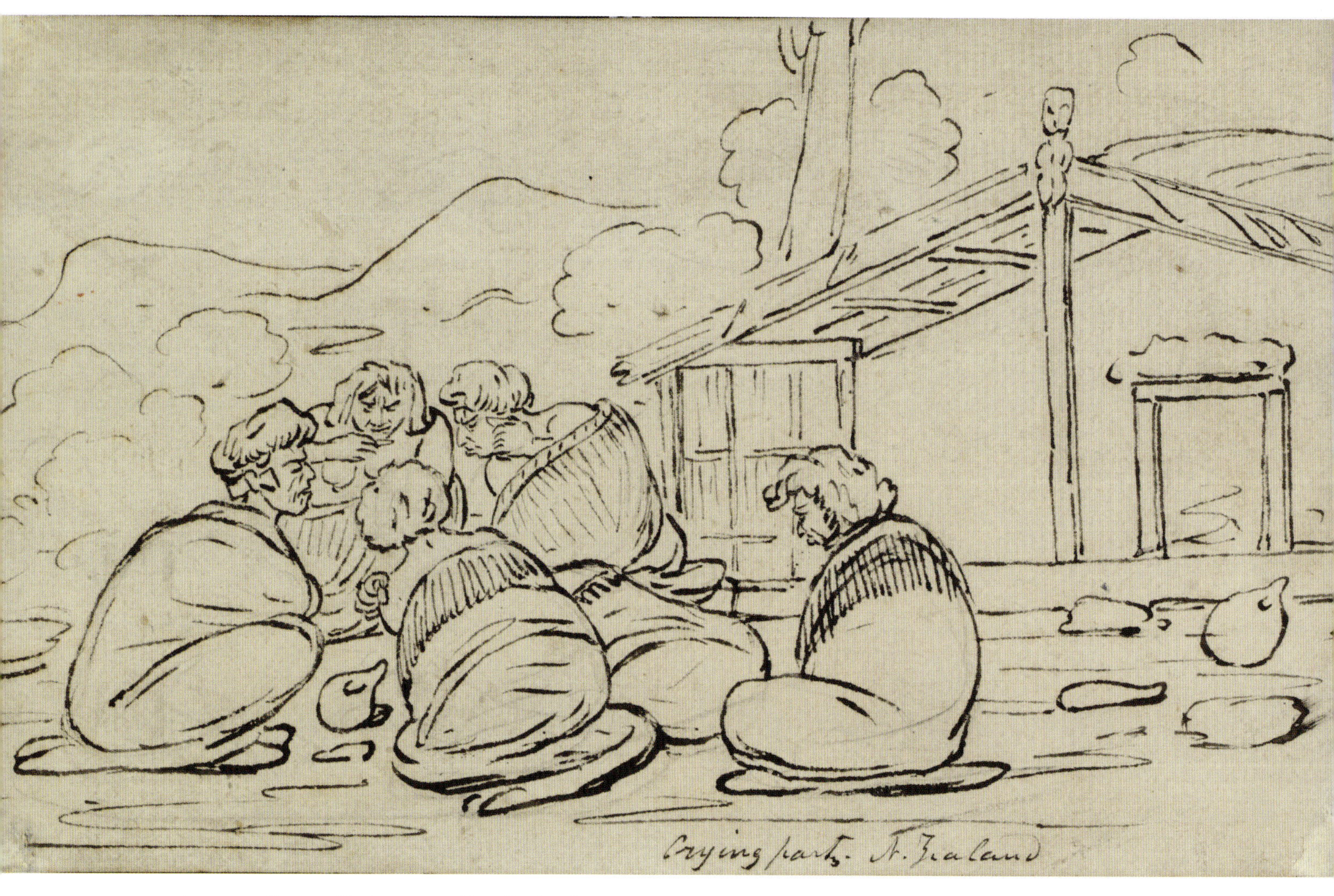

Augustus Earle – Crying party, New Zealand.

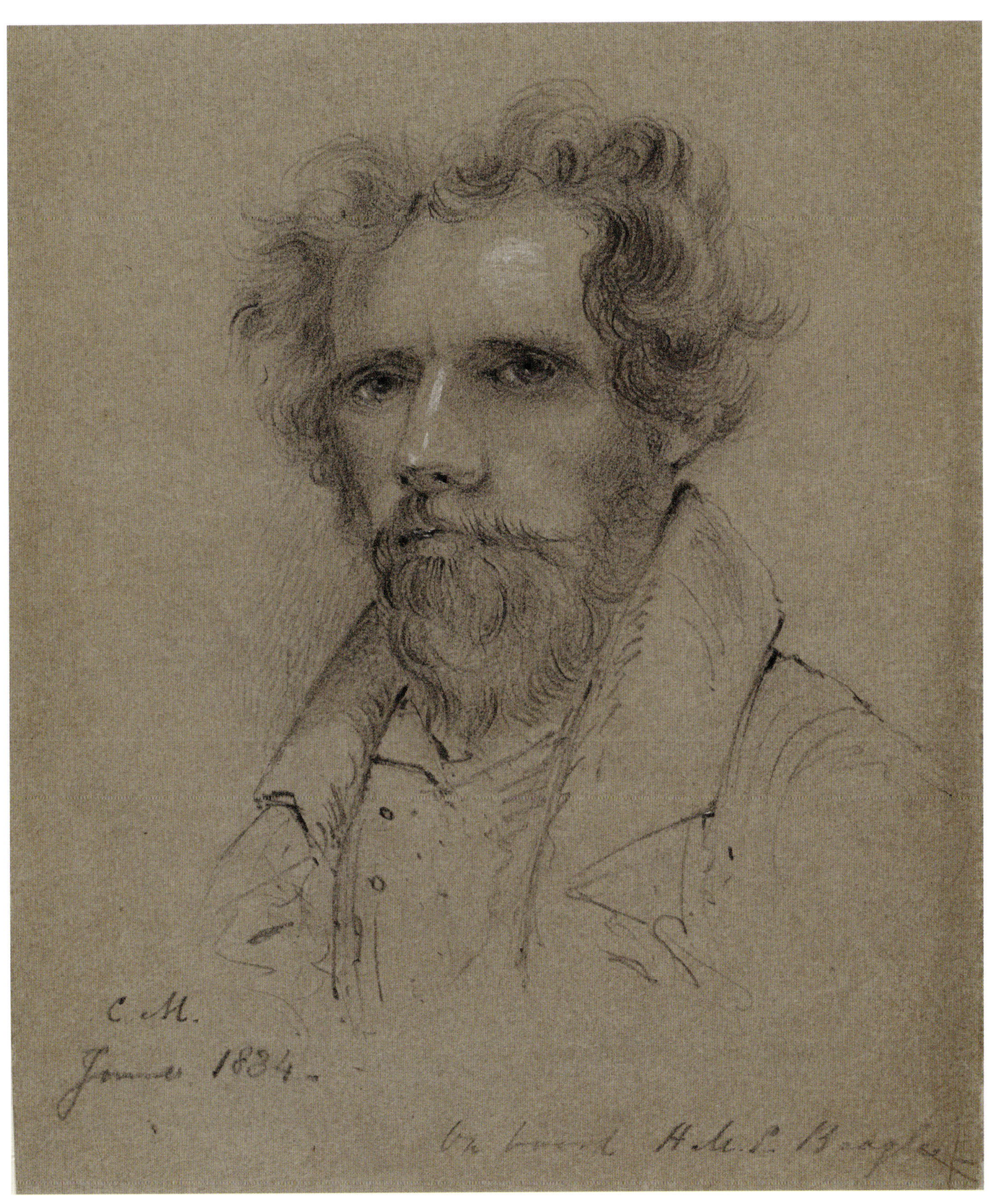

Conrad Martens – Conrad Martens on board the HMAS *Beagle*.

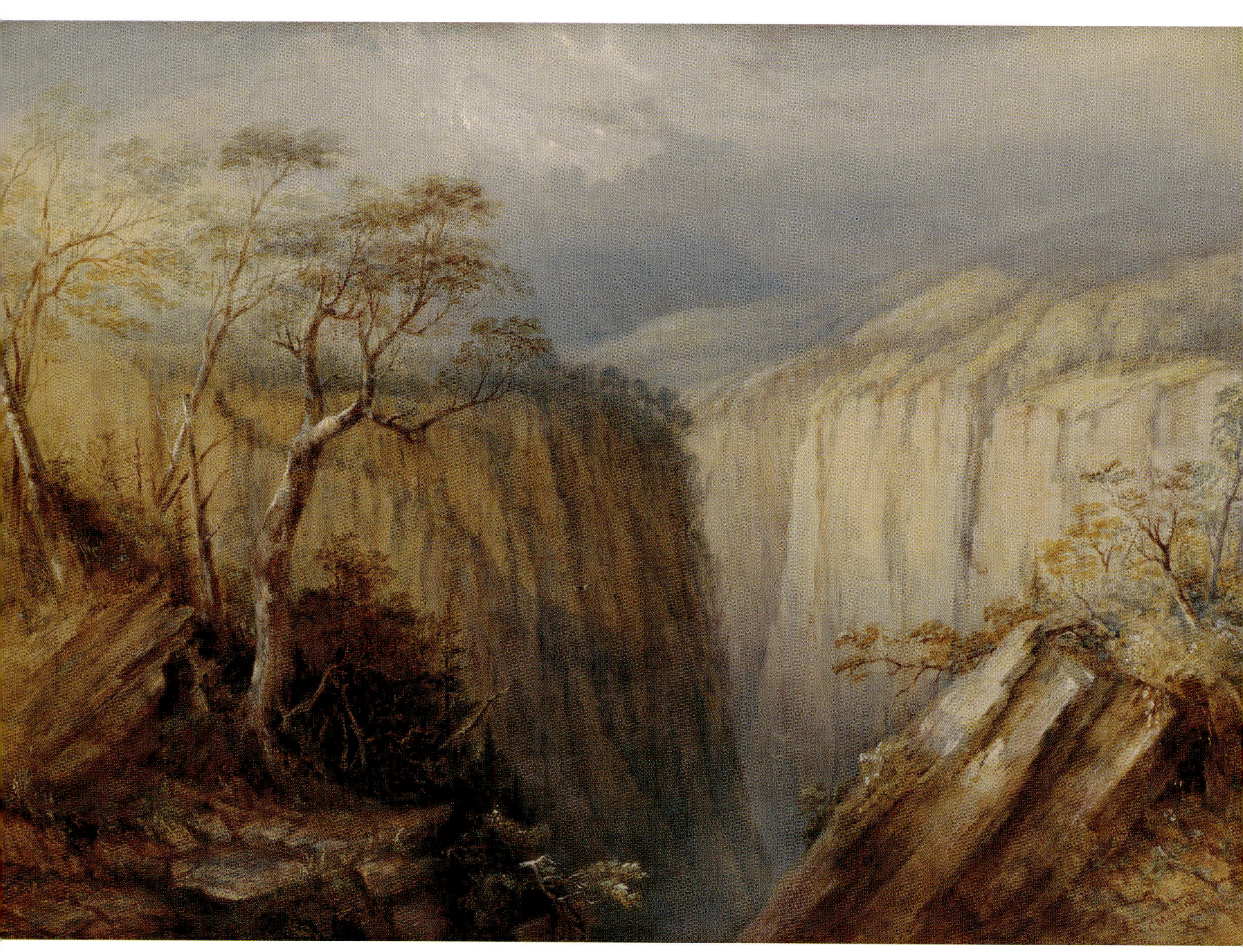

Conrad Martens – Apsley Falls, NSW.

Conrad Martens – View of Sydney Harbour.

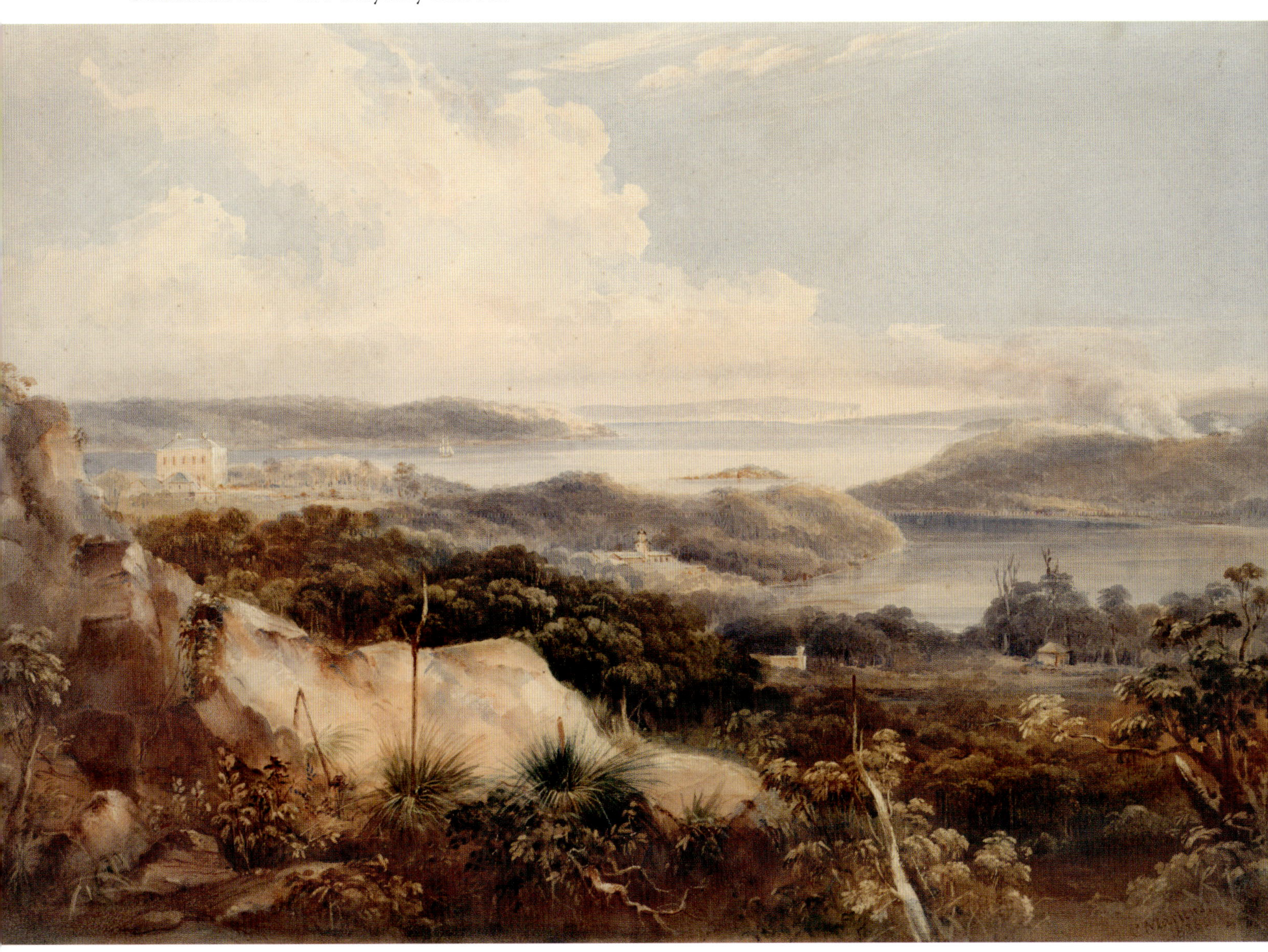

The next morning I was awakened, at daybreak, by the most dismal sounds I had
ever heard. I started up, and found it proceeded from the tribes parting with each
other. They had divided themselves into little parties, each forming a circle; and
were crying most piteously, and cutting their flesh as a cook would score pork for
roasting. On such occasions each is armed with a sharp shell, or, if he can possibly
obtain so valuable a prize, a piece of a broken glass bottle. All were streaming
with tears and blood, while Shunghie and his friends embarked in their large
and richly ornamented canoes, and sailed from our beach. After his departure, I
soon discovered that, notwithstanding their apparent affection, King George and
his friends were most happy their visitors had left them; and that it was more the
dread of Shunghie's power, than love for him, that induced them to treat him with
such respect and homage. I made several excursions into the interior, and each
confirmed me in the good opinion I had formed of the natives. I felt myself quite
safe amongst them. There is a great peculiarity in rambling quiet this country;
namely, the total absence of quadrupeds. There are abundance of birds, which are
so numerous at times as these to darken the air – many of them possessing very
sweet notes; and wild ducks, teal, &c. cover the various streams. Wherever I went
I did not discover any grass; almost every part being covered either with fern or
Flax; the former yielding the natives their principal article of food, and the latter
their clothing. To this dearth of animals may be attributed the chief cause of their
ferocity, and propensity to cannibalism.

Returning to Sydney, Earle finally headed home in late 1828, stopping at Guam, the
Caroline Islands, Manila and Singapore, before visiting Madras and Pondicherry, then
reaching England after a final stop in Mauritius. But the next year he was recruited
to the *Beagle* as one of the natural history artists. The main task of HMS *Beagle*,
captained by Robert Fitzroy, was to continue the extraordinarily detailed survey of
the lands of the Southern Ocean which had been supported by British Admiralty ever
since the voyages of Captain Cook more than half a century earlier. But *Beagle* carried
a passenger who was to use his study of the creatures and the lands he found in the
voyage to totally change mankind's understanding of our world – Charles Darwin.

Earle, however, was to see none of this. He fell ill, and left *Beagle* at Rio to go home.
Earle's misfortune was, however, opportune for another artist, the half German, half
English Conrad Martens, who was already working in South America. He applied for
the post, and was given it.

Martens was to record many of the places *Beagle* was surveying. But he also
accompanied Darwin when, given the slightest opportunity, the great naturalist went
ashore. He was one of the party which Darwin took 250 miles up the Santa Cruz

river and back – utterly unknown territory at the time. Martens, who contributed a significant collection of drawings and paintings to Darwin's published work, ended up in Australia, where he married and established a successful career painting Sydney scenes and landscapes.

Earle, still a relatively young man, died in 1838. But he was probably by then the most travelled English artist of any era, having ventured to the remotest places to record what he saw. And, of course, he left a vast treasury of drawings and paintings from the voyages which had taken him right round the world.

Augustus Earle – Native village and cowdie forest.

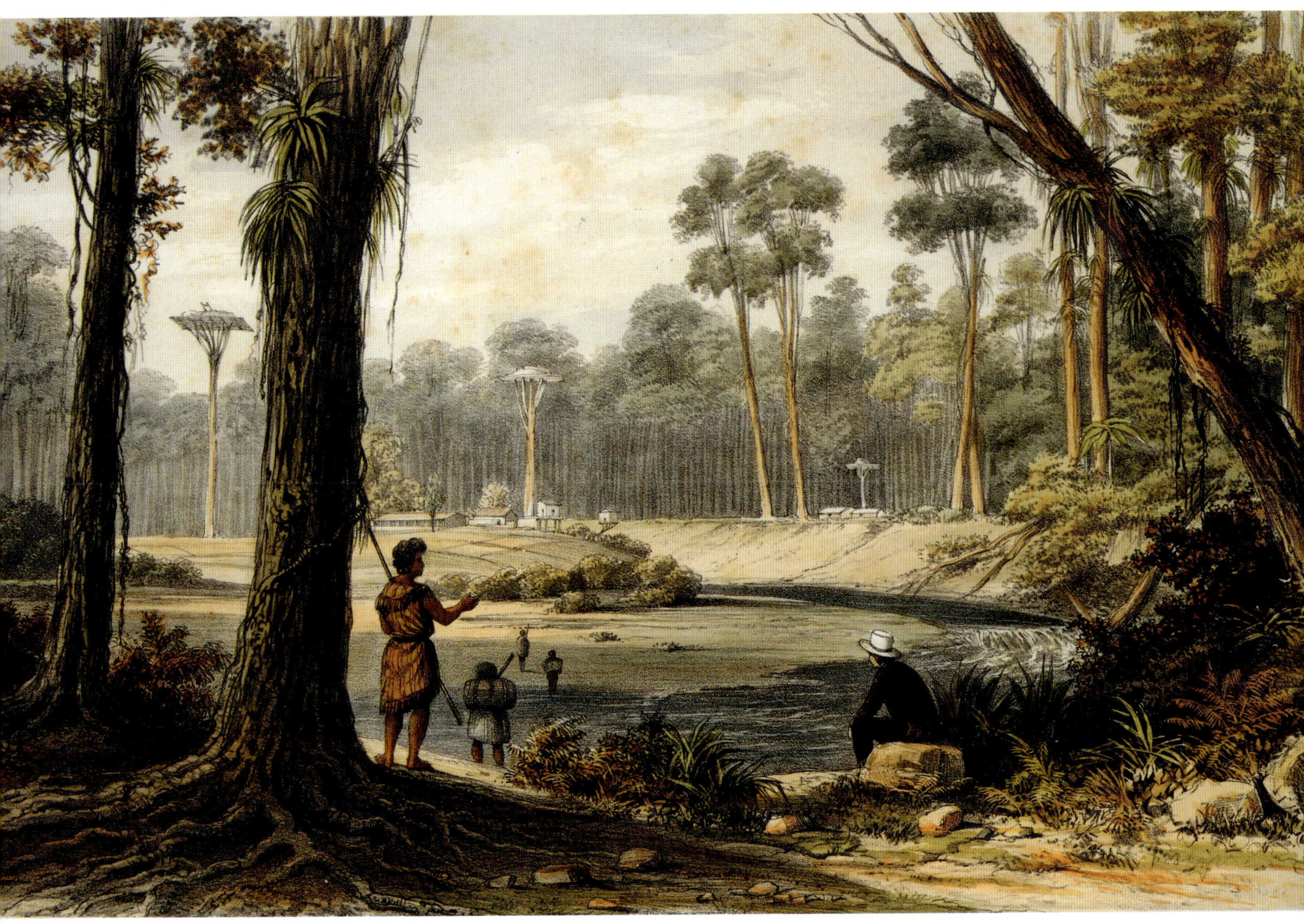

Chapter 6

Heaphy and New Zealand

Not many artists have won the Victoria Cross. And when Charles Heaphy applied in 1839 to join the determinedly commercial New Zealand Company, the requirement to exhibit valour was certainly not in the job description. It was a straightforward joint stock company with shareholders and a board of directors drawn from London city grandees and Members of Parliament. They had managed to persuade the British Government that they could buy land in New Zealand from the Māoris and lay out garden towns, with allotments of land which could then be sold to British investors and worked by emigrants, many of them convicted men, who would be allowed to earn enough to buy land themselves.

The company needed publicity back home to entice further settlers, and thus it was that Charles Heaphy found himself in the fleet of three ships which arrived in 1839, with a brief to paint the delights of this new promised land. And indeed, he soon produced pictures which proved very appealing back home in Britain. He painted what was to become the town of Nelson, apparently with rather more ships than were actually there in the harbour. His pictures of the extraordinary Mount Egmont transfixed critics in Britain. But he also showed the early settlers at work, felling the forests and clearing the land.

Heaphy remained committed to his new country for the rest of his life, undertaking expeditions, painting the then unknown west coast, joining the militia and becoming a Member of Parliament. It was as a militiaman that he was called up for one of the Māori wars and earned his Victoria Cross by protecting and rescuing a wounded comrade under intense attack from Māori warriors.

Heaphy was still a teenager when he arrived in New Zealand. But he immediately started not only painting and sketching his new found land, but also recording in diary form the situation he found there, for example the fractious and difficult relationship between Māoris and missionaries.

The new settlers, under the auspices of the New Zealand Company, established a convention by which land was bought from the Māoris while continuing to protect their rights. Heaphy's pictures reflect how rapidly this system allowed the new economy to grow. The felling and working of the kauri trees show the production of spars and planking, which were already in demand by ships going to and from Australia and the

Opposite: Charles Heaphy – Te Puni Māori Chief.

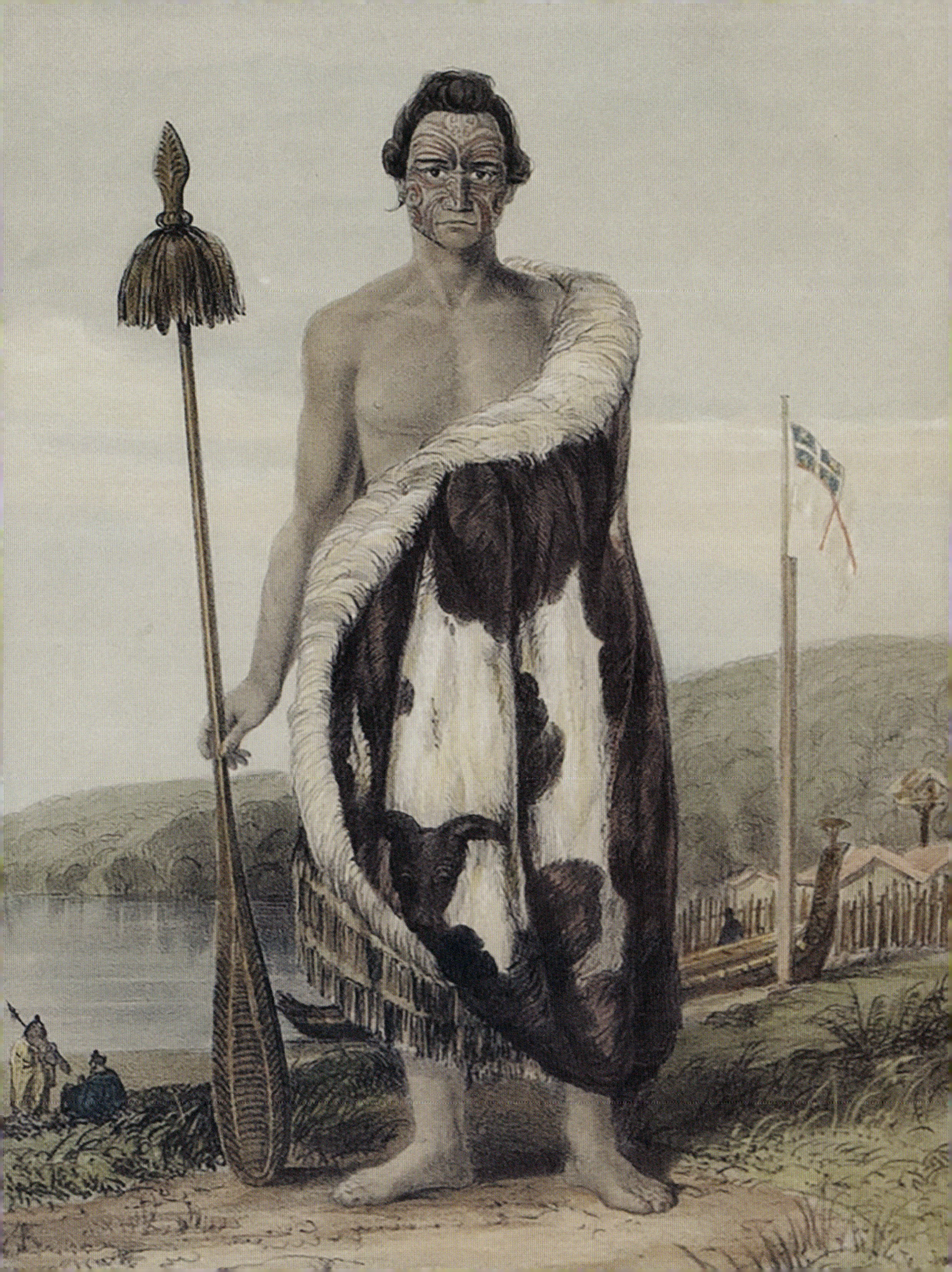

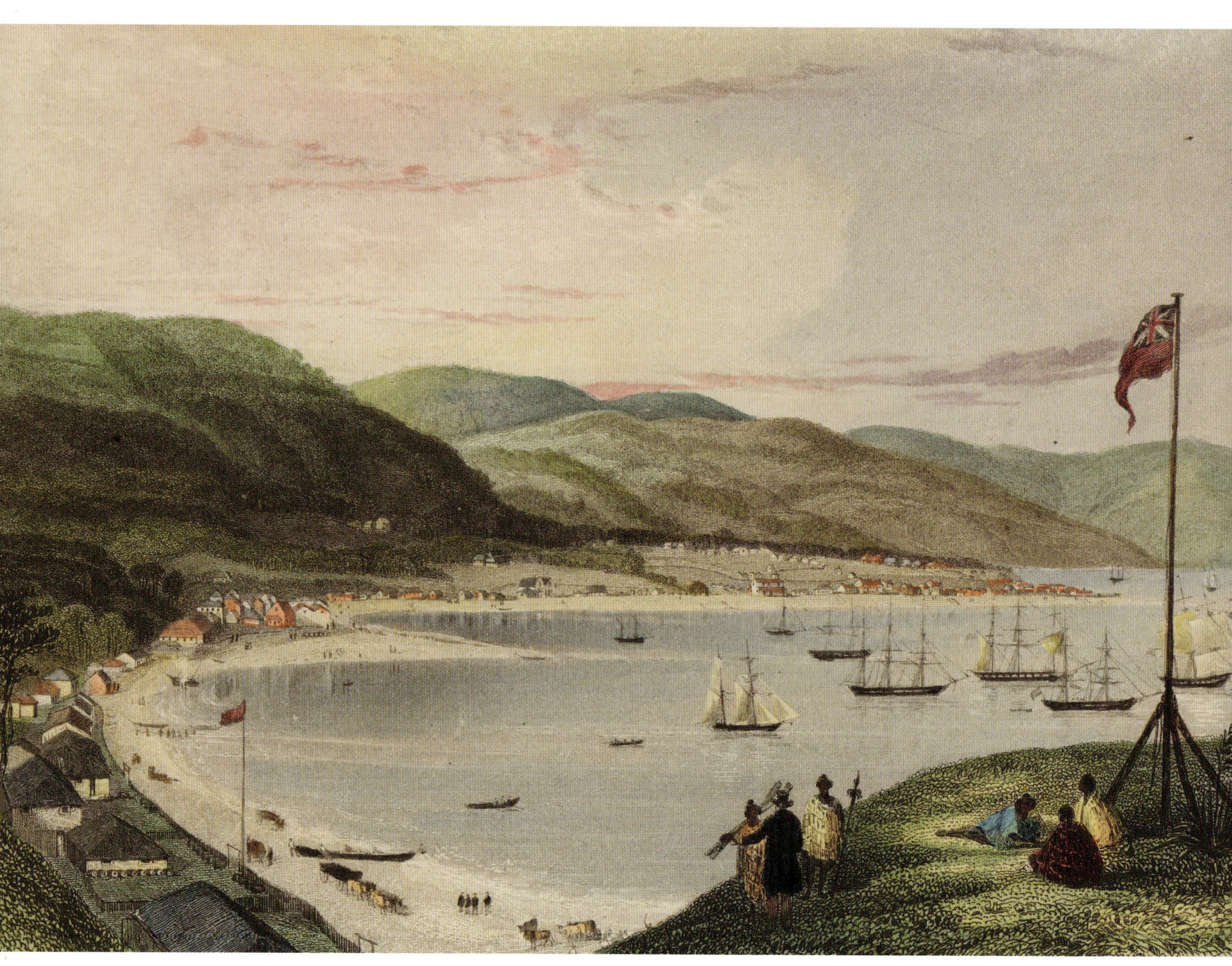

Charles Heaphy – Part of Lambton Harbour, in Port Nicholson, New Zealand; comprehending about one third of the water frontage of the town of Wellington.

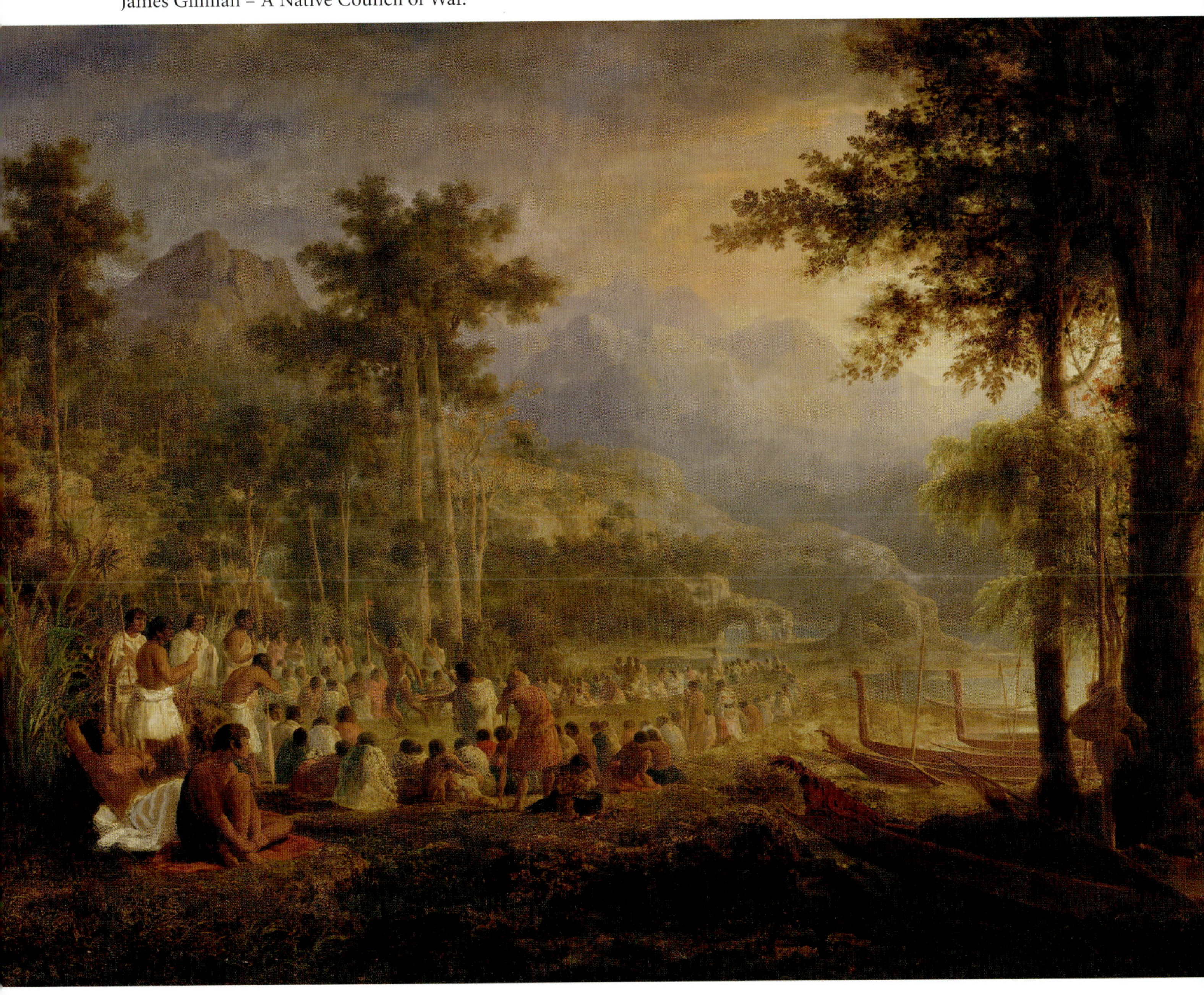

James Gilfillan – A Native Council of War.

Southern Ocean. His picture of Wellington Harbour, perhaps a little exaggerated, shows an already busy port.

These were the images which within months were being shipped back home and used to entice what soon became a flood of emigrants to the new colony. Heaphy's pictures reinforced the vision of New Zealand as a fertile land of bucolic bliss and a cooperative, unthreatening native population. He was of course to discover for himself the fragility of such assumptions. The Māori wars, in which he was to find himself involved and ultimately decorated with the Victoria Cross, displayed the ferocity and determination which the Māoris could command.

Other artists, too, beguiled by the alluring tales and inspiring pictures of the colony, were tempted to try their luck in this farthest land. James Alexander Gilfillan was already an established artist in Britain; indeed, he had been appointed Professor of Painting at the University of Glasgow, after serving for eight years in the Royal Navy. Yet in 1841 he persuaded himself that New Zealand offered better prospects. He embarked with his wife and four children on the dauntingly long trip and was duly rewarded with an allotment of more than a hundred acres in what became known as the Matarawa Valley. By 1847 the family had established a successful farm there.

Then in the middle of April, with signs of unrest among the Māoris at this occupation of their land, the farm was attacked. Gilfillan seems to have believed that he was the intended target, having been a vocal spokesman for the new colonists in the area. So he made his way to nearby Wanganui, where there were armed police and troops, believing that the Māoris would not hurt his womenfolk. But when he came back the next day he found his wife and three daughters murdered and a fourth badly injured.

Not surprisingly, Gilfillan abandoned the farm and left for Australia, where he became a respected figure in the art world. However, the picture that first made his name there was a large, peaceful scene of a Māori Native Council, with no hint of the shadow and violence that the Māoris had inflicted on the artist's own life.

*   *   *

Although a generation had passed since Augustus Earle recorded his journeys through the unknown land of New Zealand, there was still much wild country which Heaphy was determined to portray. The mountain which became known as Egmont was an early subject:

> On visiting the northern parts of the island, which we did after having acquired the various districts around Cook's Strait most suitable for colonisation, it became apparent to us that the country beyond Mount Egmont, or, at the farthest, Kafia,

was not at all adapted for immediate settlement, on account of the absence of good harbours. The land around Mount Egmont was the finest which we had seen in New Zealand; but in consequence of the insecurity of the anchorage, many objections presented themselves to its immediately becoming the scene of the Company's operations.

But Heaphy was fascinated by how the skills of carpentry, forestry and even quite ambitious ship-building had established themselves in the early colonist communities:

From the Kauarapawa settlement upwards, the scenery on both sides of the river is most magnificent. Sometimes on one side, sometimes on the other, huge amphitheatrical ridges rise from the water's edge to the height of 800 or 1,000 feet, covered with nothing but fern, except close to the water, where a little terraced flat leaves room, in places, for a few stunted trees and a native plantation of corn, kumeras [sweet potato] or potatoes. On the opposite side a hill rising more gradually to an equal height is clothed, from its top to the water's edge, with the most magnificent specimen of New Zealand forest, except where the native's axe had cleared a patch for cultivation, or where a cliff of white sandstone peeps through the foliage. Here and there, of course, you open a gulley or valley, according to the size of the watercourse, which either brawls over the blocks of stone which it has rolled to its mouth, or trickles from the face of an overhanging cliff covered with moss; and in other places, at a bend of the river, the mountainous ridge strikes straight across, leaving a semicircular flat varying in size from four to twenty or even 100 acres. On these flats there is generally a settlement and plantations. Picture to yourself this scenery, enlivened by the Indian corn and potato fields of the natives on either side; the little villages varying from two or three huts, to the fortified pah on a terraced hill, which can muster its 100 fighting men; and canoes resembling the Canadian 'dug-out' loaded to the water's brim with pigs, potatoes, fern, kumeras, corn, pumpkins, calabashes, water-melons, and baskets full of the kernel of the krakaberry, which meet you in every reach, with the everlasting greeting of 'Naumai, or 'tena-koit-ou, 'welcome' or 'hail to you, and exchange, as they pass, the news up and down the river. The part of the river here described is from forty to seventy miles distant from the sea: beyond this the country opens on each side of the river, disclosing the Tongariro, rising isolated from the centre of an immense plain.

Heaphy was contracted to provide illustrations which would attract a full range of colonists, people who might establish businesses which could deliver serious dividends

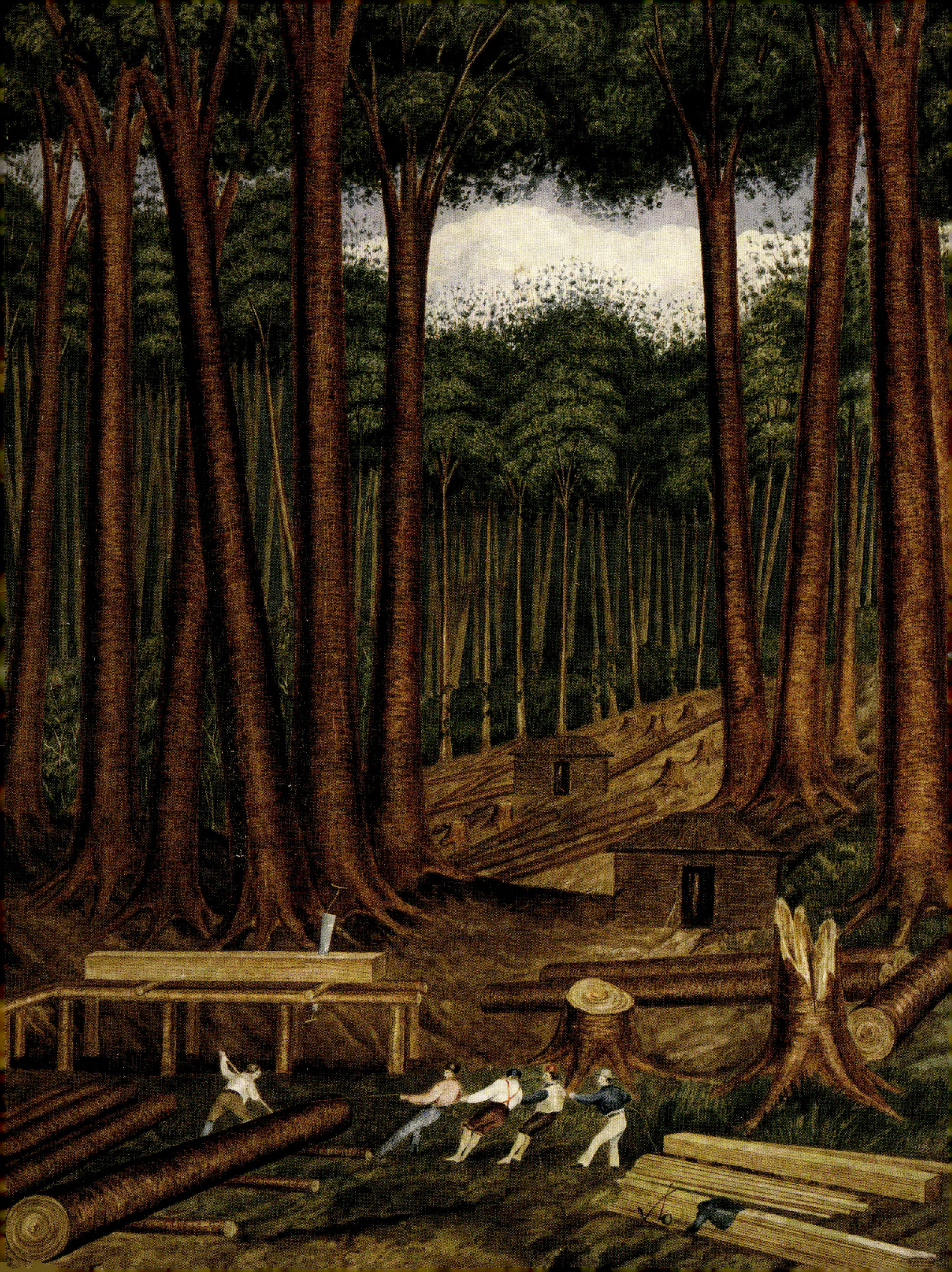

to the shareholders back home in England. Hence the harbours which would become
Nelson and Wellington were drawn in the most appealing way, and his overhead view
of Port Nicholson suggests an already comfortable, settled landscape.

His painting of the kauri forest workers is a hive of activity. In the foreground are
five men moving a log with ropes. Beyond them is a saw-pit with prepared timber, and
there is further timber cut into planks in the right foreground, with two axes and a
jacket. There are two millers' huts, many trunks and tree stumps, and large stands of
kauri trees.

Towards the end of his life Heaphy reflected on the changes he had seen since he
arrived as a young man:

The forest was more undisturbed. Along the eastern shore, from the mouth of the
Hutt River to outside of Ward Island, the forest was uninterrupted, and the trees
overhung the water, giving shelter to great numbers of wild fowl.

The forest was then teeming with birds. Of twelve or fourteen species of small
birds that were then to be seen in every wood, only the tui, the fly-catcher, and the
wren, with the sandlark, in the open, are now common, while the robin, the bell-
bird, the titmouse, the thrush, the popokatea, the tiraweke, and the riroriro, are
rarely seen or have entirely passed away.

Charles Heaphy concluded his account of the country as follows:

From my statements and descriptions contained in the preceding pages, it may be
imagined that I am prejudiced against the Local Government in New Zealand, as
also against the settlement which it has founded; and that the same cause has led
me to condemn the missionaries.

This, however, is not the case. The conduct of Capt. Hobson and his subordinates
is alike censured in every part of the country, and the dislike and dissatisfaction
evinced by all classes in the colony, amounts to something more than the effects of
mere prejudice. Can any of Capt. Hobson's party state where he is popular? At Port
Nicholson, the seat of half the white population of the island? It may be that he is
popular there, but it scarcely appeared, on their visits to that place, that either he
or his Colonial Secretary were. Is he beloved at the Bay of Islands? His suppression
of the people's press there was not the way to ensure their attachment, and the
letters which are continually being received, by the Wellington settlers, demanding
their commiseration and support, do not lead us to suppose that his method has
succeeded.

Opposite: Charles Heaphy – Kauri forest, Wairoa River, Kaipara.

Are the settlers at Nelson predisposed in his favour? It is undoubtedly true that to his throwing obstacles in the way of their location at the place proposed, they are indebted for the discovery of the splendid district which they now occupy; but this fortuitous circumstance is not the result of any great regard for their welfare.

Turn to his own fostered settlement: no doubt the officials there are friendly to themselves, but are the inhabitants generally? If the paper there is a popular one, (and unless supported by Government it is impossible for any other to exist in a colony), he is not even in Auckland esteemed in his public capacity; as all the political articles in that paper are condemnatory of his measures and government.

Amongst whom then is he popular? With none but his dependants.

Never had a governor better opportunity of cultivating the esteem of those whom he was appointed to govern. On his arriving in the country, the settlers – who had so long been beyond the protection of the British law, whose property had been insecure, and whose land was until then comparatively worthless – hailed the event as most propitious to their interests, and received the representative of the Crown with every demonstration of respect and support: now, it is not too much to say that three-fourths of them most fervently desire his removal. This must be the effect of real oppression; not of imaginary grievances.

That I am prejudiced against all but the Company's settlements I most decidedly deny. I believe Auckland to be well situated, and that it will, in all probability, become an important and valuable colony; and I think it likely that if the locality had not been pre-occupied it would have been chosen as the site of New Plymouth, or some other of the Company's townships; but I cannot think that it is a proper place for the seat of government, nor do I believe that it will, for any length of time, remain the capital. I consider, also, that the other settlements in the northern part of the island will prosper: they each possess a valuable article for exportation, immediately attainable, which will support them through the first years of their existence; and although there may be attendant disadvantages, they present many inducements to the immigrant.

As to the missionaries, although the objects of the society in England are undoubtedly praiseworthy, all who are acquainted with must condemn their practices in the colony. Every one, not connected with their interest, who has returned from New Zealand, can bear witness to the fact that the natives have received no physical benefit from their religious instruction. If, in the course of twenty-eight years, the missionaries, who have spent as much money on their colonial establishment in New Zealand as the settlement of Wellington cost founding, have been unable to ameliorate the condition of the aborigines by the operation of their plan, which is to teach them doctrine and 'chance' their improvement, it is time that they should adopt the other principle, of civilizing them first, and then improving their morals.

As regards the parts of New Zealand, or the various settlements, which offer the most advantages to the immigrant, persons who have seen the country may hold various opinions, but they all agree that it is well adapted generally for colonisation. For my part, I am of opinion, that to the agriculturist, or breeder of stock, the settlements around Cook's Straits offer at present the most advantages.

To the immigrant of small capital, the country by the Wanganui river, or at Nelson, is the most suitable, as it can be cleared and cultivated with the least outlay. To the settler possessed of more means, and who are not necessitated to look for immediate dependence to the soil, I would recommend the country around Port Nicholson, as being preferable on account of its extreme fertility. For rearing herds, the countries of Nelson, Wanganui, Manewatu, and New Plymouth are best adapted; and to this branch of farming I think the settler should particularly direct his attention, as it is a pursuit which, I am confident, will always prove of profit to himself, and of service to the community.

There are now no apparent obstacles to the progress of the Colony. At Wellington, in particular, the settlers have had much to discourage them; but the crisis is now past, and every thing appears in a fair way for the speedy realisation of their prospects. As in all new colonies, capital is wanted in the various settlements; but the establishment of a loan bank, which is in contemplation, for advancing money upon landed security, will much assist the small capitalist, and cause the whole of the available land around each township speedily to become settled, and of value.

It is satisfactory to find, that of seven persons now in England who have been resident in Wellington, four intend immediately returning, being perfectly satisfied with the present state of the colony, and confident of its future success. I have no hesitation in saying, that in all the Company's settlements the same sentiments prevail: a few there are, undoubtedly, who are dissatisfied, and who do not neglect to send home grievous accounts of the state of things; but these are invariably men whose irregular course of life in England rendered any change of country, however short the duration, a matter of expediency – persons whose habits caused them to be unfit to remain at home, and whose want of industry and application renders still less fit for a colonial life. I am also certain, that all of those who, after due deliberation, emigrated to New Zealand, with fixed views and intentions respecting their proceedings in that place, and who, since their arrival, have, by an industrious life, endeavoured to realise their expectation, do not now regret the change, but in every way prefer their adopted country.

Chapter 7

North America

Expertise with pencil and brush was highly valued and greatly encouraged by the British Army. Precise and accurate renderings of the terrain over which troops might have to march and fight were of huge advantage to military commanders. Young officers at the Royal Engineers headquarters at Woolwich were given extensive training in cartography, and over the centuries a number of these soldiers proved to be notable artists. Their duties often meant they were among the first to visit the new worlds which were attracting the interest of European explorers, and their pictures were often the first guides to these new lands.

The picture by Captain Thomas Davies is the first known painting of what came to be called Niagara Falls in North America. It is a view from the east side and includes the almost permanent rainbow which crowned the Falls, but it is also a carefully rendered study of two Native Americans. The local people were still a mystery to Europeans when this painting was executed in 1762. The Falls are, of course, now a mark of the frontier between Canada and the United States. But in 1762 they were a prominent feature of the territorial struggle between Britain and France, centred on the fur trade.

Thomas Davies spent several years in these North American landscapes, participating in a number of encounters with the French. But, besides Niagara, he produced admired paintings of a range of American scenes, including the burning of the city of Grimross, and cascade paintings of Casconschlagon.

And he was perhaps the first to convey in his pictures the extraordinary array of autumn and spring colours which, to this day, are the great tourist attraction of the Canadian forests.

Much of Canada remained unknown or unexplored until very late in the nineteenth century. Lucius O'Brien's painting, 'View of the Rockies', was made when he was one of the first travellers on the newly completed Canadian Pacific Railway in 1886. Up to then there had been no route, road or track across the country to the province of British Columbia. Getting there from Ottawa meant a long sea voyage. The new railway had to make its way through Blackfoot Indian country – only after protracted negotiations with the tribe – and then through precipitous Rocky Mountain passes and ravines, and Kicking Horse Pass.

Captain Thomas Davies – An east view of the Great Cataract of Niagara.

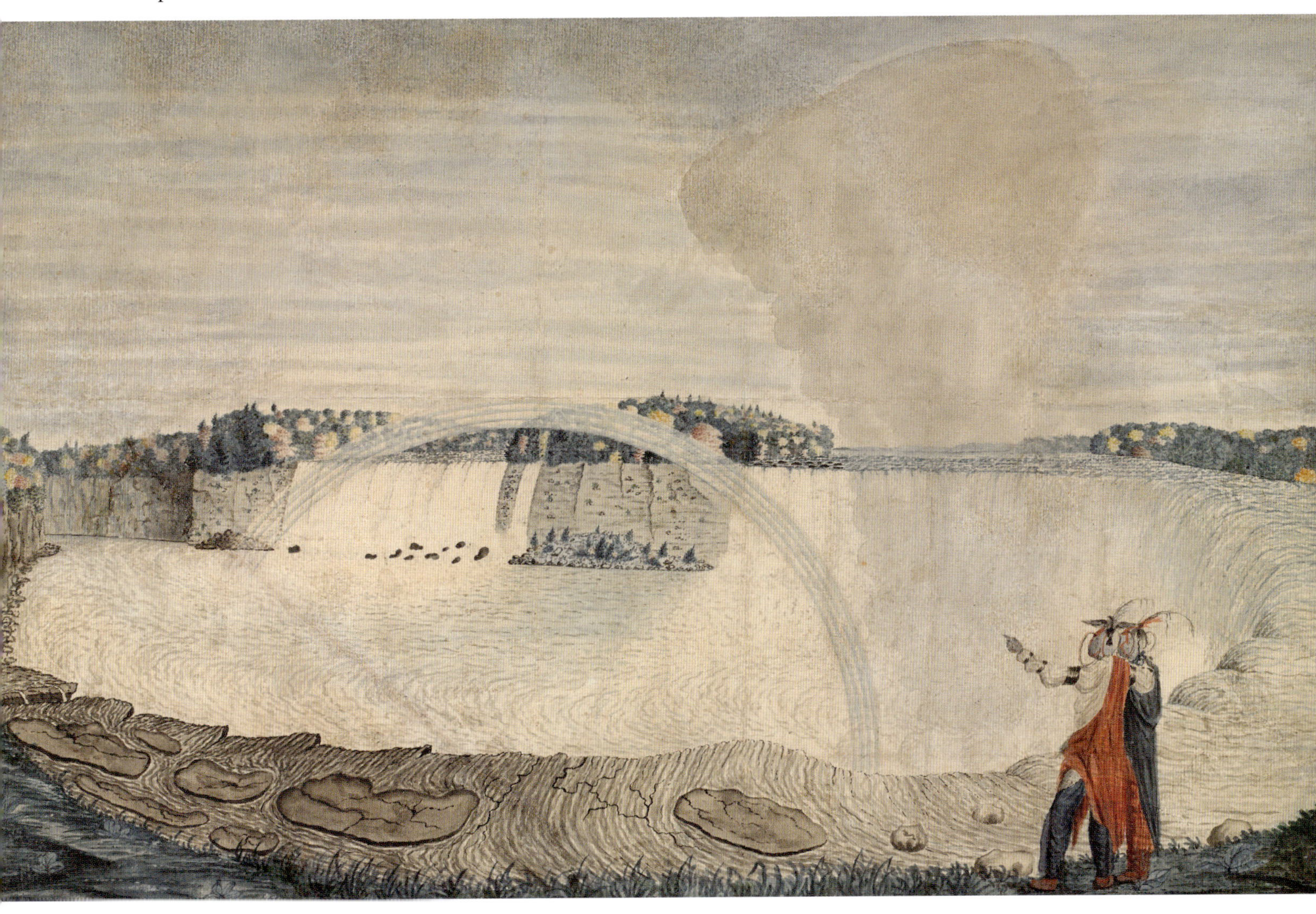

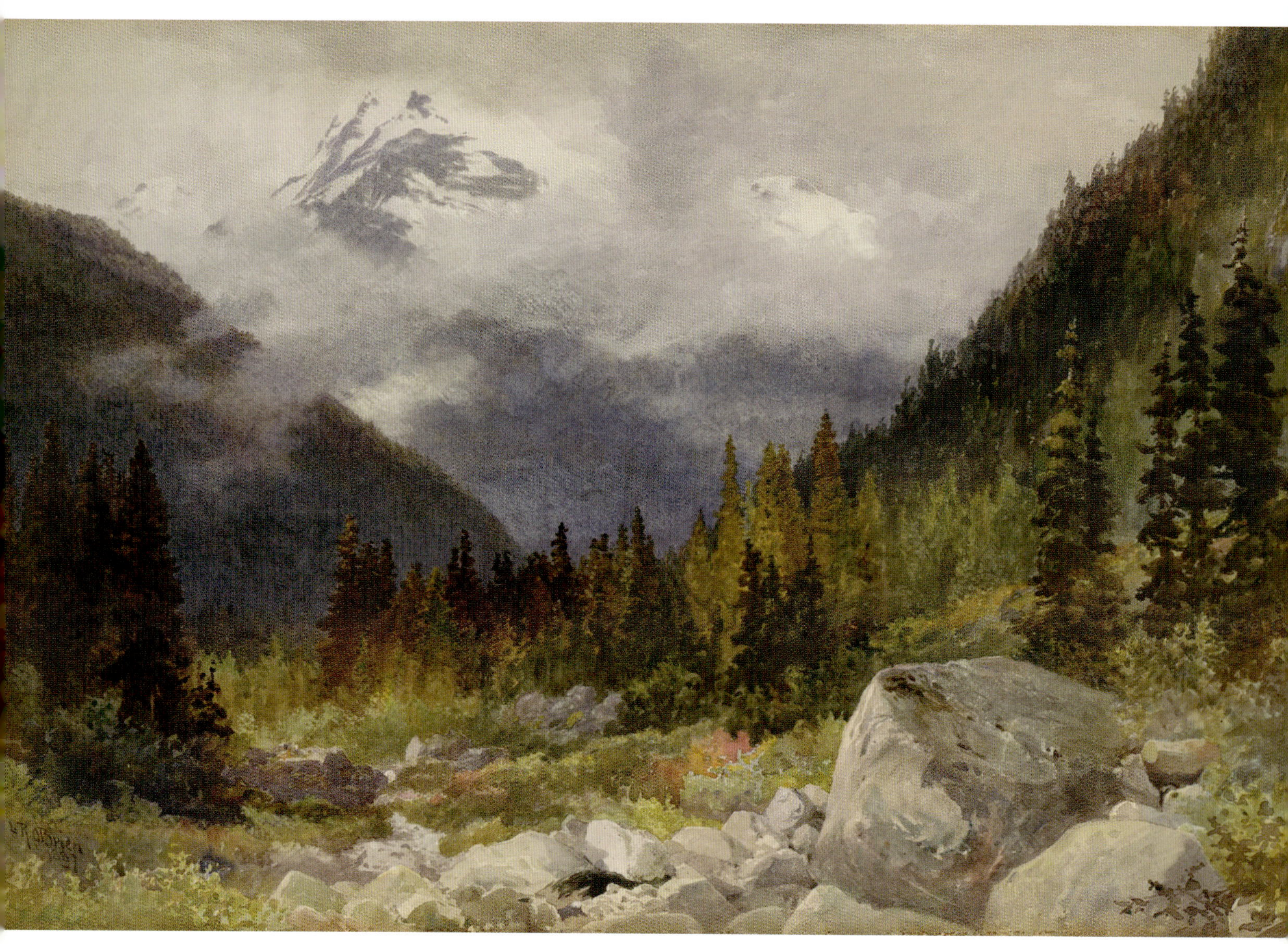

Lucius O'Brien – View of the Rockies.

John Arthur Fraser – Summit Lake near Lenchoile, Bow River, Canadian Pacific Railway.

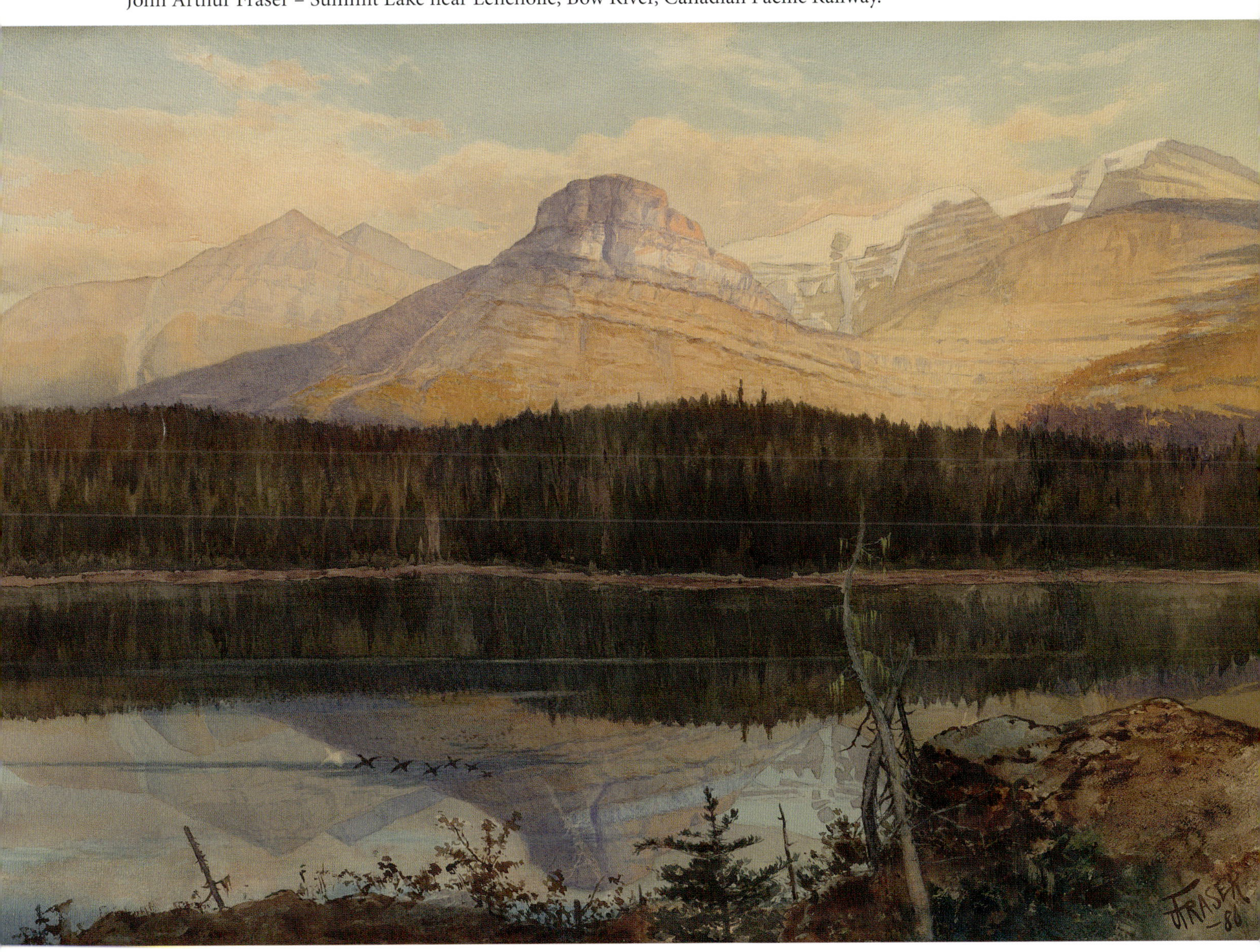

More than 17,000 navvies – mainly Chinese coolies – were employed as the Canadian government tried to deliver on its promise of an overland link to the new province. The O'Brien pictures showed a landscape unknown not only to Europeans, but also to the citizens of eastern Canada.

The railway management, after seeing O'Brien's work, offered free rail passes to a number of artists, including Thomas Mower Martin and John Arthur Fraser, in order to help generate passenger traffic. Fraser travelled all the way to Vancouver and back and produced a host of drawings and paintings which were exhibited in Britain and New York as well as in Canada. His 'Summit above the Bow Lake' was painted at Lenchoile, and such paintings were used by the agents of the railway in Europe to attract immigrants, who were sold a package consisting of a transatlantic ticket on a CPR Liner and a railway ticket on the Canadian Pacific, along with the right to purchase virgin land along the track at 2 dollars 50 cents per acre.

*　*　*

From Viking times, or even earlier, Europeans knew that there was a vast icy landmass to the north. But throughout more than three centuries, as Columbus and his successors tried to find a northern route around the Americas, the Arctic remained impenetrable and mysterious.

The search for a north-west passage to shorten the time it took to get from Europe to the Indies by sailing through the Arctic ice began within a century of Columbus finding America. Exploration in the region went back to the days of the Venetian John Cabot in the late fifteenth century, The English sailor Martin Frobisher, a contemporary of Drake, was the first to set out with that specific aim in mind, although there is reason to suppose that the Vikings, already knowing of Greenland, had made landfall in what is now the Hudson Bay Area. For three hundred years, however, successive attempts by other mariners failed in dramatic, tragic or mysterious ways which entranced the public in Britain, Europe and the United States, and by the early nineteenth century finding the north-west passage was one of the great challenges remaining for explorers.

Having joined the Royal Navy at the age of fourteen, John Franklin served at the Battle of Trafalgar and subsequently became one of the most famous names in polar exploration. In 1818 he was commander of the *Trent*, with orders to sail to the North Pole and thence into the Bering Strait, searching for a route which would connect trade between the Atlantic and Pacific via the Arctic. Knighted in 1829, Franklin was a founding member of the Geographical Society of London, a recipient of the Gold Medal from the Société de Géographie of France, and a natural choice to lead the new expedition in *Erebus* and *Terror* in 1845.

Franklin's ships were last seen by a whaler off Baffin Bay in August 1845, when they had enough supplies to last until summer 1848 – longer than the two summers thought necessary for the exploration of the north-west passage. It is perhaps not surprising that John Ross's initial offer to search for Franklin in January 1847 was rebuffed by the Admiralty, who countered that they had 'unlimited confidence in the skills and resources of Sir John Franklin'. Shortly afterwards, traces of Franklin's expedition began to be found, and the graves of three of the crew, who had died in early 1846, were discovered on Beechey Island. In 1850 a squadron of four vessels led by HMS *Resolute* was dispatched, using dog sleds and even primitive hydrogen balloons with messages attached, to look for Franklin – although, unbeknownst to those at home, Franklin had died some three years earlier. The Admiralty planned one final search the next year, but having become ice-bound, *Resolute* and her squadron had to be abandoned in 1854. She was later found drifting some 1,000 miles east in the Davis Strait. Discovered by an American whaler, the ship was refitted and presented as a gift to Britain.

The Admiralty abandoned its search in January 1854, *The Times* declaring that the expeditions were by now 'wasting time upon a search for dead men's bones'. Lady Franklin nevertheless continued to fund missions in search of her husband and his crew, defending them against lurid rumours of cannibalism and seeking proof that their exploration had not been in vain. Although none of Franklin's crew was rescued alive, numerous traces were found (and later exhibited in London), and the missions produced valuable information which helped to map northern Canada.

In one sense the search for Franklin never truly ended. The three graves on Beechey Island were exhumed in the 1980s and the bodies found in a miraculous state of preservation. The island was designated a National Historic Site of Canada in 1992. It was only in 2014 and 2016, using state-of-the-art technology, that the wrecks of *Erebus* and *Terror* were found off King William Island. *Terror* was in a remarkable state of preservation – indeed, some of her recovered timbers were made into a desk which was presented to the White House in Washington. As climate change disrupts ice in the Arctic, the north-west passage has today become navigable for small ships.

Franklin's expedition, the countless searches to find him, and later the tragic fate that befell his men caught the imagination of the Romantic movement, finding their most shocking depiction in Edwin Landseer's 'Man Proposes, God Disposes' of 1864. Millais' painting, 'The North West Passage', an uninhibitedly romantic piece, was a huge public success, with its old sailor and young girl looking at maps while the ship is already on its fateful way in the distance. When no news of *Erebus* arrived in the years after 1845, the magazines were full of imaginative drawings. But the most celebrated was Landseer's large painting of *Erebus* with a broken mast, and polar bears chewing at the corpse of a fallen seaman.

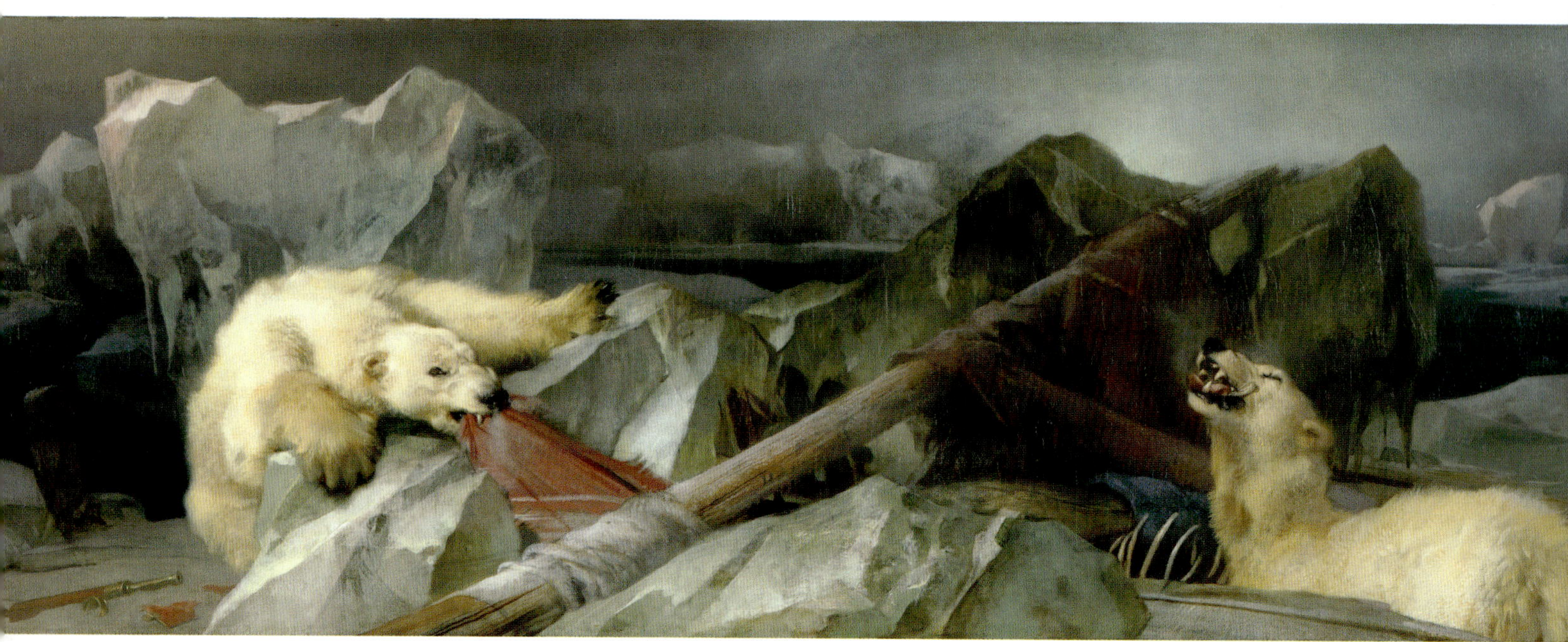

Edwin Landseer – Man Proposes, God Disposes.

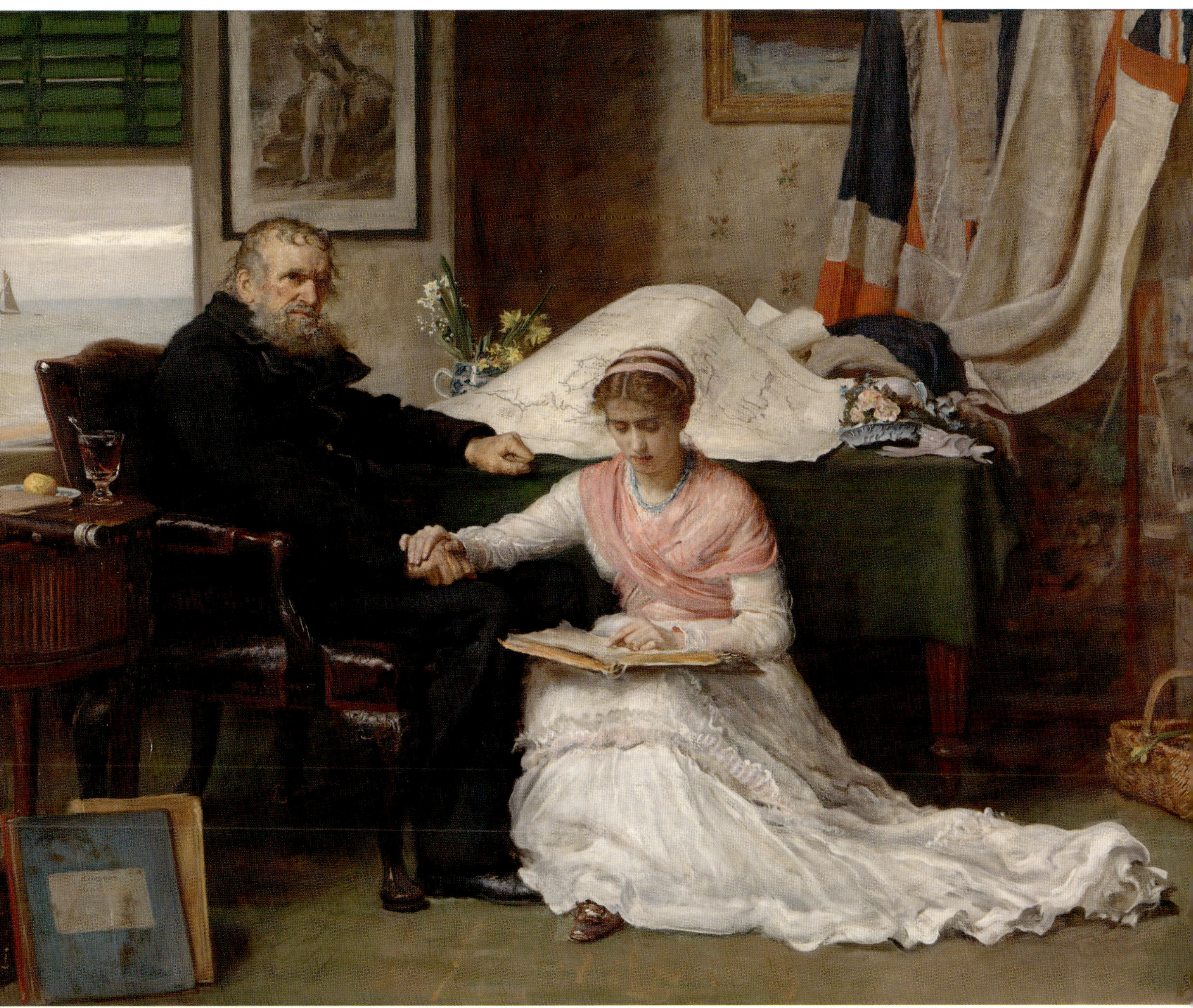

John Everett Millais – The North-West Passage.

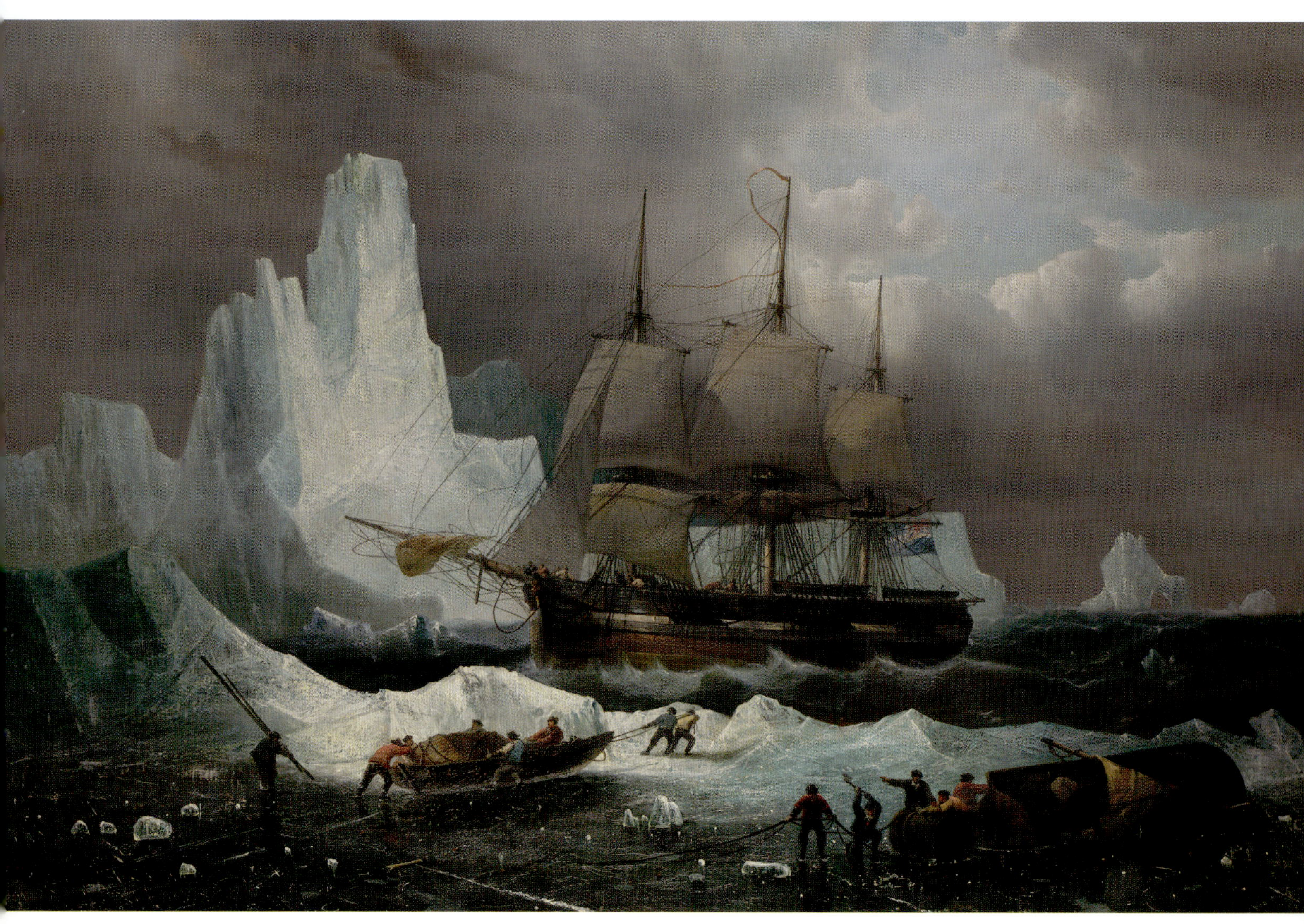

Francois Musin – HMS *Erebus* in the ice.

François Musin – HMS *Resolute* in search of Sir John Franklin.

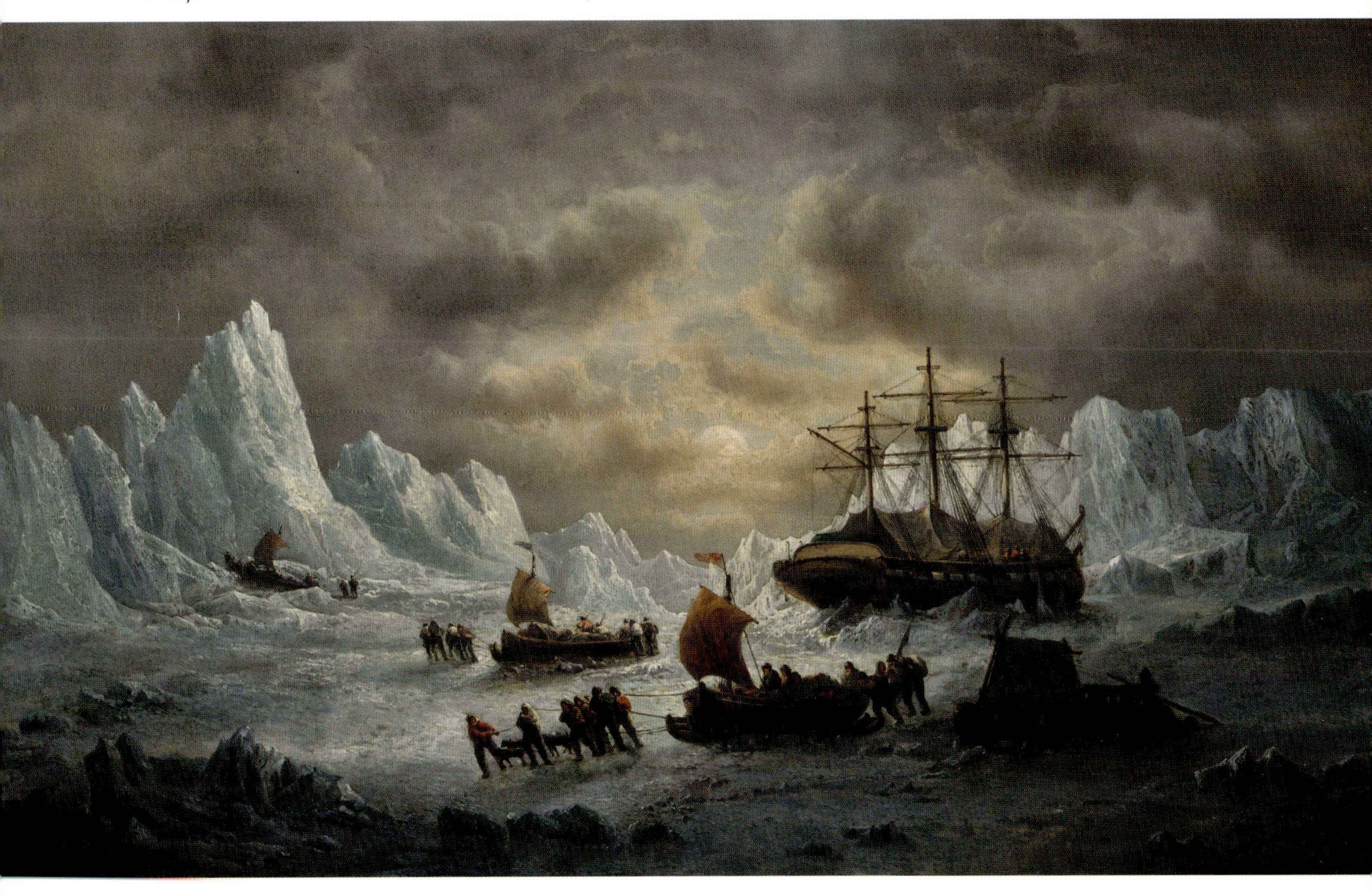

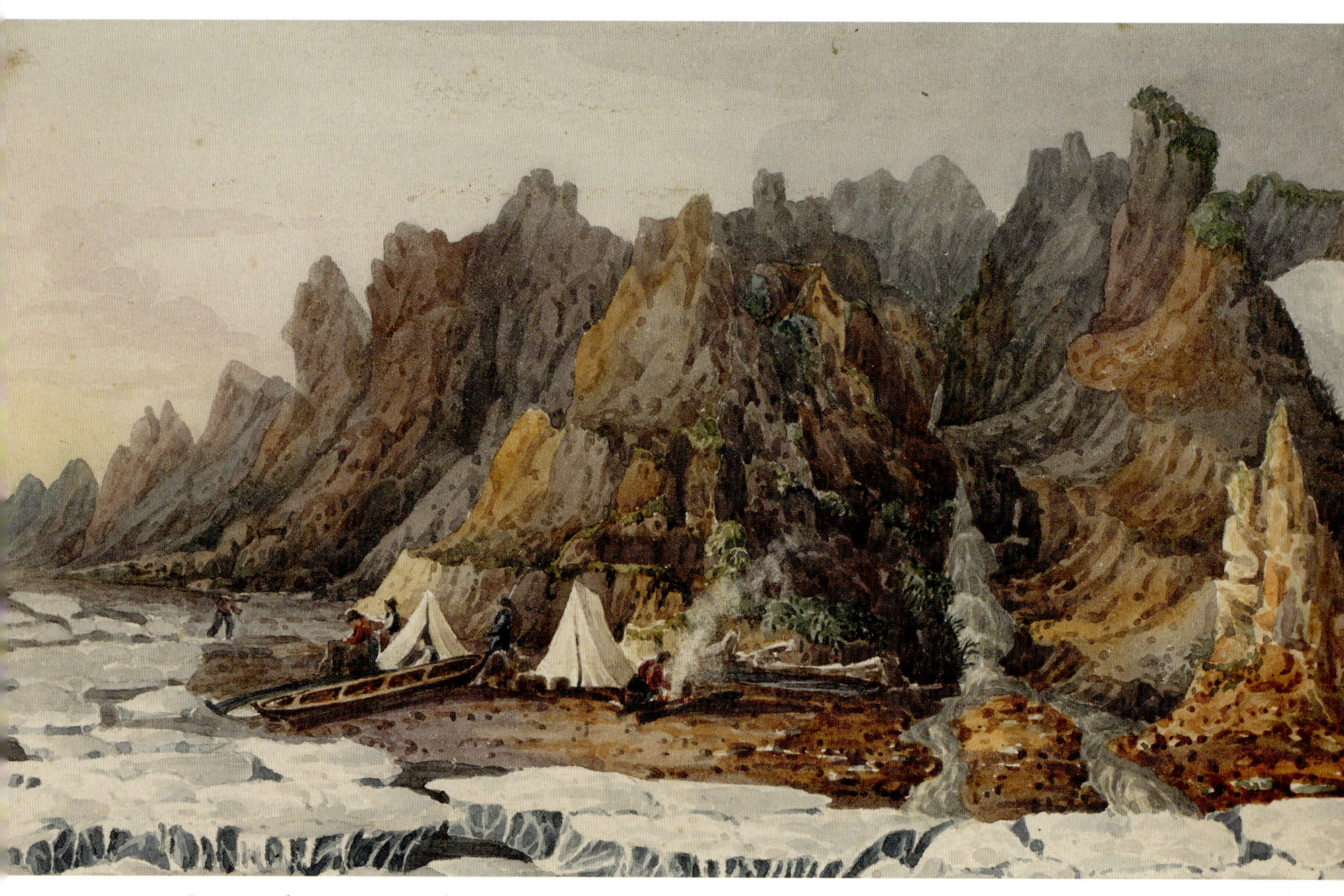

George Back – Encampment between Points King and Sabine.

George Back – Tower of ice with HMS *Terror*.

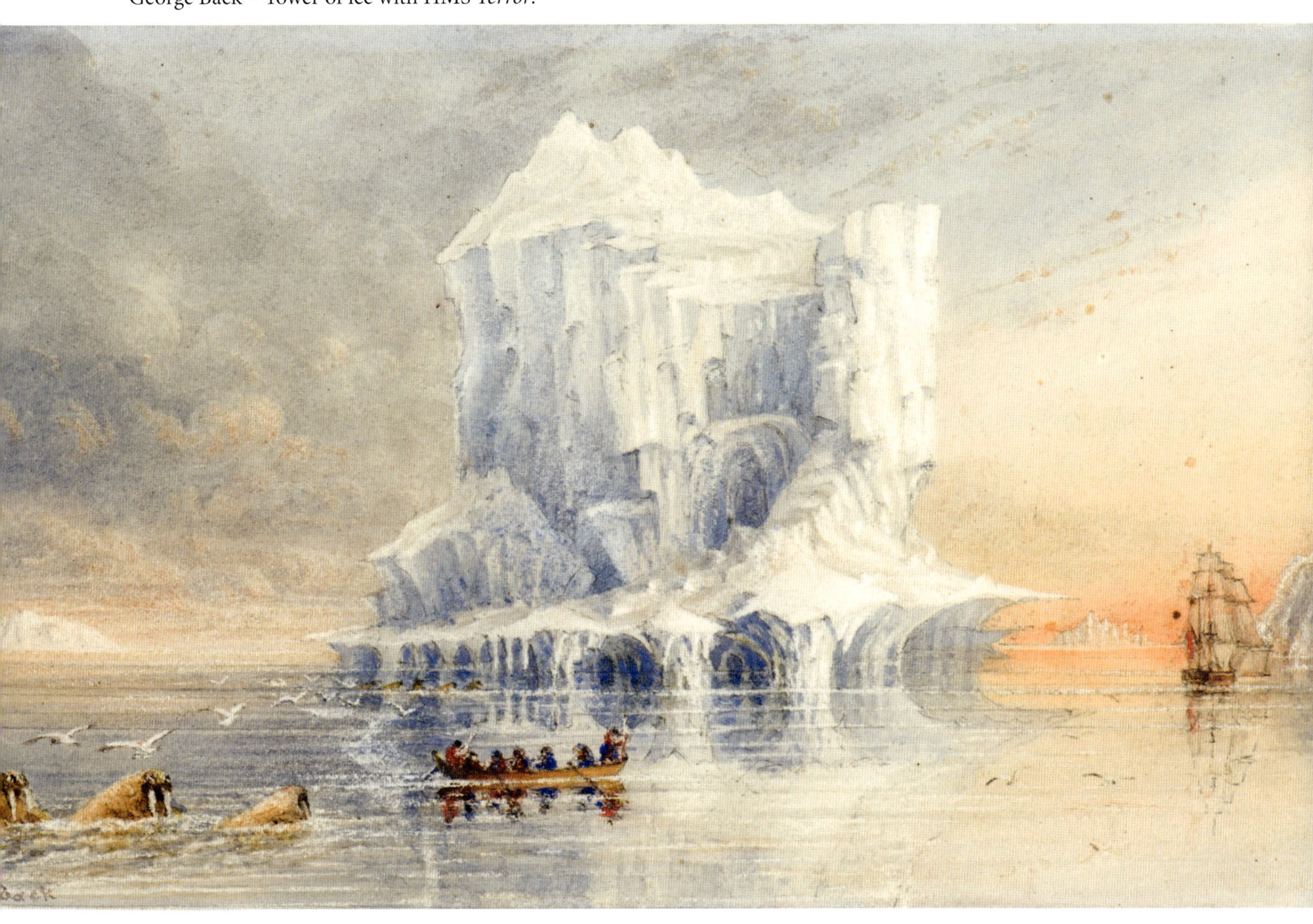

The Belgian painter François Musin, who was known for his seascapes and
patronized by, among other dignitaries, the Kaiser, spent some time in England and
seized on the commercial opportunity offered by the Franklin mystery. His paintings of
Erebus and of *Resolute* show why he had such an eager clientele. Born in Ostend, Musin
came to public prominence as a marine painter in 1840 and went on to enjoy a highly
successful international career. His success in Britain led him to stay in the country
until 1849. Only one other similar subject is known: 'HMS *Erebus* in the Ice', in the
National Maritime Museum, Greenwich. The work was acquired by Sir James Caird in
1930, and bequeathed along with his collection to the museum which he had a key role
in founding.

Throughout the expeditions which continued to search for the north-west passage
artists tried to show the reality of confronting the great icebergs and solid sea ice which
were to doom every effort until the early twentieth century.

George Back was only in his mid-twenties when he joined Franklin's first expedition
in 1818. But in 1834 he was given command of HMS *Terror* to survey the land beyond
Hudson's Bay. His picture of the ship dwarfed by a giant iceberg stretched credulity, and
his paintings of the mountain camp at Points King and Sabine were just as compelling.
Yet *Terror* was subsequently to sail all the way back across the Atlantic, buckled and
crippled by the ice which had captured the ship and had barely melted by the time she
reached Ireland.

Back began what was to prove a phenomenal career in modest circumstances in
Stockport, Cheshire. Boy sailors were still accepted by the Royal Navy, and Back was
only twelve in 1807 when, with the war with France still raging, he volunteered and
was posted to HMS *Arethusa*. The ship was ordered to proceed to the Bay of Biscay and
shell the French-occupied Spanish coast, and during one of these encounters Back was
captured. He was then to spend the next five years a prisoner in Verdun. According
to his later memoirs, fellow prisoners there taught him the practicalities of navigation
and chart-making. At Verdun, too, he refined and developed his skills in drawing and
painting.

When he was finally released after the 1814 peace negotiations, Back possessed
skills which made him very welcome in the Royal Navy. He served as a midshipman
aboard two ships before, in 1818, making another fateful decision, to volunteer for John
Franklin's first Arctic expedition. Franklin clearly valued the young man's skills, and
took him as a map-maker on two overland expeditions, including the venture to the
Mackenzie River.

In 1833 another British explorer, John Ross, had apparently disappeared in the
Arctic, and Back, by now a Commander, was tasked with putting together an
expedition to find him. Soon after he reached the Arctic, Back received news from the

Admiralty that Ross was safely back in England, but he was instructed that he could use his resources to explore what was known as the Fish River. However, as the weather turned, he decided to return home.

Back retired as a full Admiral, but spent much of his time in the newly developing Canada, including being commissioned to depict the completion of the Canadian Pacific Railway on its almost unimaginable route through the Rocky Mountains, over rivers and across the emerging prairies. And when he first came to Canada, he also painted landscapes of the interior: the Clarence River, the Slave Falls and the encampments at Point King and Sabine.

*　*　*

The union of the vast lands north of the United States into what became known as Canada took more than a century after the American War of Independence. It was only towards the end of the nineteenth century, after the Canadian Pacific Railway joined the Atlantic to the Pacific, that the numbers of Europeans arriving to seek their fortunes in this new land began to expand, although unlike many other new colonies, few painters were producing pictures to entice immigrants.

The appeal of wealth in the form of major gold rushes in the early nineteenth century in what became known as British Columbia on the Pacific coast, and above all the fur trade, had been the early magnets for voyagers to the American north. Trade came to be monopolized by the Hudson Bay Company, which formed in effect the government of these great stretches of new land. Though settlers did establish themselves along the coasts of Hudson Bay, the main business of delivering furs to the eager markets of Europe was conducted through trading posts. These small collections of huts along river banks and in the forest attracted the eye of the first European artists. This was where the Indians came with their beaver skins and other furs to be exchanged for knives, tools and practical items. It was usually a peaceful trade, and the furs were dispatched down the rivers to the Hudson Bay ports and thence to Europe. Furs were, indeed, the principal foundation of what became the great Canadian federation.

Romantic painted landscapes of Canada, delivered back to Europe, were muted in their appeal to immigrants. But when artists did arrive they were entranced by the small communities they visited, far from European contact. Josephine Crease depicted the appeal of one of these little settlements.

Emily Carr, working well into the twentieth century, captured the uniqueness of the land she found: blue skies; the huge lone trees vaulting towards those skies; and the Indians with whom trade seemed more profitable than war.

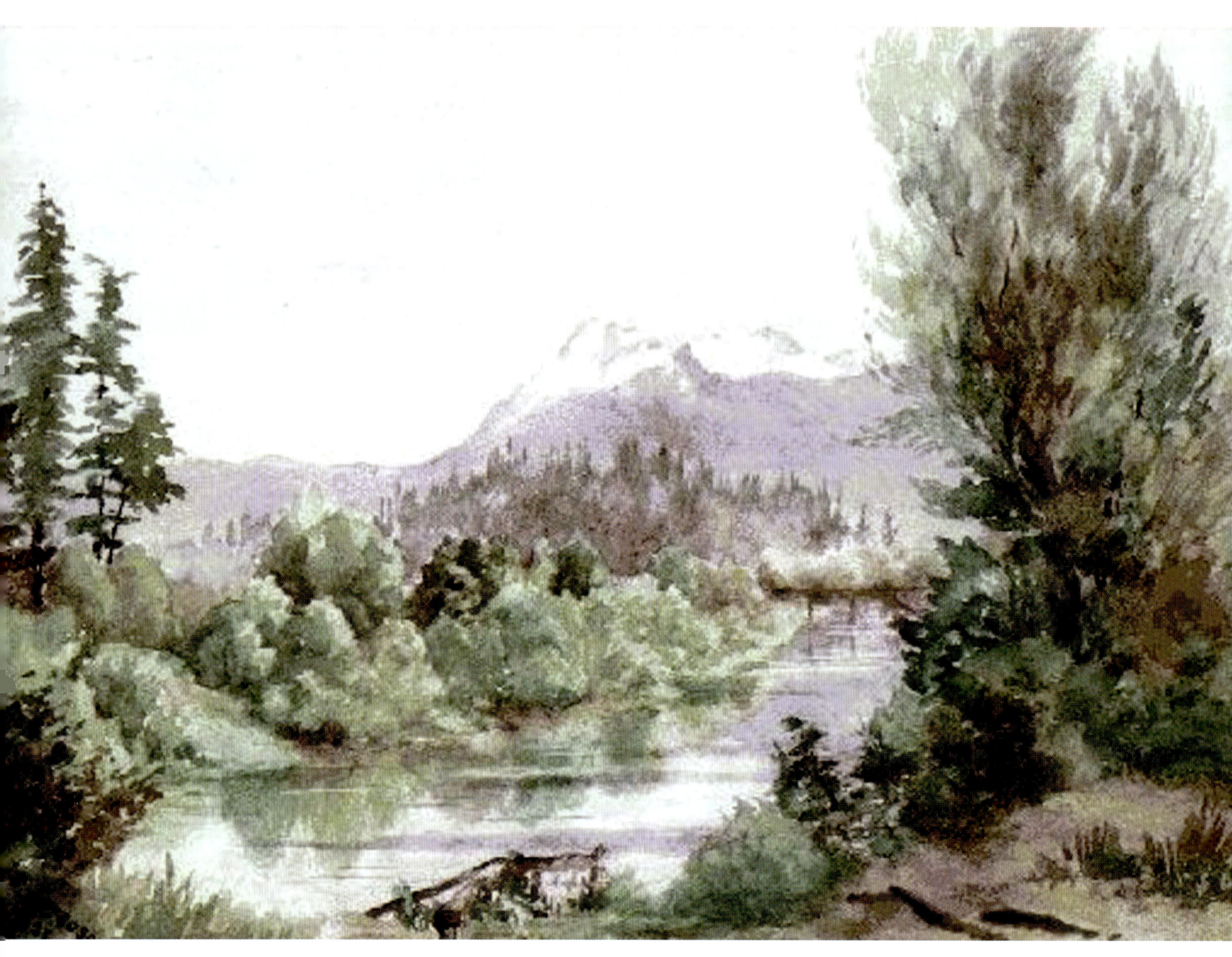

Josephine Crease – Canada.

Opposite: Emily Carr – Blue Sky.

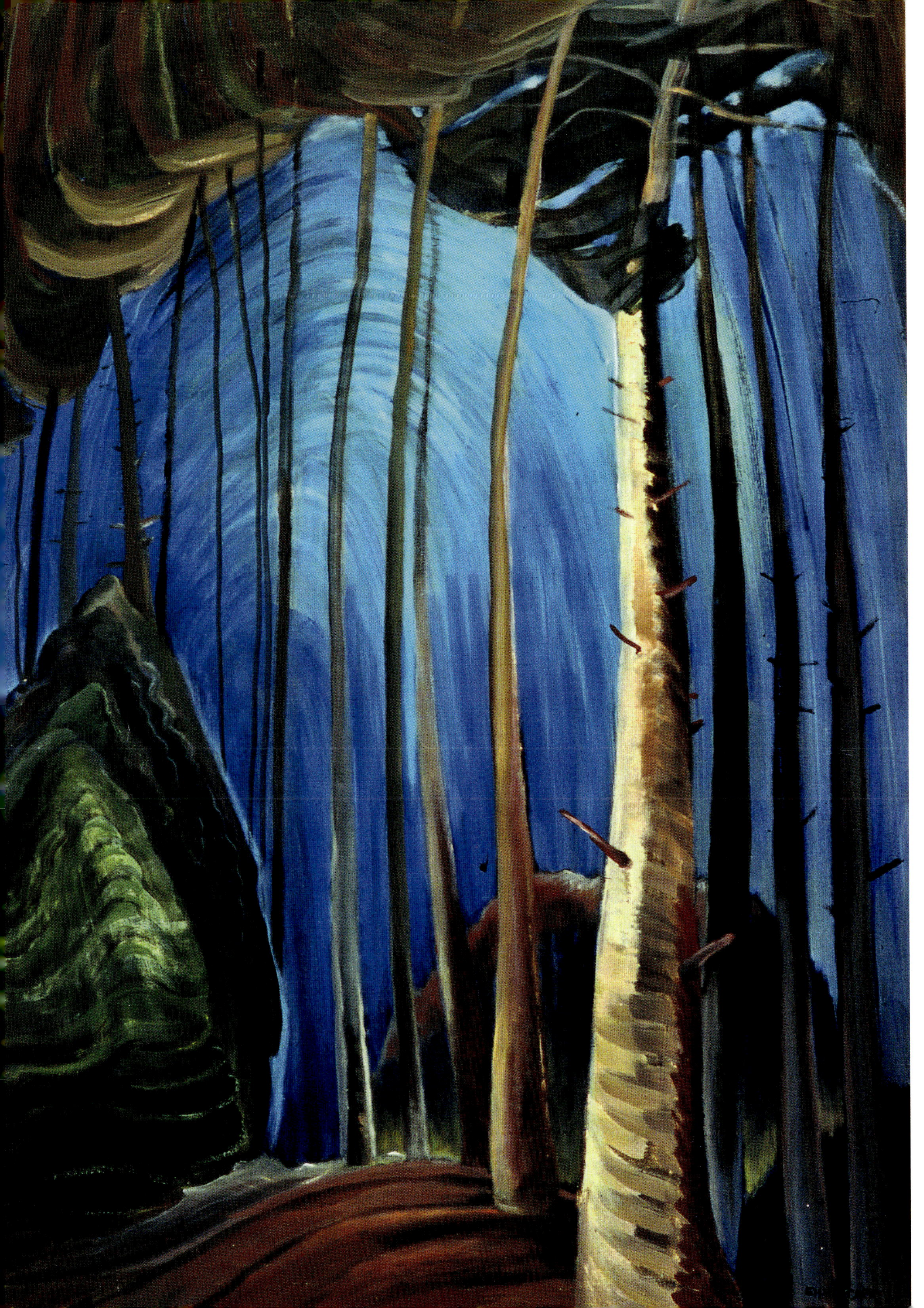

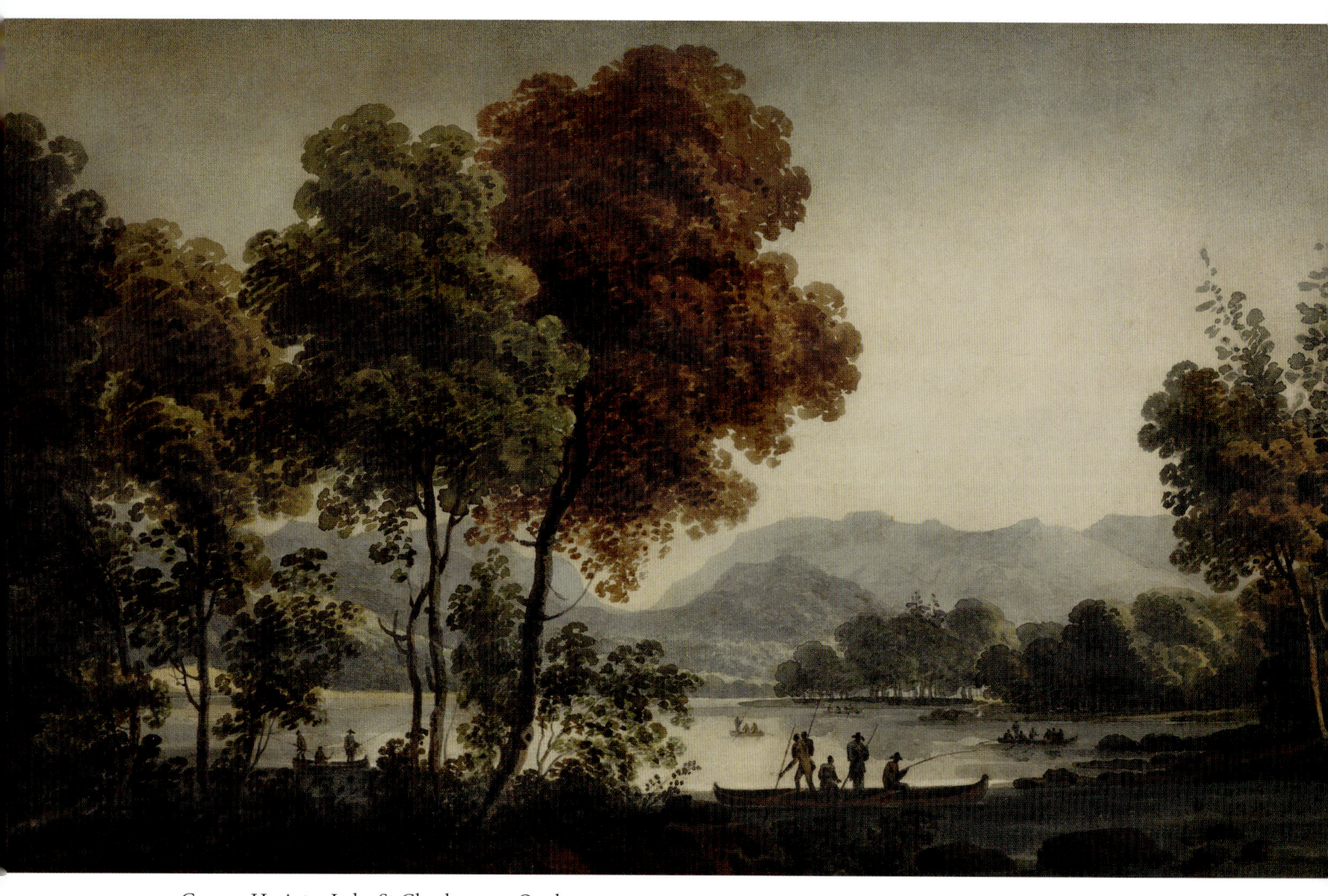

George Heriot – Lake St Charles near Quebec.

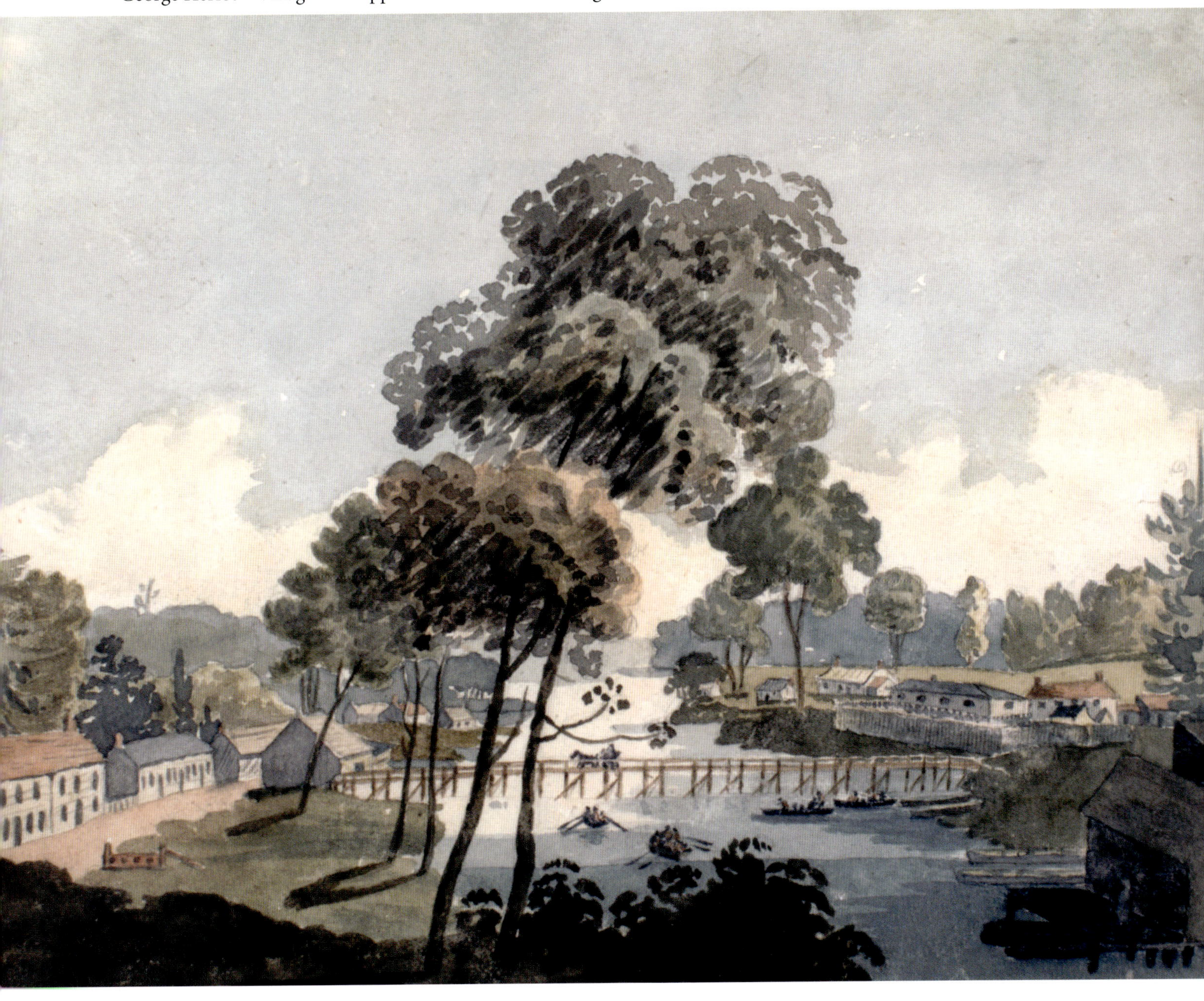

George Heriot – Village of Chippawa near the Falls of Niagara.

George Heriot arrived in Canada in 1792. Although already a successful artist in England, he had family connections in Canada which allowed him to secure a series of jobs as a postmaster and storekeeper. He became a determined traveller in the interior, publishing in 1807 a book entitled *Travels through Canada*, which carried a series of his own illustrations. He made drawings of Mohawk Indians, and travelled as far south as Niagara, showing the King's Bridge at Chippewa. After four years he returned to England in order to submit pictures which were shown at the Royal Academy. He then returned to Canada and produced the series of paintings of rural Quebec which were to adorn his book. Another woodland scene of Lake St Charles has a group of natives in the foreground – a common feature of his work.

Chapter 8

Talbot Kelly and Burma

The motives which underlay European exploration – colonizing new lands, finding gold and treasure, expanding empires – were well understood and embellished by the artists, who were often explorers themselves. But artists were also quite consciously feeding the curiosity which consumed the many people at home who did not or could not travel. This curiosity helped to produce a great market for the many magazines and journals of the nineteenth and early twentieth centuries, which often funded artists to travel the world for them.

It was A. & C. Black, publishers of *Encyclopaedia Britannica*, along with many travel books, who persuaded an initially reluctant Robert Talbot Kelly to leave his beloved Egypt and explore Burma, a country already under the control of the British but largely unknown. Talbot Kelly was keen to dispense practical advice to fellow travellers to Burma:

A solar topee is imperative. A very good helmet can be bought at Port Said for a few shillings, the best pattern being a wide, quilted one of khaki which, if ugly, is I think the most serviceable.

Silk suits are essential, and may be procured in Rangoon.

A supply of quinine is required – to prevent fever, not to cure it.

Provisions can be best obtained from Barnett Brothers in Fytche Square in Rangoon. Bedding, mosquito nets, come from Rowe and Company in the same square. A riding suit of hard light material will be required for a forest journey, and I found putties preferable to leggings.

The forest and the natural scenery were to feature in many of the paintings which Kelly made while deliberately setting out to depict life in Burma at the very beginning of the twentieth century. But it was scarcely two decades since the British had summarily dethroned Thebaw, King of Burma, and spirited him off to permanent captivity in India in what became known as The Glass Palace.

Thus another nation was added to the British Empire. Talbot Kelly was fascinated by how totally the British had managed to establish their authority, and how a mere handful of British managers could control enormous enterprises. He frequently came

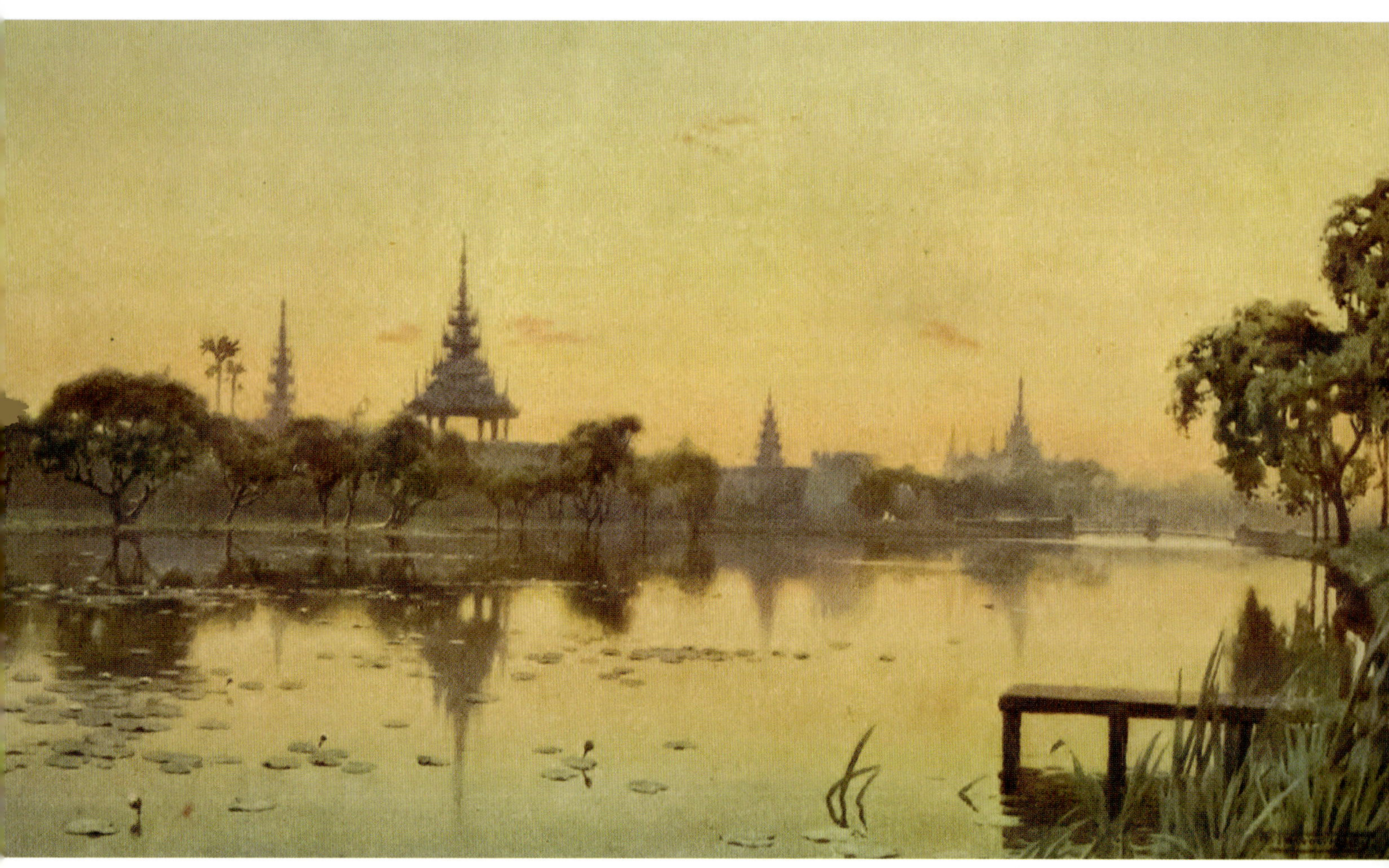

Robert Talbot Kelly – The Moat at Mandalay.

Robert Talbot Kelly – Jungle at Delanchoon.

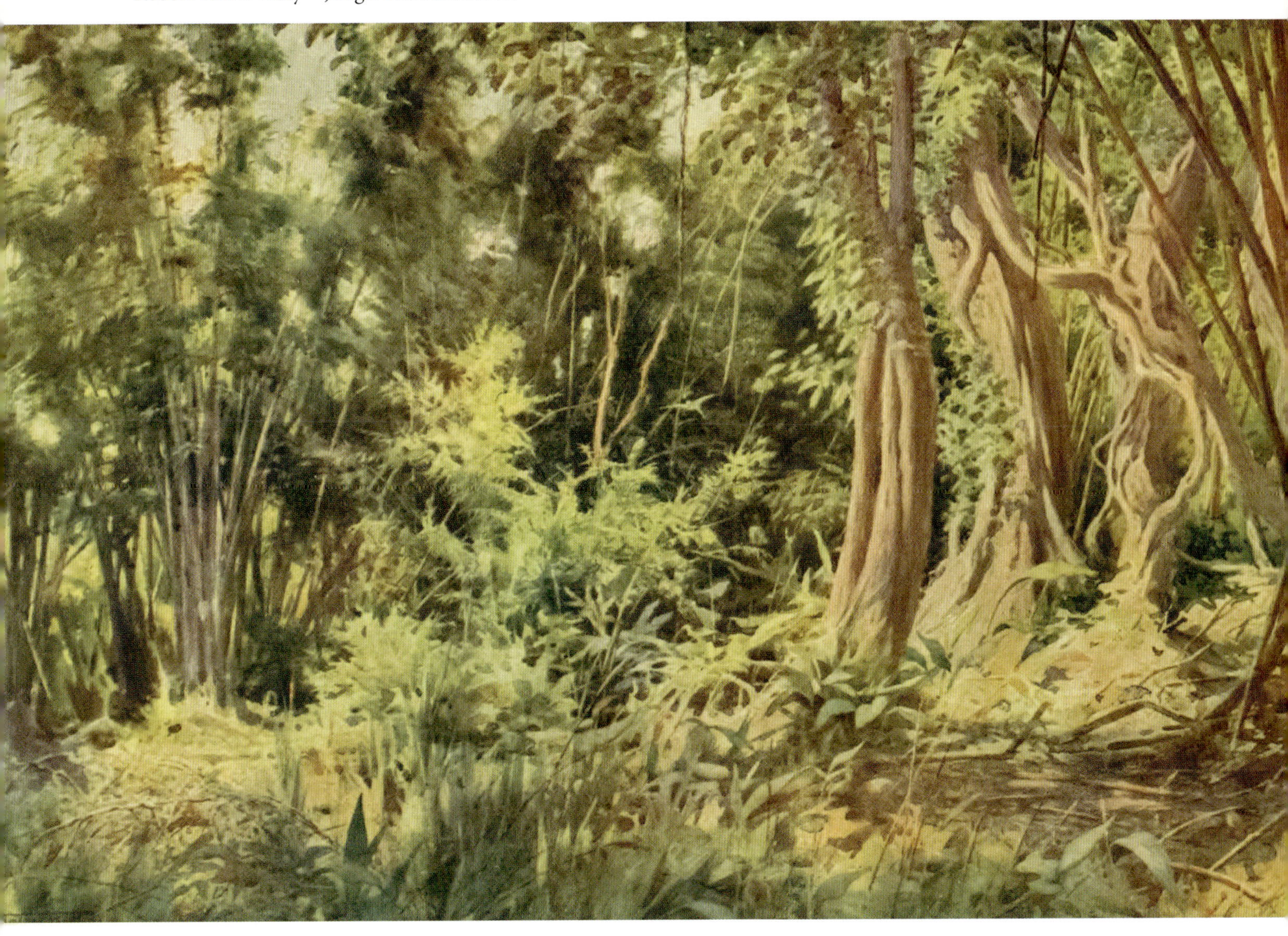

across vast logging or mining operations, often deep in the jungle or forest, with only two or three British men in charge.

When he reached Mandalay and started to paint the magnificence of the palace and fort – today sadly diminished by fire and neglect – he was again beguiled by the confidence of his compatriots. Only twenty-five years earlier, the emissaries of the Viceroy of India, he reminds us, had been forced to remove their boots and kneel at the threshold of the largest of the palace audience chambers in order to negotiate with King Mindon Min, who surveyed them with opera glasses from his throne at the far end of the chamber.

Now that great room had become the British Upper Burma Club. 'I was much amused,' he relates, 'on one occasion, while looking at the British newspapers, to see the doors of the throne fly open and a lady tourist, clad in helmet and white duck, step on to the dais. She seemed very surprised to find herself so suddenly introduced to a room full of men, and retired precipitately.'

The Burmese, Kelly notes, much disliked this usurpation of the palace, and occasionally tried to set fire to it.

In that surge of late Victorian imperial energy, the British had already built a railway almost to the Chinese border. Kelly found a special railway car bestowed upon him by the local agent, Captain Kincaid, which could be attached to and detached from any passing train to take him to anywhere along the line where artistic inspiration might strike. It was fully equipped with bedding and furniture, and stocked with provisions, and they duly set off for the Shan Hills. At one point a station master asked Kelly if he would mind being detached and waiting for the next train, so that the engine could negotiate a steep slope. With his newly acquired imperial hauteur, he declined. As a result, he relates, a whole carriage full of third-class passengers was detached and shunted into a siding, so that Kelly and his personal carriage could continue unimpeded.

The country was already endowed with bungalows and rest stations, fully equipped for use by European travellers. When the railway temporarily ran out and Kelly was obliged to abandon his personal carriage and proceed to a river on the other side of which the new headquarters of a silver mine was being established, his companion simply fired a few revolver shots. In response, a rope ferry appeared and they were welcomed to the bungalow of Mr Park, the mine's chief engineer, an amenity as yet incomplete but comfortable enough for Kelly to relax in a cane chair, quaff a bottle of Bass Pale Ale and contemplate what he would paint.

A year before, he tells us, the area had been uninhabited waste. Now the population of the village was roughly 1,000, 'composed of Indian coolies, Shans, Kachins, Chinese and Burmans, all perhaps bad specimens of their race, but here apparently living on

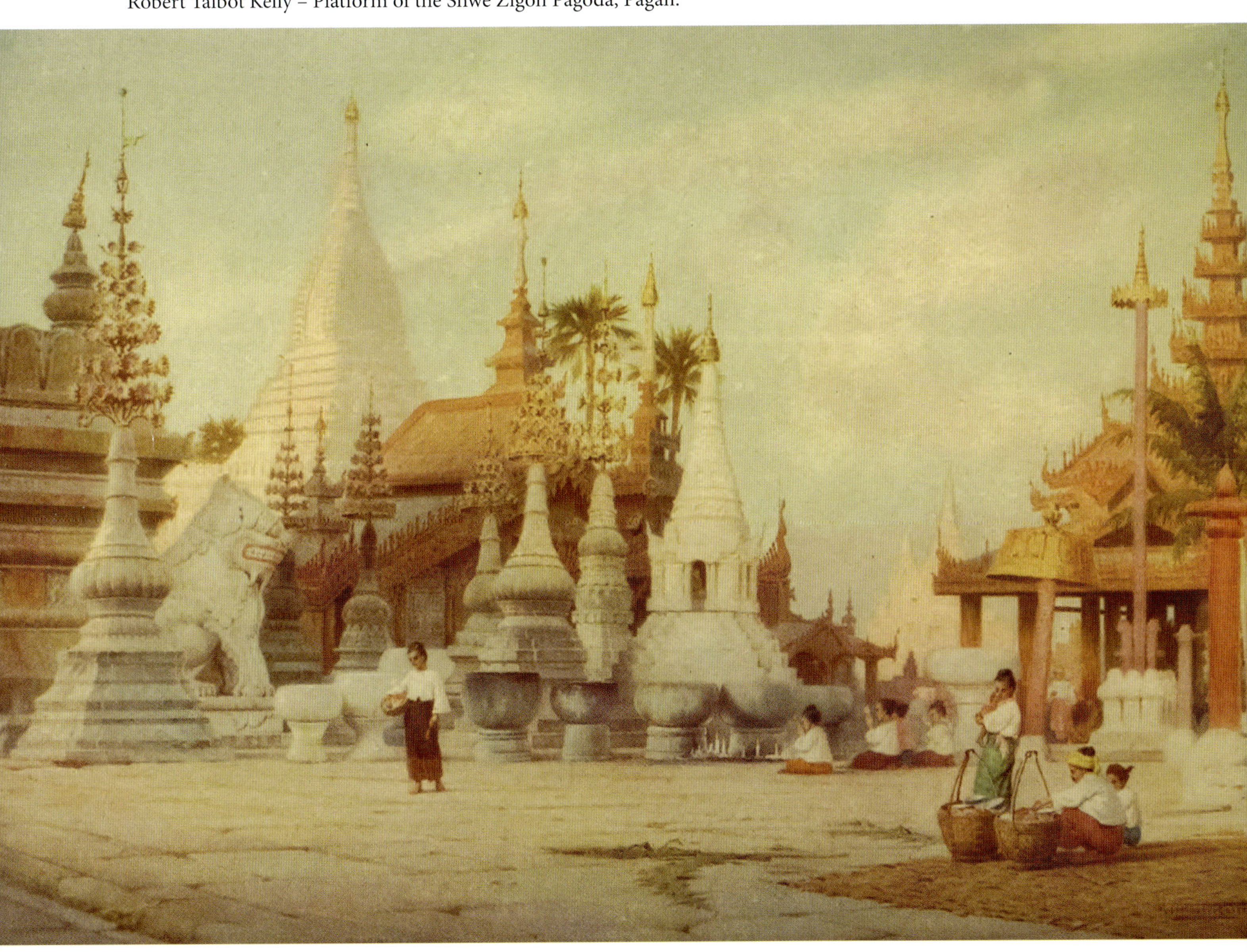

Robert Talbot Kelly – Platform of the Shwe Zigon Pagoda, Pagan.

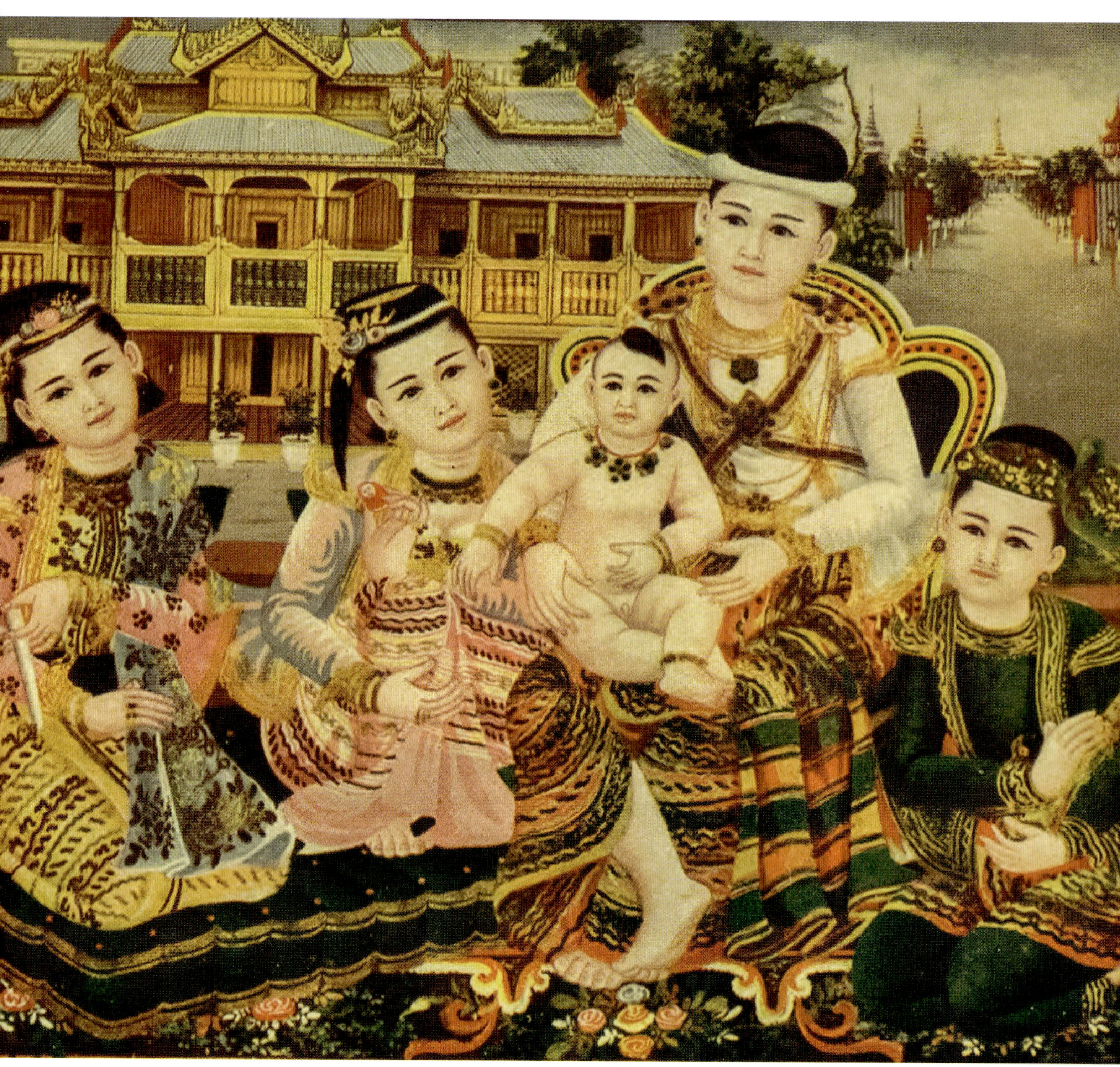

Robert Talbot Kelly – Domestic Felicity (from a Burmese Painting).

good terms with each other, and all submitting to the quiet domination of two young Englishmen.'

Only days before, the Chinese gambling house had stayed open beyond permitted hours. The two Englishmen, wielding only riding whips,

> raided the place, confiscating both money and appliances, and clearing it of its half drunk and fully armed habitués. Needless to say, their lives were absolutely at the mercy of the crowd, to whom the adjacent Chinese frontier offered an easy asylum, but grit and personal force of character accomplished more than many a fully armed party would have risked.

Kelly proceeded to paint a number of pictures which showed the natural challenges of mountain, gorge and forest which the two young Englishmen were committed to overcome in bringing the railway to the mine. 'I was strongly impressed', Kelly recalled, 'by the combination of pluck and good humour by which Messrs Sulman and Park maintained discipline and exacted honest work from the motley crowd of more or less lawless men and women over whom they had no legal authority.'

Apart from the natural world of Burma, and its imperial servants, Kelly was most enthralled by the temples and pagodas. As soon as he was settled in the imperial Strand Hotel in Rangoon, he went off to see the great Shwe Dagon pagoda. These two buildings remain to this day among the chief glories of Rangoon, now Yangon.

His favourite view of the Shwe Dagon was from Dalhousie Park and its Gymkhana Club.

> The Club is large and airy and well supplied with card and reading rooms, the ground floor being almost entirely occupied by its fifteen or sixteen billiard tables. In front is the cricket field where many hard fights take place. The lawn is dotted with the tea tables of members and their wives. Behind are tennis courts and stabling. The ladies have their own reading and billiard rooms, and once a week an impromptu dance takes place in the recently added ballroom.

Kelly was to paint many pagodas, from the extraordinary deserted city of Pagan, with its hundreds of temples, some of a size to rival St Paul's in London, to Mandalay, and the ones he encountered in a long journey by steamer up the Irawaddy River. Their glittering decorated beauty never palled for him. And the Burmese who made their devotions and celebrations there contributed to his valedictory view that 'The Burmese are a people infinitely attractive, Burma a country which is a garden of wonderful beauty, and inhabited by a race entirely in harmony with its surroundings, and who understand what is meant by the joy of living.'

Kelly was to spend more than seven months trekking through the jungle, making his way a thousand miles up the Irrawaddy and fighting off tropical afflictions, in order to bring back the great store of pictures which be exhibited in London in 1912. For all the rigours he had to endure, his pictures, which received a warm reception when London audiences first saw them, display the wonder and affection he felt for an idyllic land.

Chapter 9

North Africa

Seeking new worlds and exploring the farthest lands produced martyrs and heroes, from Captain Cook to Captain Oates, but it also drew the adventurers into conflict and conquest, defiance and rebellion. The sword was needed as well as the sail. From New Zealand to China, in India and Africa, the artist explorers found themselves portraying military scenes as well as acts of greeting and friendship.

Indeed, for the last thirty years of the nineteenth century the British found themselves almost continually involved in the north-east of Africa. A dispute with Abyssinia was caused by a British businessman being taken hostage. The Suez Canal, cut through Egyptian territory and partly owned by the French and the British, provoked hostility from the Ottoman Turks. But above all, the Nile, running for 1,000 miles south down to the Mediterranean and endowing its banks with great fertility, was a focus of conflict. Explorers travelled up the river as far as they could. But its upper reaches remained virtually unknown.

French explorers pushing eastwards from the Congo aimed to establish a base on the Nile, for transport and commercial shipping. For the British in Egypt, the push was southwards down the Nile to the Sudan. The British reaction, when their rival expedition met the French, led to what became known as the Fashoda Incident, with threats that nearly resulted in war. Britain's ventures were conducted primarily by the military, trying to make their way through powerful and well armed Islamic kingdoms and local Arab princes. The process was hazardous and there were setbacks such as the killing of General Gordon in Khartoum, which dismayed the British public at home.

Only in 1899 did the decisive moment come with the Battle of Omdurman, which allowed the British commander Kitchener to ride into the city of Khartoum. Winston Churchill was a young cavalryman in the battle, and British cavalry were shown in Woodcote's famous painting. Churchill was later to describe in his memoir *The River War* the nature and importance of the Nile country and his experience of battle:

The town of Khartoum, at the confluence of the Blue and White Niles, is the point on which the trade of the south must inevitably converge. It is the great spout through which the merchandise collected from a wide area streams northwards to the Mediterranean shore. It marks the extreme northern limit of the fertile

Soudan. Between Khartoum and Assuan the river flows for twelve hundred miles through deserts of surpassing desolation. At last the wilderness recedes and the living world broadens out again into Egypt and the Delta.

Through the desert flows the river – a thread of blue silk drawn across an enormous brown drugget; and even this thread is brown for half the year.

Where the water laps the sand and soaks into the banks there grows an avenue of vegetation which seems very beautiful and luxuriant by contrast with what lies beyond. The Nile, through all the three thousand miles of its course vital to everything that lives beside it, is never so precious as here. The traveller clings to the strong river as to an old friend, staunch in the hour of need

All the world blazes, but here is shade. The deserts are hot, but the Nile is cool. The land is parched, but here is abundant water. The picture painted in burnt sienna is relieved by a grateful flash of green.

Churchill described the Omdurman charge as follows:

Tho trumpet jerked out a shrill note, heard faintly above the trampling of the horses and the noise of the rifles. On the instant all the sixteen troops swung round and locked up into a long galloping line, and the 21st Lancers were committed to their first charge in war. Two hundred and fifty yards away the dark-blue men were firing madly in a thin film of light-blue smoke. Their bullets struck the hard gravel into the air, and the troopers, to shield their faces from the stinging dust, bowed their helmets forward, like the Cuirassiers at Waterloo.

The pace was fast and the distance short. Yet, before it was half covered, the whole aspect of the affair changed. A deep crease in the ground-a dry watercourse, where all had seemed smooth, level plain; and from it there sprang, with the suddenness of a pantomime effect and a high-pitched yell, a dense white mass of men nearly as long as our front and about twelve deep.

A score of horsemen and a dozen bright flags rose as if by magic from the earth.

Eager warriors sprang forward to anticipate the shock.

The rest stood firm to meet it. The Lancers acknowledged the apparition only by an increase of pace.

Each man wanted sufficient momentum to drive through such a solid line.

The flank troops, seeing that they overlapped, curved inwards like the horns of a moon. But the whole event was a matter of seconds. The riflemen, firing bravely to the last, were swept head over heels into the khor [ravine], and jumping down with them, at full gallop and in the closest order, the British squadrons struck the fierce

Richard Caton Woodville – The Charge of the 21st Lancers at the Battle of Omdurman, 2 September 1898.

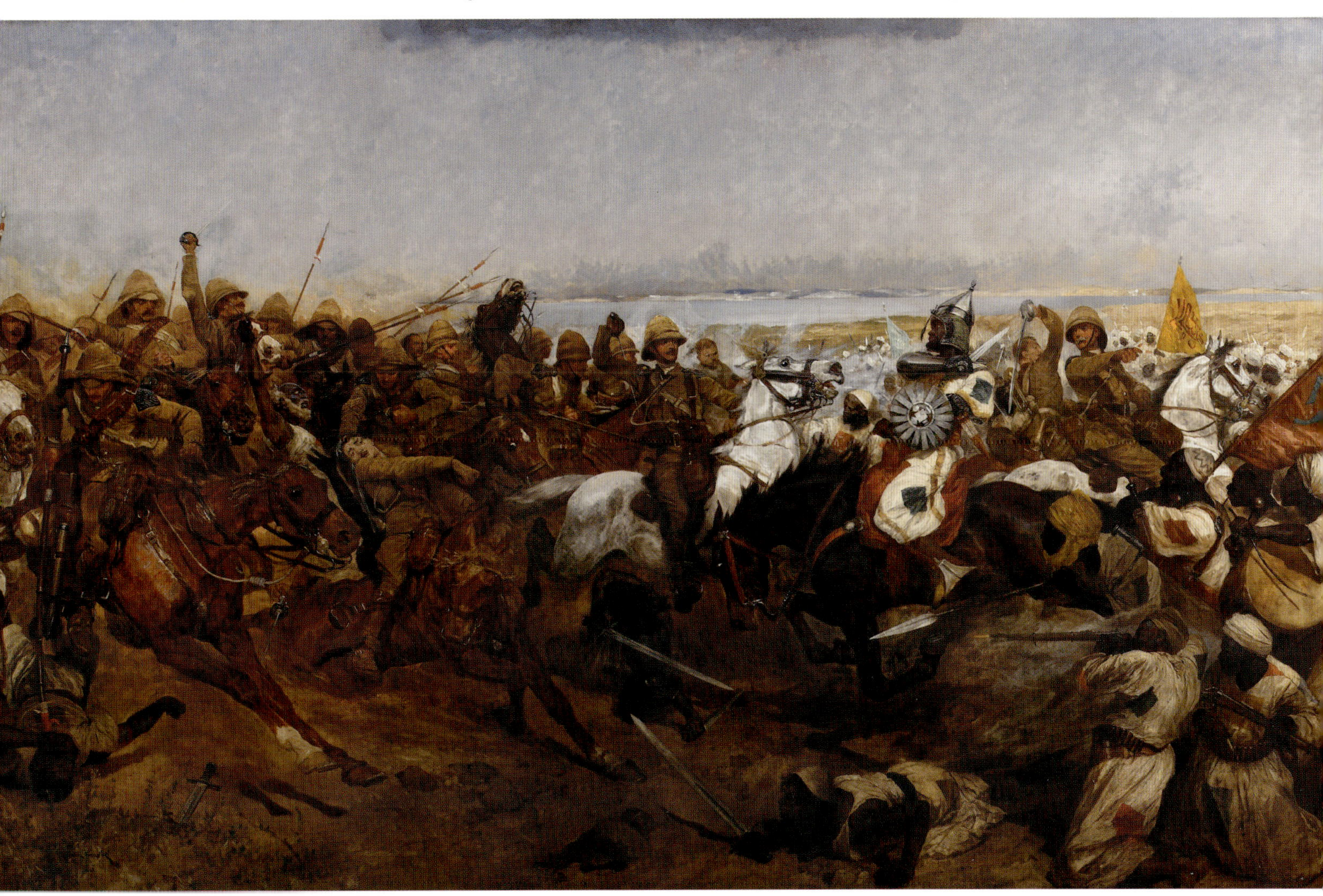

brigade with one loud furious shout. The collision was prodigious. Nearly thirty Lancers, men and horses, and at least two hundred Arabs were overthrown.

The shock was stunning to both sides, and for perhaps ten wonderful seconds no man heeded his enemy. Terrified horses wedged in the crowd, bruised and shaken men, sprawling in heaps, struggled, dazed and stupid, to their feet, panted, and looked about them. Several fallen Lancers had even time to remount. Meanwhile the impetus of the cavalry carried them on.

As a rider tears through a bullfinch [hedge], the officers forced their way through the press; and as an iron rake might be drawn through a heap of shingle, so the regiment followed.

They shattered the Dervish array, and, their pace reduced to walk, scrambled out of the khor on the further side, leaving a score of troopers behind them, and dragging on with the charge more than a thousand Arabs.

Then, and not till then, the killing began; and thereafter each man saw the world along his lance, under his guard, or through the back-sight of his pistol; and each had his own strange tale to tell.

Chapter 10

China and India

The opening-up of China to Europeans began with the British victory in the First Opium War in 1841, prompted by the Chinese government's attempt to stop the export of opium from India to China. Hong Kong had been the port through which the trade went, but it was now ceded to Britain and began to accommodate residents.

George Chinnery, already a successful artist in India, working in Hyderabad, was one of the first to seize this opportunity. He had already moved from India to base himself in China at the Portuguese colony in Macau, and then spent six months working in Hong Kong in 1846. His painting of the Spring Gardens waterfront, radiating calm and quiet, is a modest introduction to the place which was to develop so rapidly into the great commercial hub of the British China trade.

Chinnery was clearly beguiled by the life of the inhabitants of Hong Kong, as he had been in Calcutta, Hyderabad and Macau. His pictures such 'The Sampan Girl', brought home to England and widely reproduced, contributed to the lure of the Far East which was to rapidly attract the first flood of British emigration, not only to Hong Kong but also to Canton and other treaty ports.

Edward Duncan's painting is of the naval battle in which the British ironclad *Nemesis* destroyed the Chinese war junks in an encounter which marked the end of the 1841 war. The British warships were the effectively invincible weapons which were to achieve not only the ceding of Hong Kong to Britain but also the other treaty ports, including Shanghai. Indeed, the series of victories which ended with the Treaty of Nanking were achieved with minimal losses on the British side.

During his time in Calcutta, Chinnery took on a number of pupils, among them James Atkinson, who was a surgeon in the British Army but also an aspiring artist. The Army had been encouraging the practice of recording their deeds as, throughout the eighteenth and nineteenth centuries, British troops found themselves in new lands in fulfilment of their duty to protect trade and newly established colonies.

Atkinson, in his capacity as a surgeon, had found himself attached to the First Bengal Army, which in 1839 was dispatched from India into Afghanistan to oust a leader in Kabul who was judged to be too accommodating towards the Russian forces who were seen to be pursuing the Tsars' ambition to invade India. Lady Butler's picture of the lone horseman in 'Remnant of an Army' was to become the saddest memorial of British

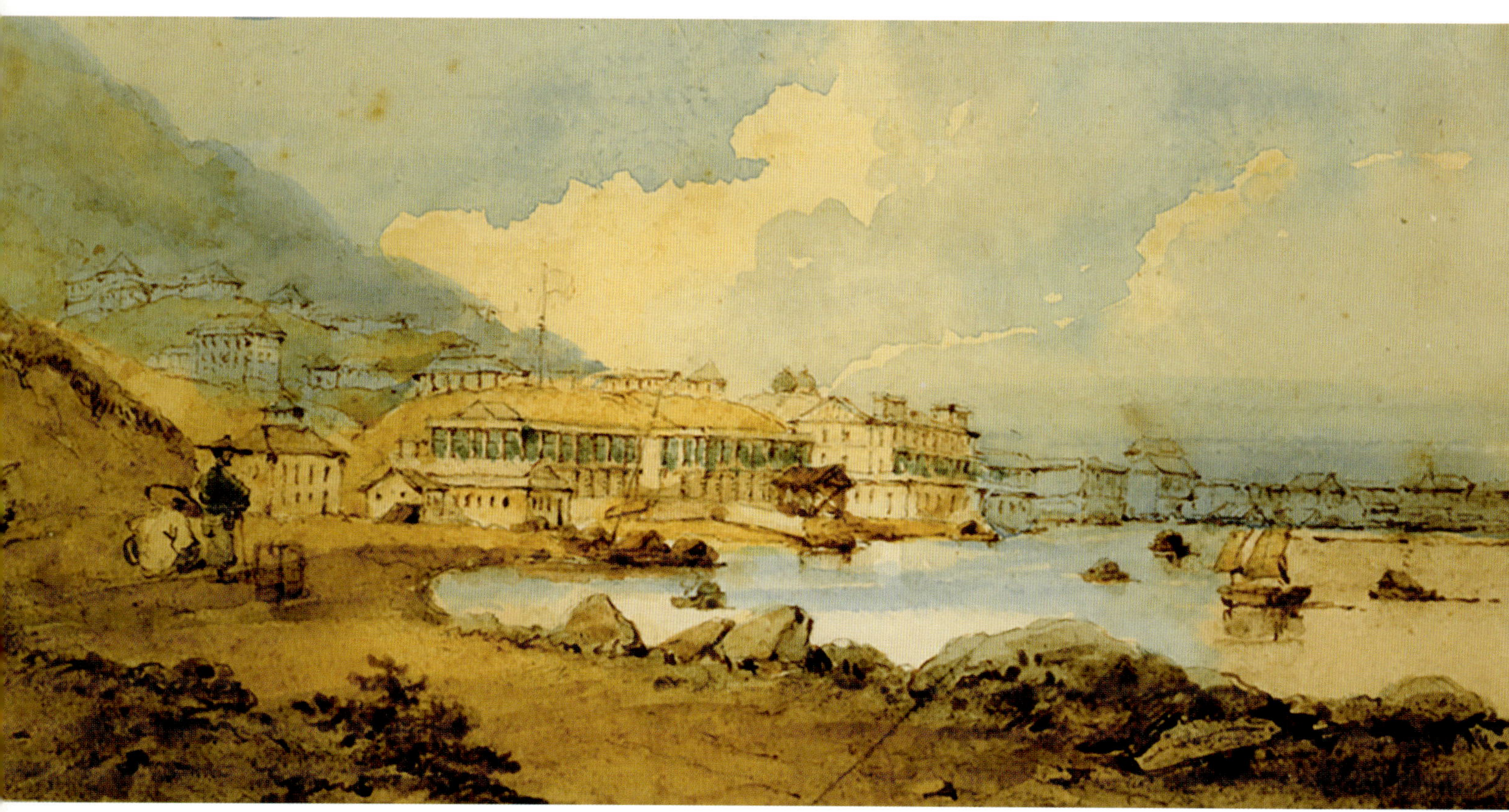

George Chinnery – Spring Gardens.

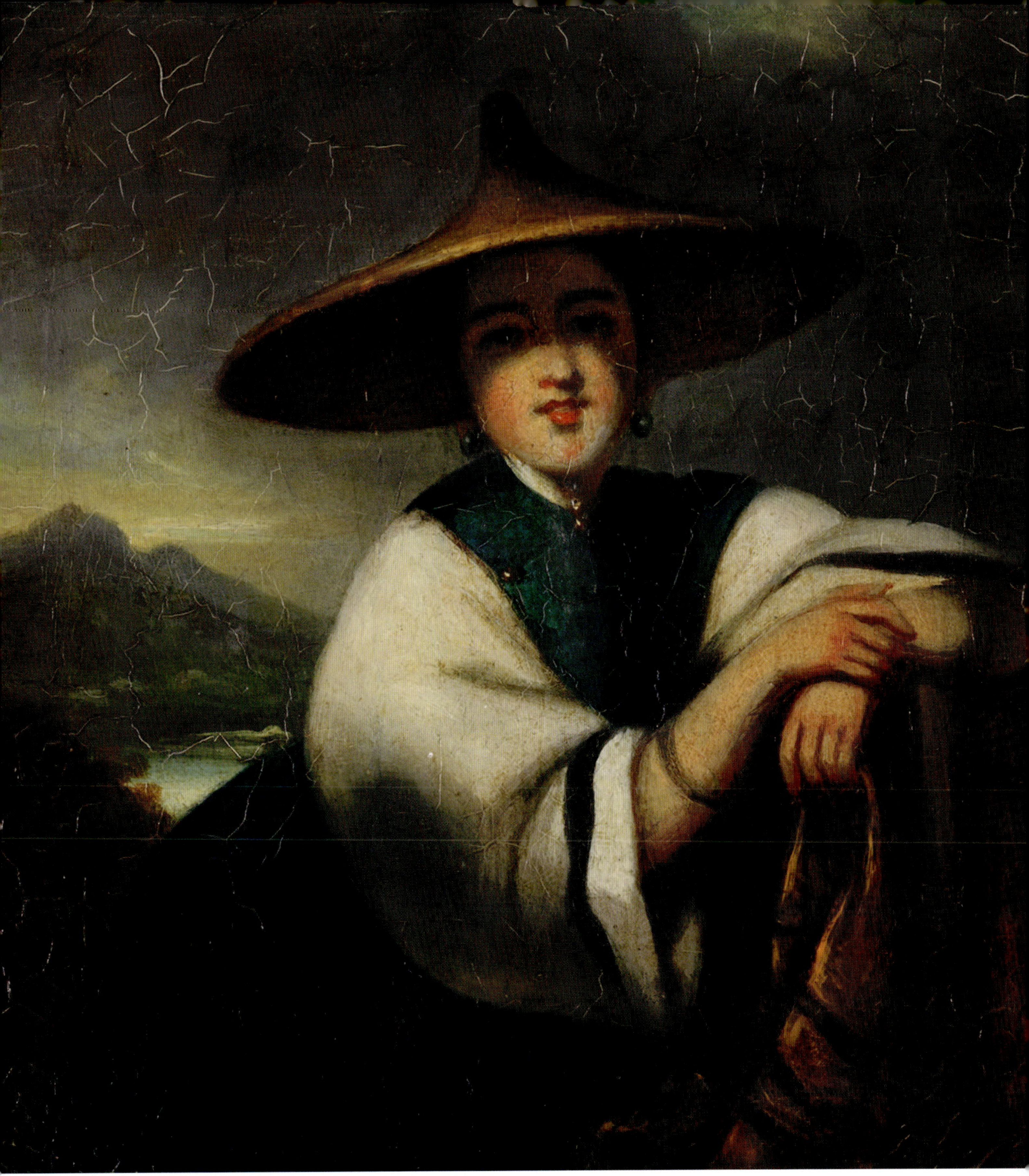

George Chinnery – China Sampan Girl.

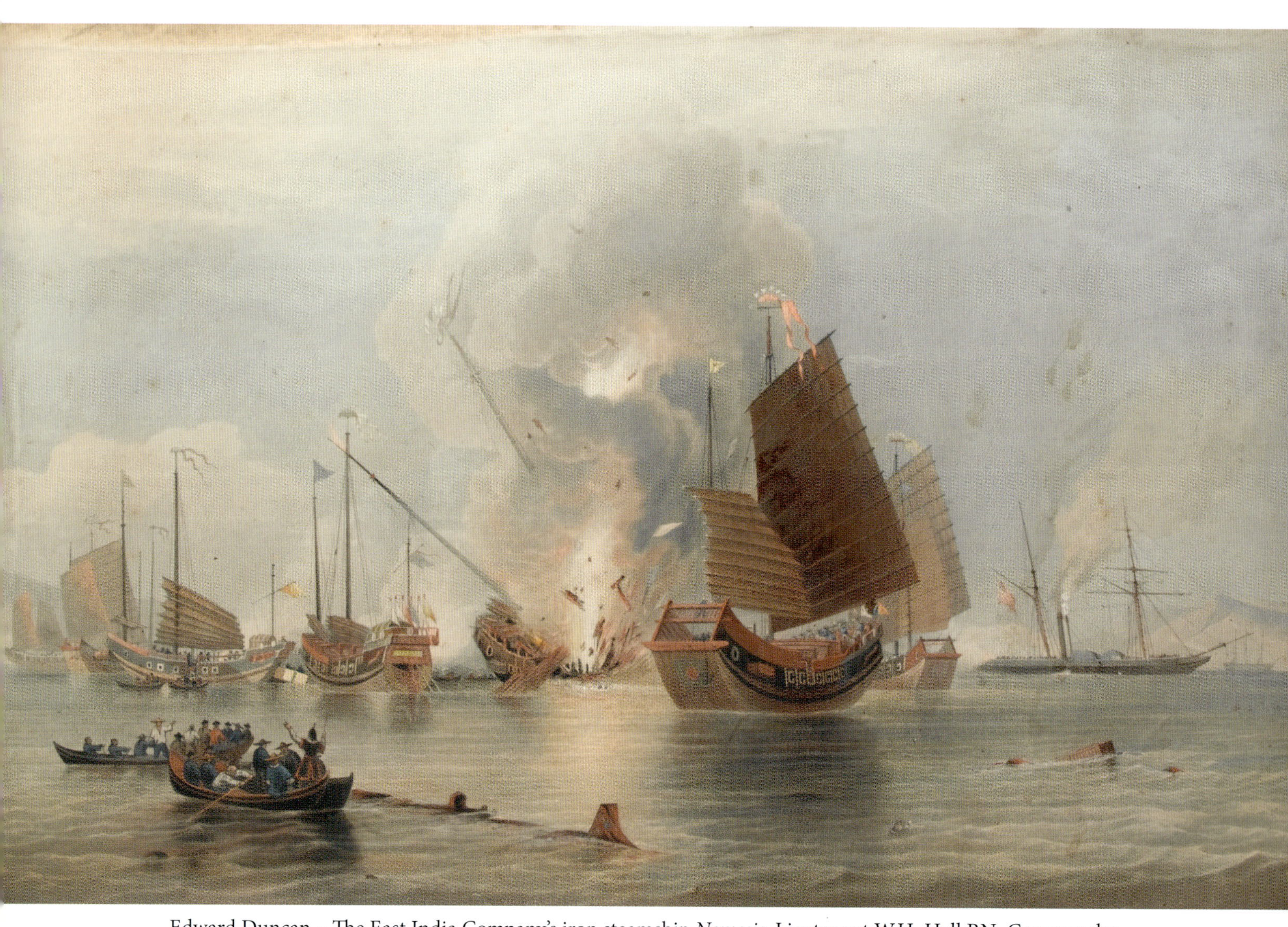

Edward Duncan – The East India Company's iron steamship *Nemesis*, Lieutenant W.H. Hall RN, Commander, with boats of *Sulphur*, *Calliope*, *Larne* and *Starling* destroying Chinese war junks in Anson's Bay, 7 January 1841.

James Atkinson – The Maidan Valley (Afghanistan). Tower on right, British officer mounted on camel, and fruit-seller. Army passing along valley on left towards Arghandi.

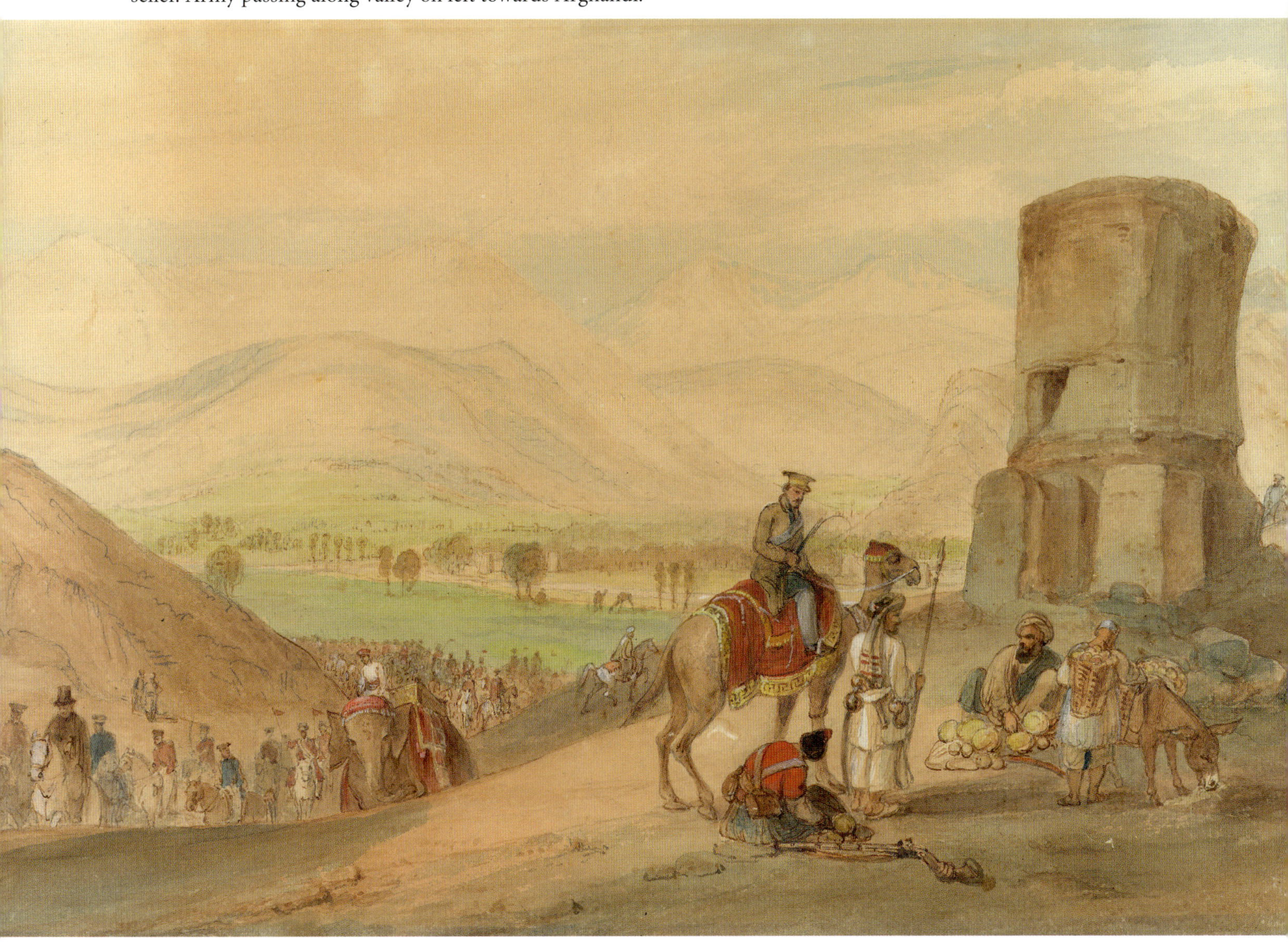

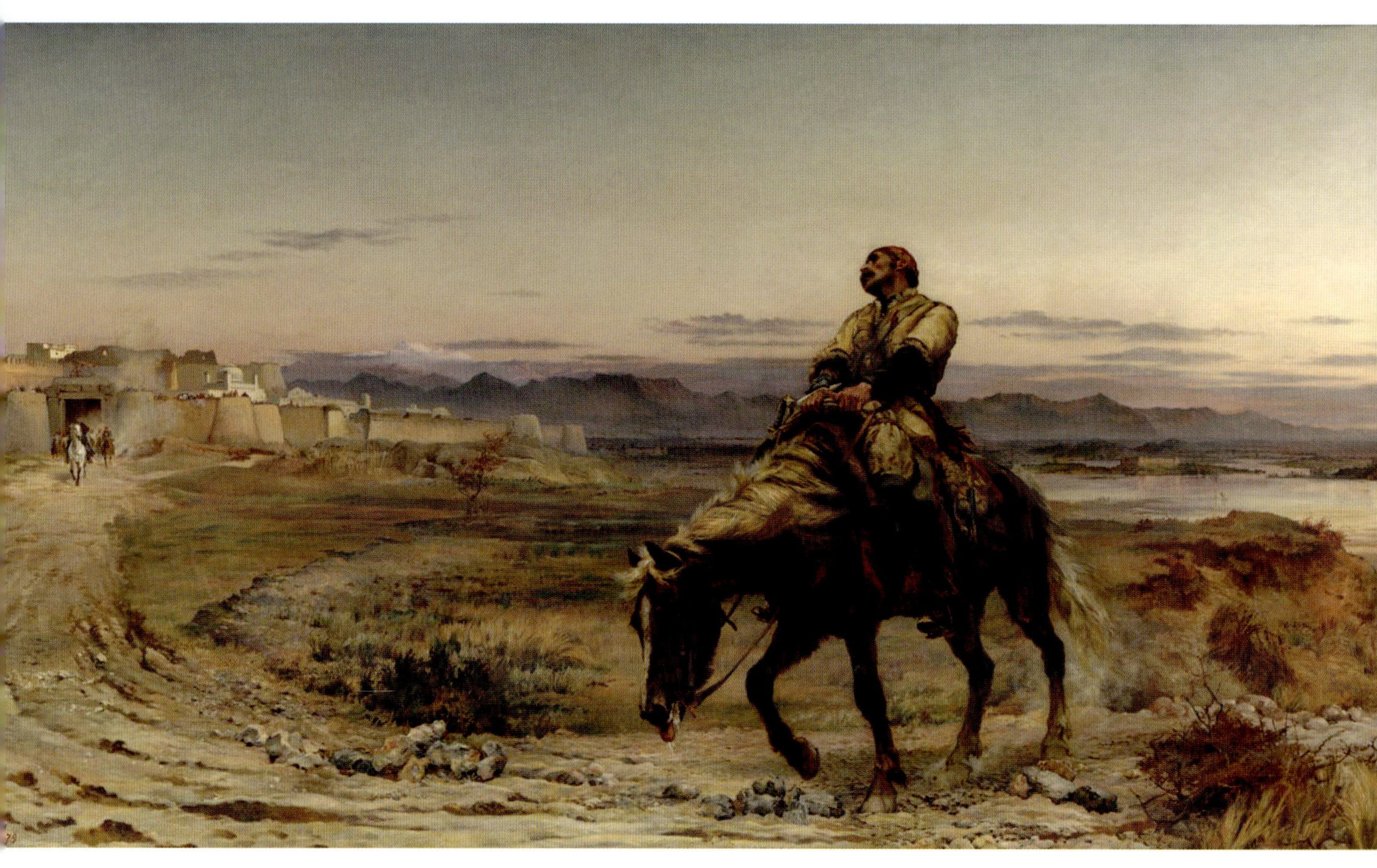

Lady Elizabeth Butler – Remnant of an Army.

defeat in that campaign. But Atkinson produced a number of more assertive pictures of what became known as the First Afghan War, which he sent back to London for publication.

His son, George Franklin Atkinson, also became a noted chronicler of the military in India, particularly as he lived through the Indian Mutiny in 1857. George brought out an edition of his work at this time accompanied by a fulsome dedication to Queen Victoria:

To Her Most Gracious Majesty the Queen,

MADAM

WHEN a remorselessly treacherous and rebellious foe sought to uproot the British Power in India, and by acts of deliberately-planned ferocity and fiendish cruelty strove to destroy every European and Christian in the land, the devoted heroism of a small but resolute force, who fought to maintain the rights of their Sovereign and the honour of England, was so far crowned with success as to stay the arm of the destroyer, wrenching from his grasp the stronghold of rebellion, and winning for them not only victory in the crime-stained streets of Delhi, but the proud satisfaction of YOUR MAJESTY'S gracious approval and heart-felt sympathy.

Though opposed to all but overpowering numbers, in long-continued, close, and deadly conflict, amidst scorching heat and withering pestilence, by night and day, that band of heroes, when the fate of India vibrated in the balance, would not suffer a thought of any other result than, under the blessing of Almighty God, a victorious one, that should re-establish the sway of YOUR MAJESTY's sceptre in the most splendid province of the Empire.

Undeterred by the protracted hardships of the siege, assault, and capture of Delhi, the glorious victors hastened to the rescue of their beleaguered countrymen and their families in Oude, gathering fresh laurels on the way, and taking share in the rescue of the suffering but heroic garrison of Lucknow.

The following Sketches, imperfect as they are, which, by permission graciously accorded, I respectfully dedicate to YOUR MAJESTY, will perhaps afford a faint idea of some of the scenes which that gallant force went through in honour of their country and for love of their Queen.

I am,
    MADAM,
    With the most profound respect,
    YOUR MAJESTY'S most faithful and devoted
    Subject and Servant,
    GEORGE FRANCKLIN ATKINSON,
    Captain, Bengal Engineers.

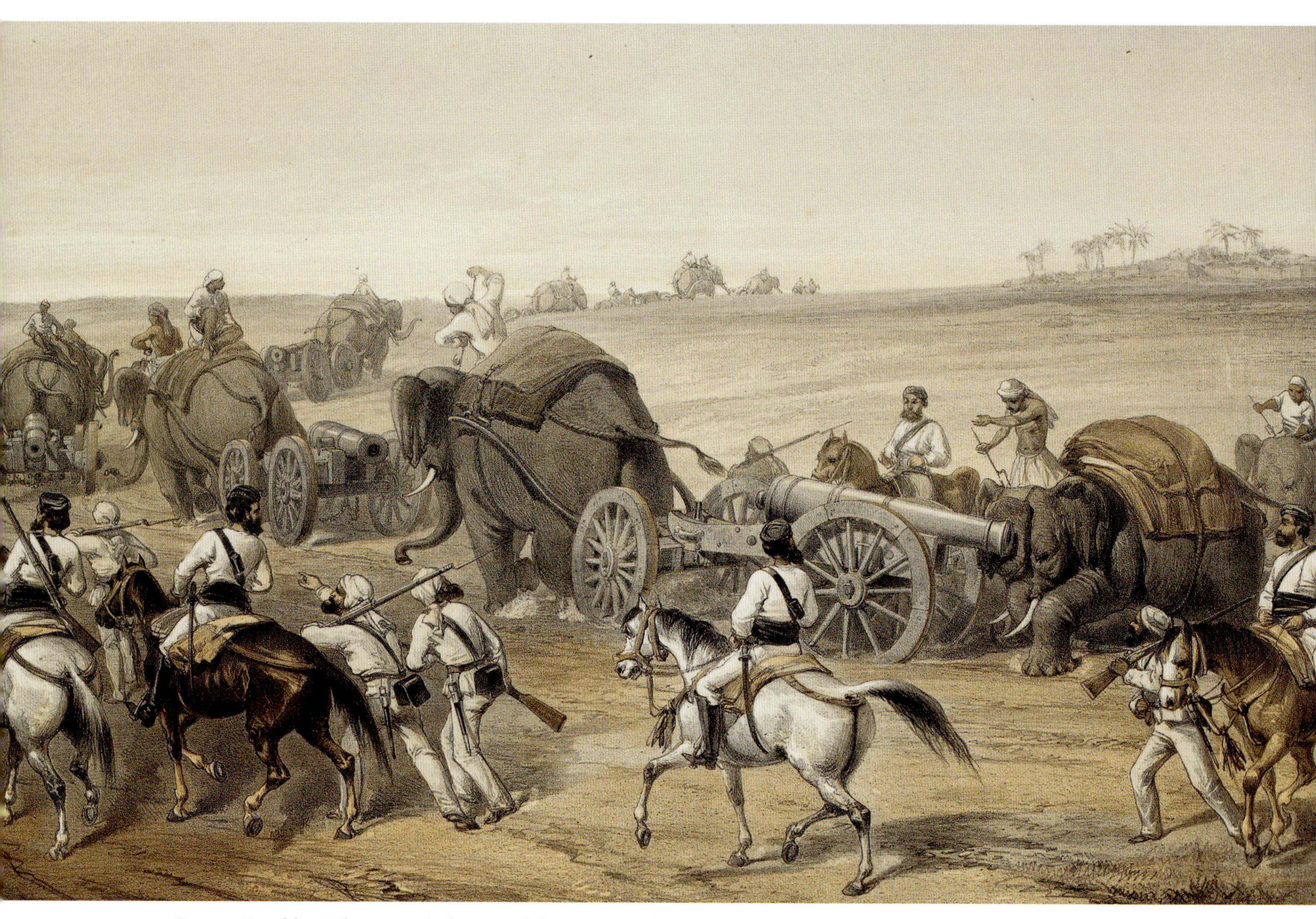

George Franklin Atkinson – 'Advance of the siege train', showing heavy guns on their way to Delhi being drawn by elephants, from *The Campaign in India*.

George wrote about his picture of the attack to retake Delhi:

A new siege-train was ordered to be sent from the arsenal of Ferozepore [Firozpur].

This magazine being at a distance of nearly 200 miles from Delhi, created considerable delay in the taking of the city; for nothing could be done but for our troops to maintain themselves in their position until its arrival, which was not until the 7th of September; by which time the batteries had been duly prepared for their reception.

The guns of this train were drawn by elephants, as shown in the Drawing – a single elephant attached to each; but at times, when the road was deep in sand, the assistance of a second elephant had to be brought into requisition; and, with a pad to protect his forehead, he would push the wheels, lowering himself on his knees, and showing wonderful sagacity in adopting the best mode of extricating the ponderous mass from its difficulties. The train consisted of nearly fifty pieces of heavy ordnance; and these, together with the innumerable carts of ammunition, extended over about seven miles of road, and were protected by British infantry, new Sikh levies, and some irregular cavalry.

*   *   *

Almost as soon as tales began to waft back of Englishmen growing rich in India, artists had been tempted to go out there and try their luck.

Johan Zoffany was already a celebrated portrait painter in London, with a studio in Albemarle Street, when he decided to take ship for Calcutta in 1783. Back in England, Zoffany had already painted a number of the Madras Governor Lord Macartney's friends and relations, and he was assured of a welcome when he stepped ashore. The warmest of letters of introduction eased his way into the uppermost levels of the East India Company, which ruled much of India at the time, including its grandest representative, Warren Hastings.

In the following three years Zoffany set the pattern which was to tempt so many of his fellow artists, as the British Raj continued to thrive and expand. The route to real wealth invariably began with portrait-painting. Zoffany did indeed portray Warren Hastings and Macartney, and many other notables, but it was his large family pictures and groups which seem to have proved not only popular but most remunerative.

His 'Cock Match', with a dozen swells and a fascinated crowd gathered round, was reproduced back home in England, but became, notoriously, the cause of one of the spectators' downfall. Cock fighting was immensely popular in England and India, with the results of 'mains', as the contests were called, recorded in meticulous

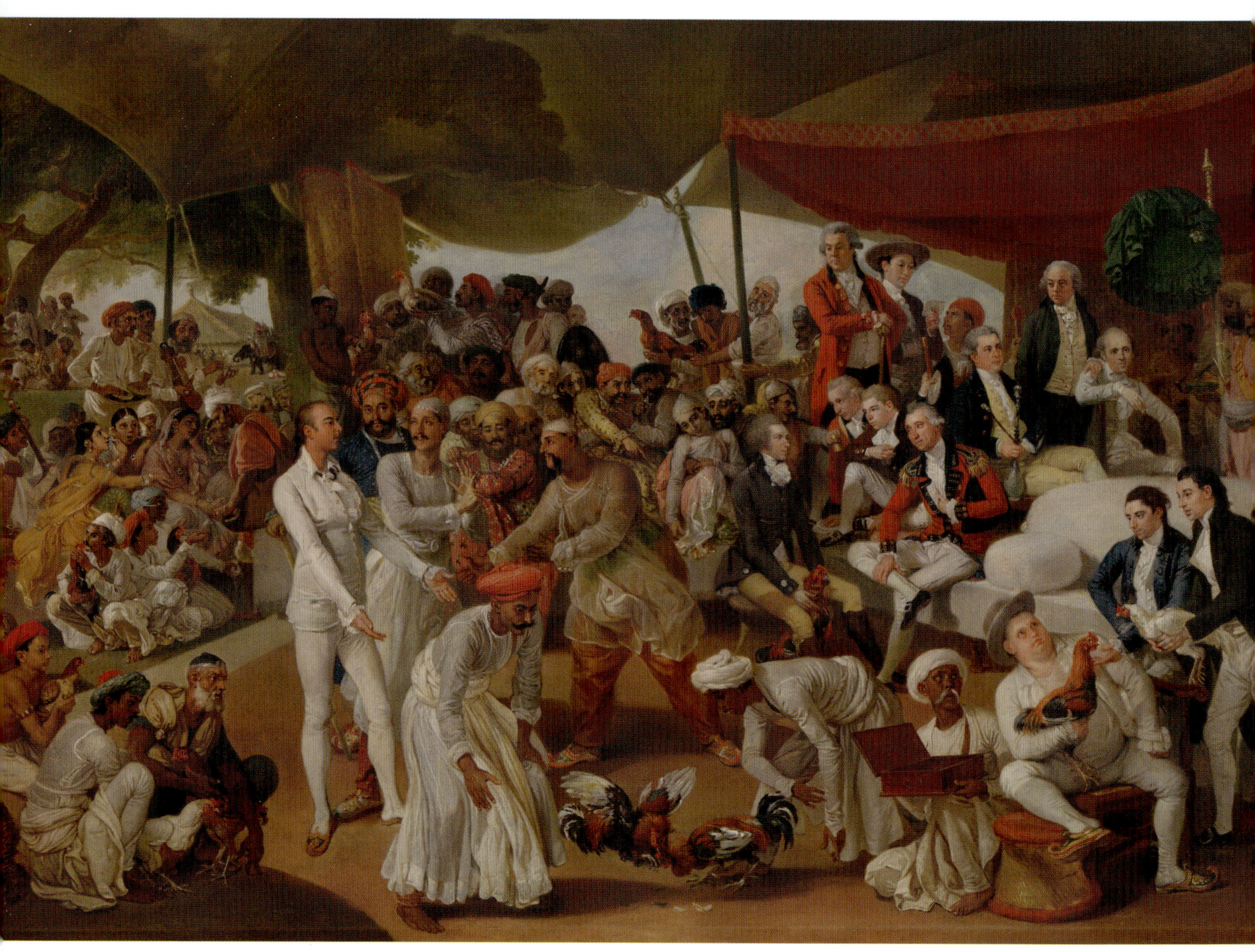

Johan Zoffany – Colonel Mordaunt's Cock Match.

detail alongside the horse racing results in the *Sporting Magazine* of the day, often accompanied by records of the eye-watering wagering that went on.

The unfortunate young man whose portrayal in 'Cock Match' proved so disastrous was Robert Gregory, the son of an Irishman who had returned home from Calcutta, but only after warning Robert that he would be cut off without a penny if he ever went to another 'main'. The story is that Gregory père was walking down the Strand in London when he saw the Zoffany picture on display in a gallery, recognized his son, made confirmatory enquiries in India, and then stood by his word and disinherited Robert from all the family Irish lands.

Zoffany returned home to England with, according to the public prints, a fortune of more than £60,000 – 'an additional spur', as a paper put it, 'to the emigration of artists'.

*   *   *

Amelia Fitzclarence Cary, Viscountess Falkland, daughter of King William IV by his mistress, the actress Mrs Jordan, might have been excused for exhibiting a certain hauteur when she stepped ashore in Bombay as the wife of the new Governor.

In fact, from the moment she arrived, she bubbled with delighted curiosity at the ways and customs of her royal relation's Indian subjects. Sketchbook and pencils in hand, she was almost immediately out, surrounded by local children, among the people and places which fascinated her through her five years in India. On her first visit to Poona (now Pune), she recalled:

I sat down in a corner, with my servant standing near me, and about to begin a very pretty picture, when an elephant passed, nearly treading on my feet. In a few minutes a large buffalo came sharply round a corner, and startled at the sight of me, turned back, raising a considerable quantity of dust. Then the children rushed out of the houses, the women came to the doors to look at me, the fakirs and their saints too stopped to wonder at me. Then a herd of cows and goats were driven by, and completely covered my paper and the inside of my colour box with dust. I went back to the carriage in despair.

Her first experience of being carried along by six men in a palanquin was, as she put it, 'fatiguing. Should you fall asleep, you are apt to incline too much to one side of the palanquin, and are sure to be immediately aroused by the bearers, as it is difficult to keep it steady under these circumstances.'

But, undeterred, the Viscountess, sketchbook at the ready, forthwith set about quizzing the bearers about how they worked. It was a family business conducted by

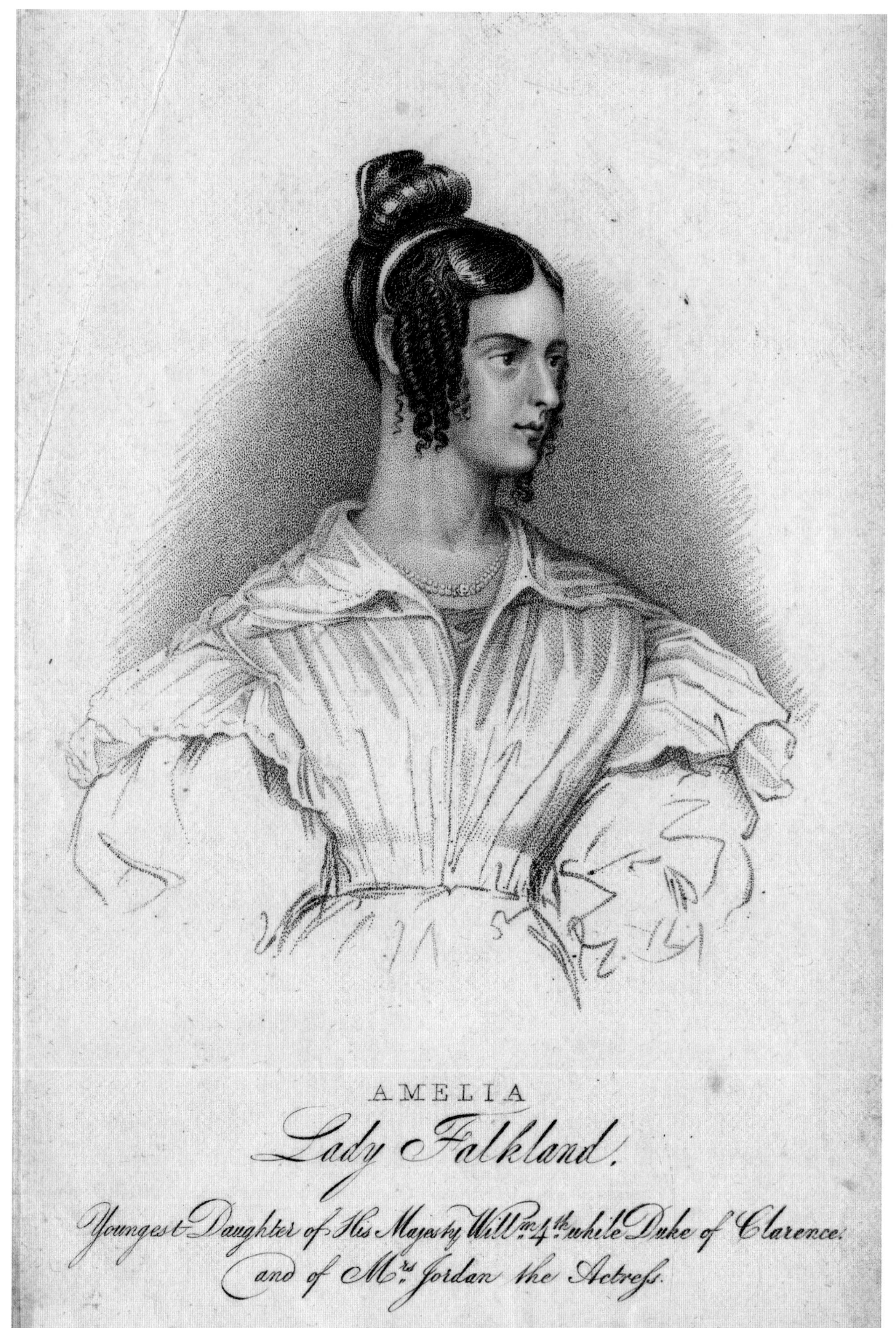

Amelia Lady Falkland – Youngest daughter of His Majesty Willm. 4th while Duke of Clarence and of Mrs Jordan the actress.

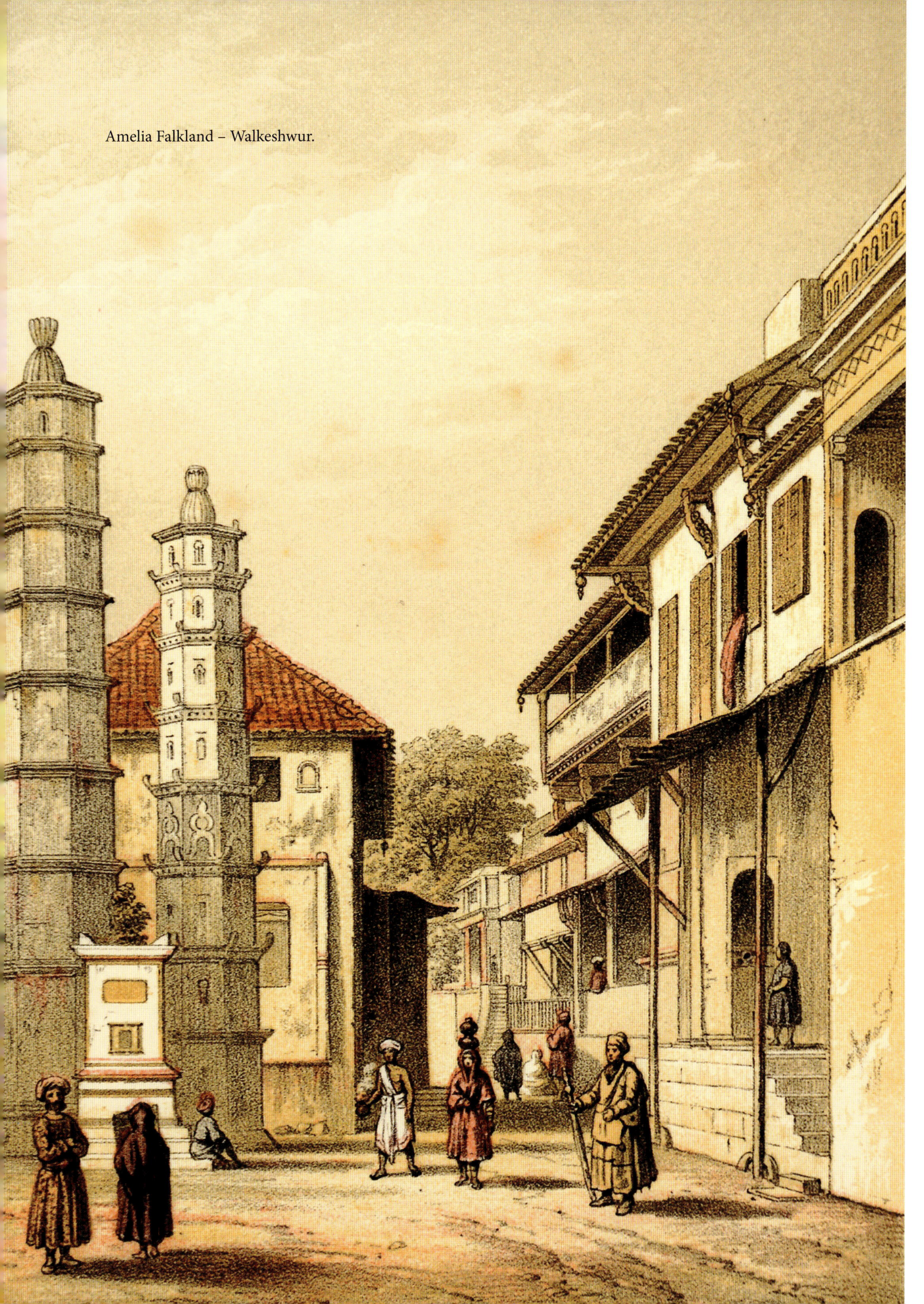
Amelia Falkland – Walkeshwur.

teams of twelve; six worked at any one time, while the other six rested. When a man became tired, he would lie face down and one of his fellows would walk on his back to massage him.

Amelia's informant explained: 'We size ourselves carefully before starting, and make up for difference in height by pads on the shoulders. We can go 18 coss [two miles each] at one run. We hold ourselves answerable for any loss by theft. I have been at work 17 years and never knew of a loss.'

Amelia was just as absorbed by the grander Indians she met. When she and the Governor retreated to the hills, she was visited by three relicts of the Rajah of Satara:

We could see the approach of the three widow Ranees. There were flags flying, banners streaming, prancing horses, stately elephants, tall camels with their heads towering over everything, soldiers on foot, tomtoms, discordant horns.

We saw maids of honour running by the side of the closed palanquin in which the princesses were carried. They were kept shut up till a wall of red cloth could be held up on each side of the entrance to our residence.

When all was ready, the princesses crept out of the palanquins and were received by the Governor. They were concealed in splendid sarees which covered them from head to foot – not even the tip of a finger was visible.

Amelia was later to make a return visit, without her husband, and finally, where no men intruded, see the three widows unveiled. Throughout her husband's five-year tenure she drew and sketched wherever she could, and also kept as vivid and illuminating a journal as any of the imperial ladies of her time.

Chapter 11

Wilson and the South Pole

Edward Wilson was to die in his tent with Captain Scott of the Antarctic, having accompanied him, hauling their sledge all the way to the South Pole and then agonisingly back to within eleven miles of the cache of food supplies that could have saved them.

When their bodies were found, Scott's arm lay across the chest of the man of whom he once said, 'Words will always fail me when I talk of Bill Wilson. He really is the finest character I've ever met.'

Ten years earlier, Wilson had been the first man to bring the colour and nature of Antarctica to western audiences. In 1902 Wilson, a medical doctor as well as an artist, was appointed to Scott's first expedition to Antarctica in the ship *Discovery*. In those early years of the twentieth century there was no effective colour photography, so Wilson's paintings and watercolours were celebrated and much copied when Scott and *Discovery* returned to Britain.

By the beginning of the twentieth century the icy outlines of Antarctica and its winter and summer growth and retreat were reasonably well known to mariners. Indeed, steamships had come close to being trapped at the wrong time of year. But no boot of man had trodden the hundreds of miles of snow and ice towards the South Pole. Geographers knew exactly where this very bottom of the earth had to be, and there was notable public interest in Europe in when the first human being might actually stand at the pole and who it might be.

In the 1902 expedition Wilson executed a number of paintings which captured the daunting demands made on the men as they dragged their sledges through the snow. In 1912 Scott was using dogs and ponies, but human traction proved the most effective, though, in the end of course, not enough.

The wildlife they were fascinated most by was the emperor penguins, which Wilson painted against the harshest of Antarctic landscapes, provoking astonishment that these birds actually found the means to stay alive. His picture 'Midnight' showed a scene he also described lyrically in words:

Stayed on deck till midnight. The sun just dipped below the southern horizon. The scene was incomparable. The northern sky was gloriously rosy and reflected in the

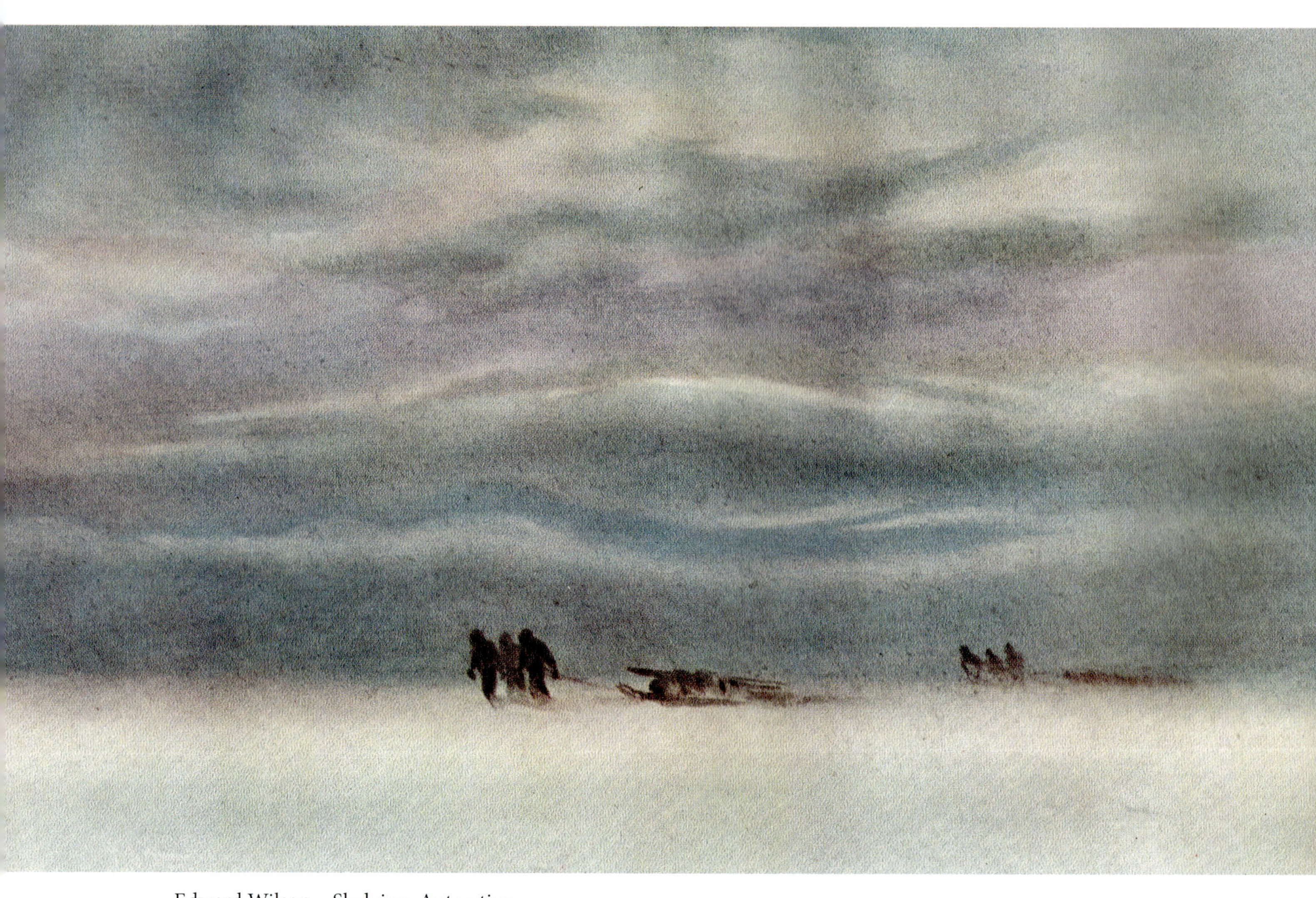

Edward Wilson – Sledging, Antarctica.

Edward Wilson – Emperor penguins.

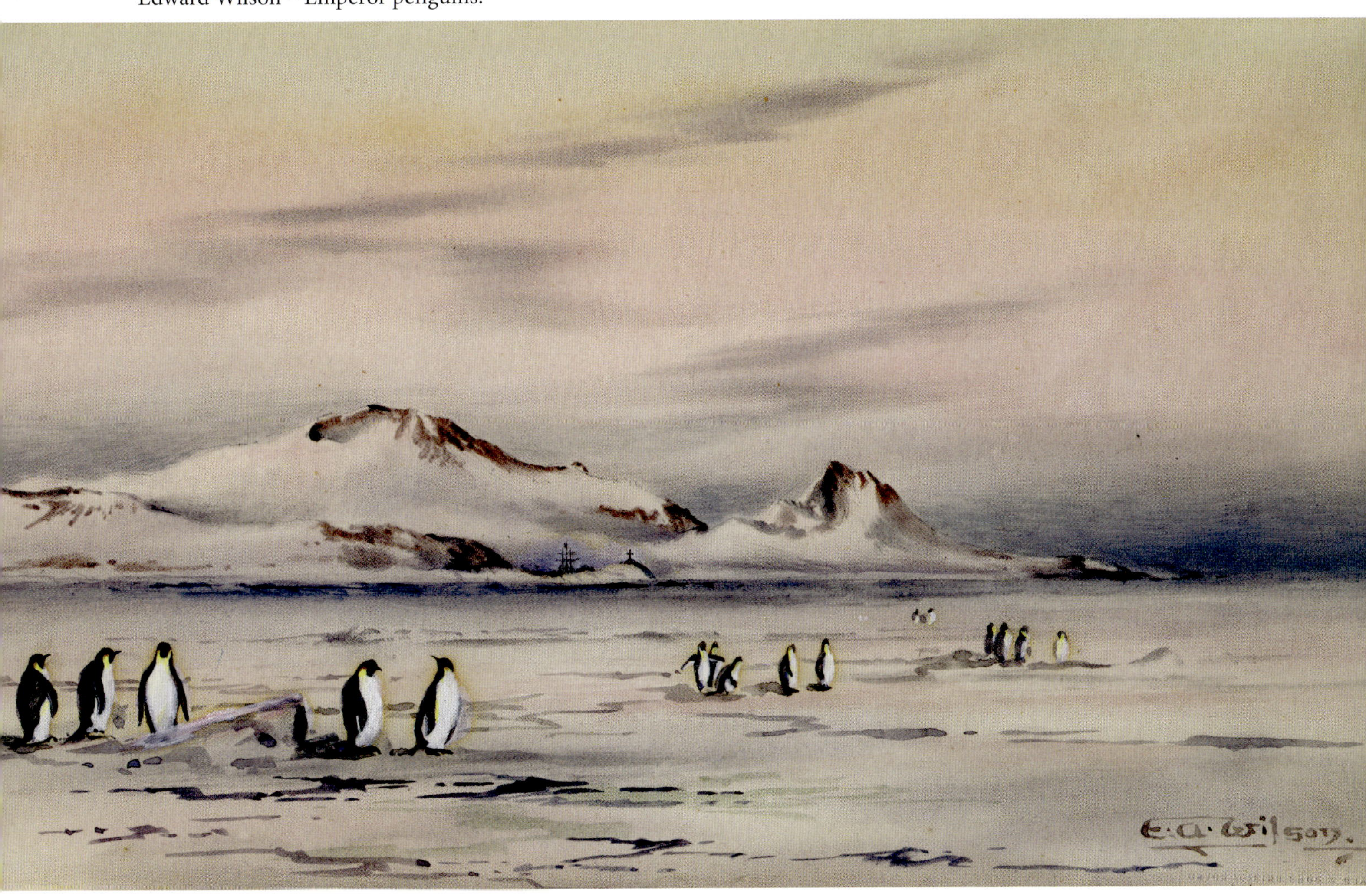

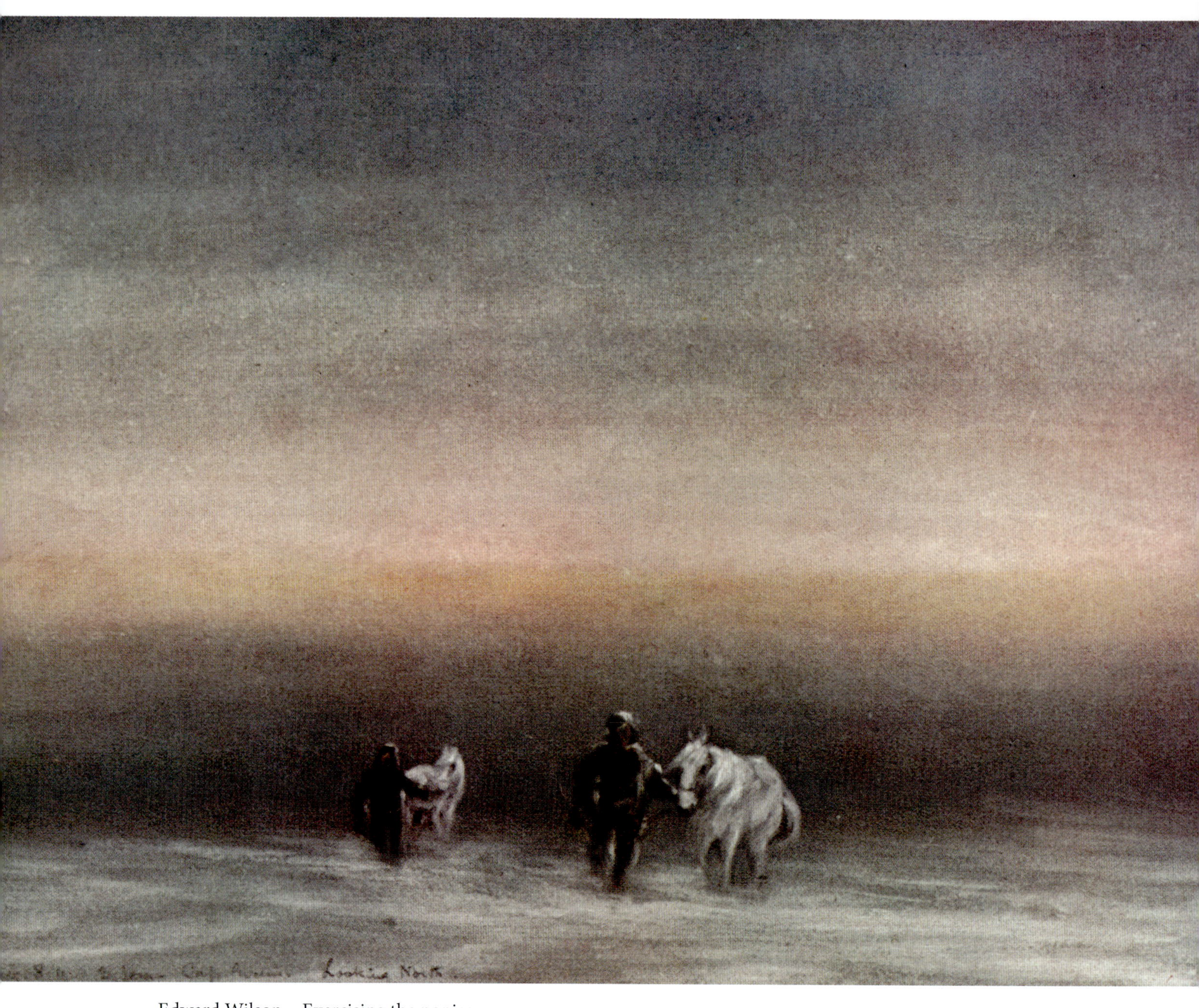

Edward Wilson – Exercising the ponies.

Opposite: Edward Wilson – Midnight at Hut Point.

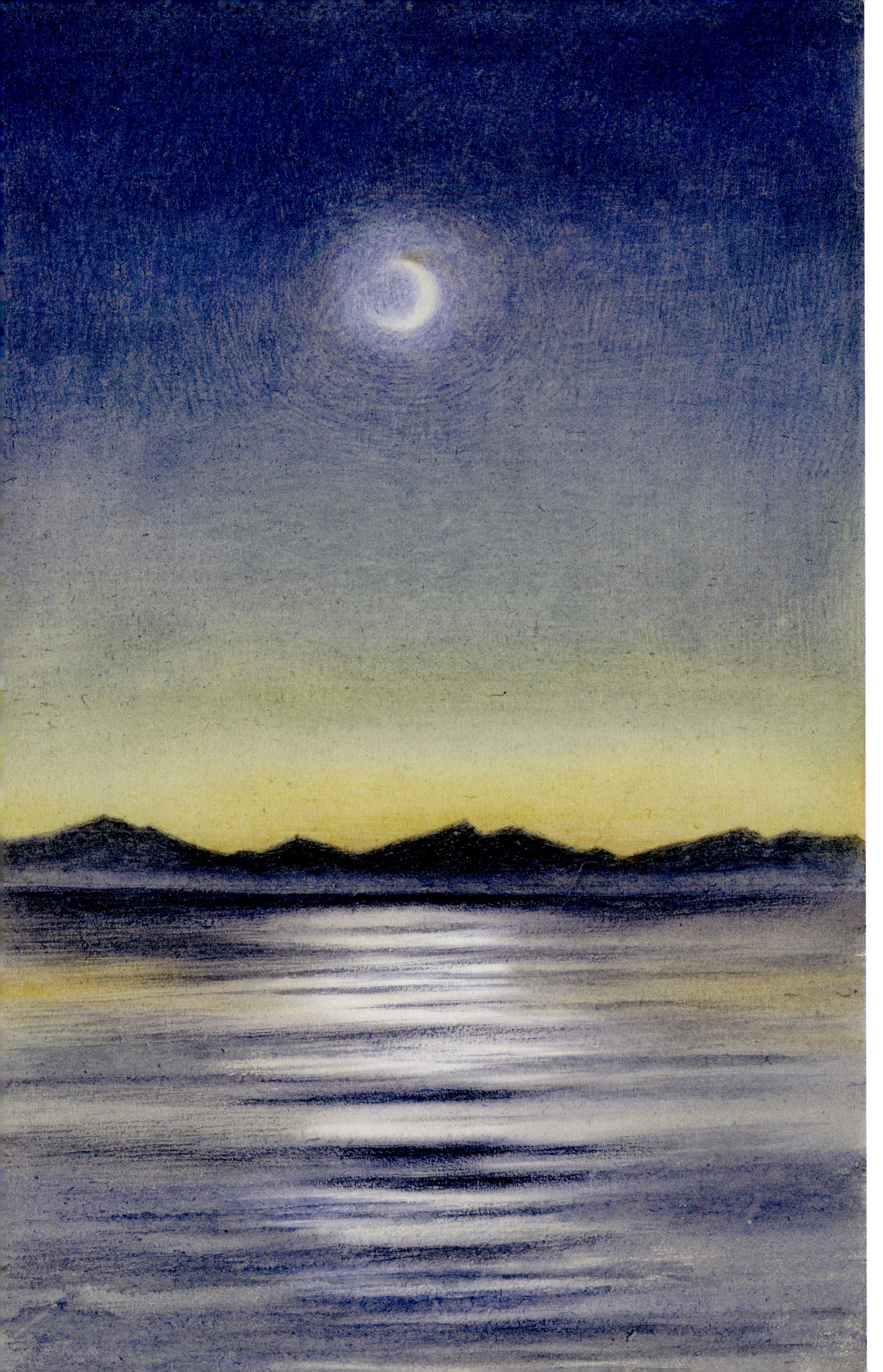

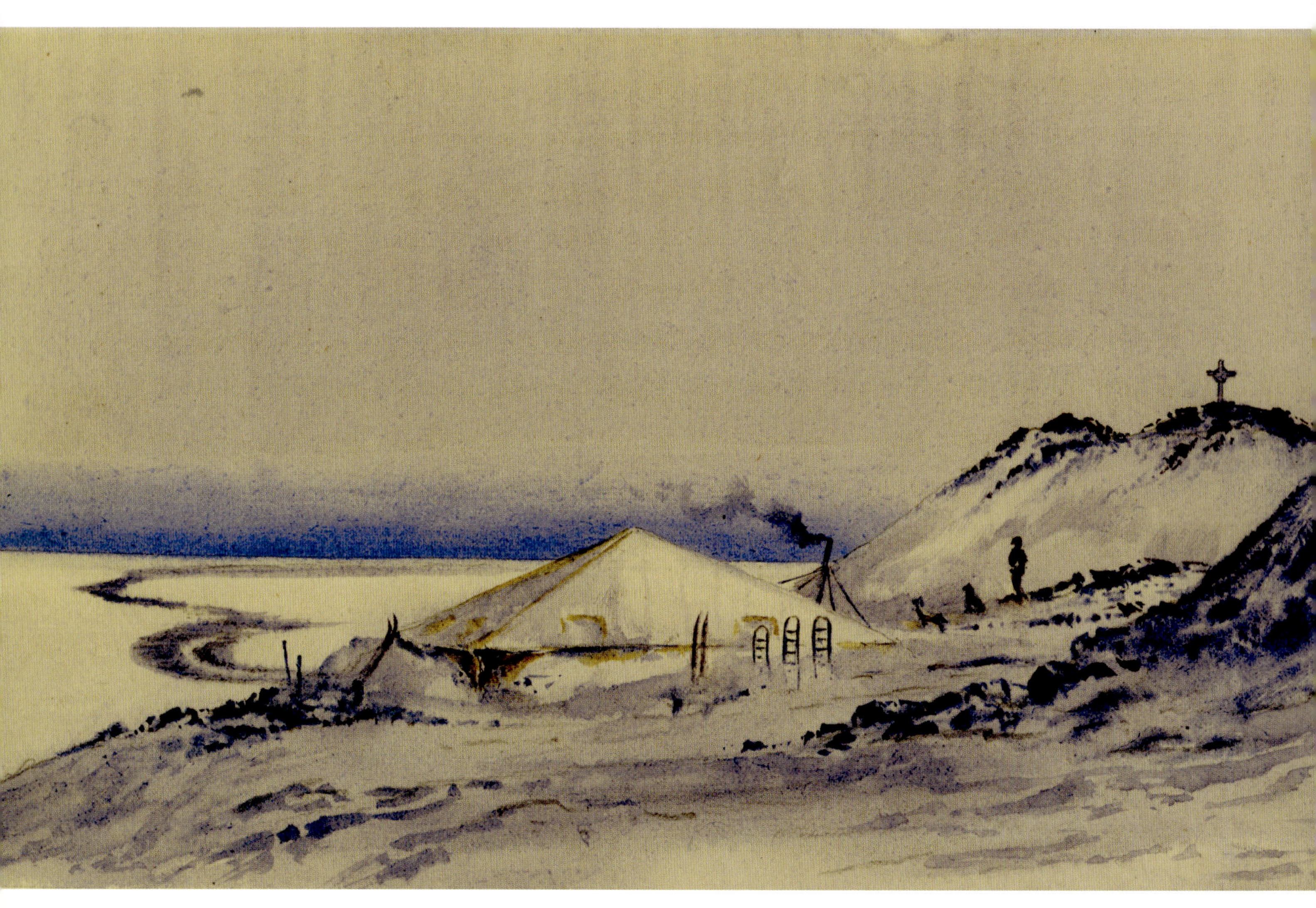

Edward Wilson – Hut Point.

Edward Wilson – The Great Ice Barrier, looking east from Cape Crozier.

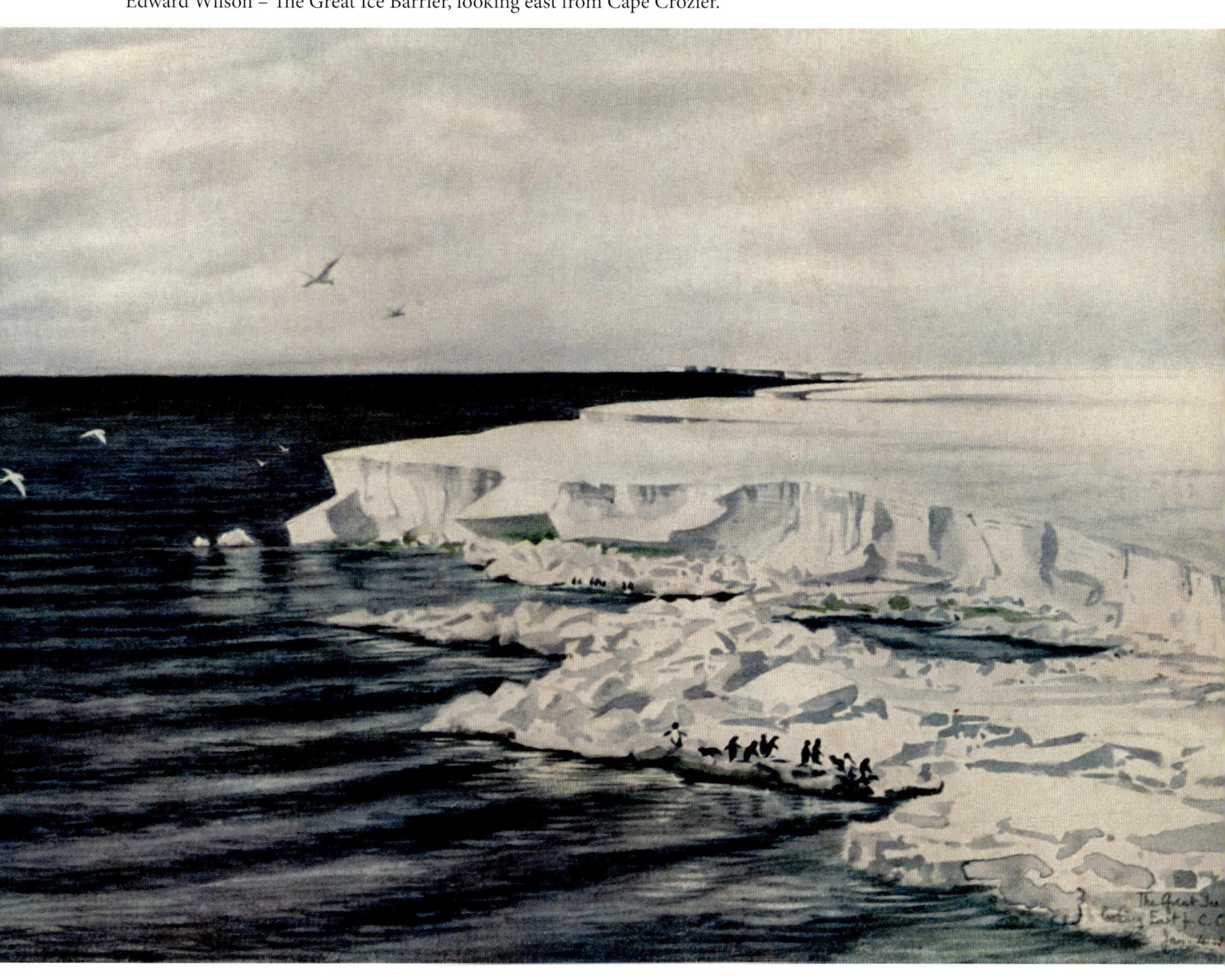

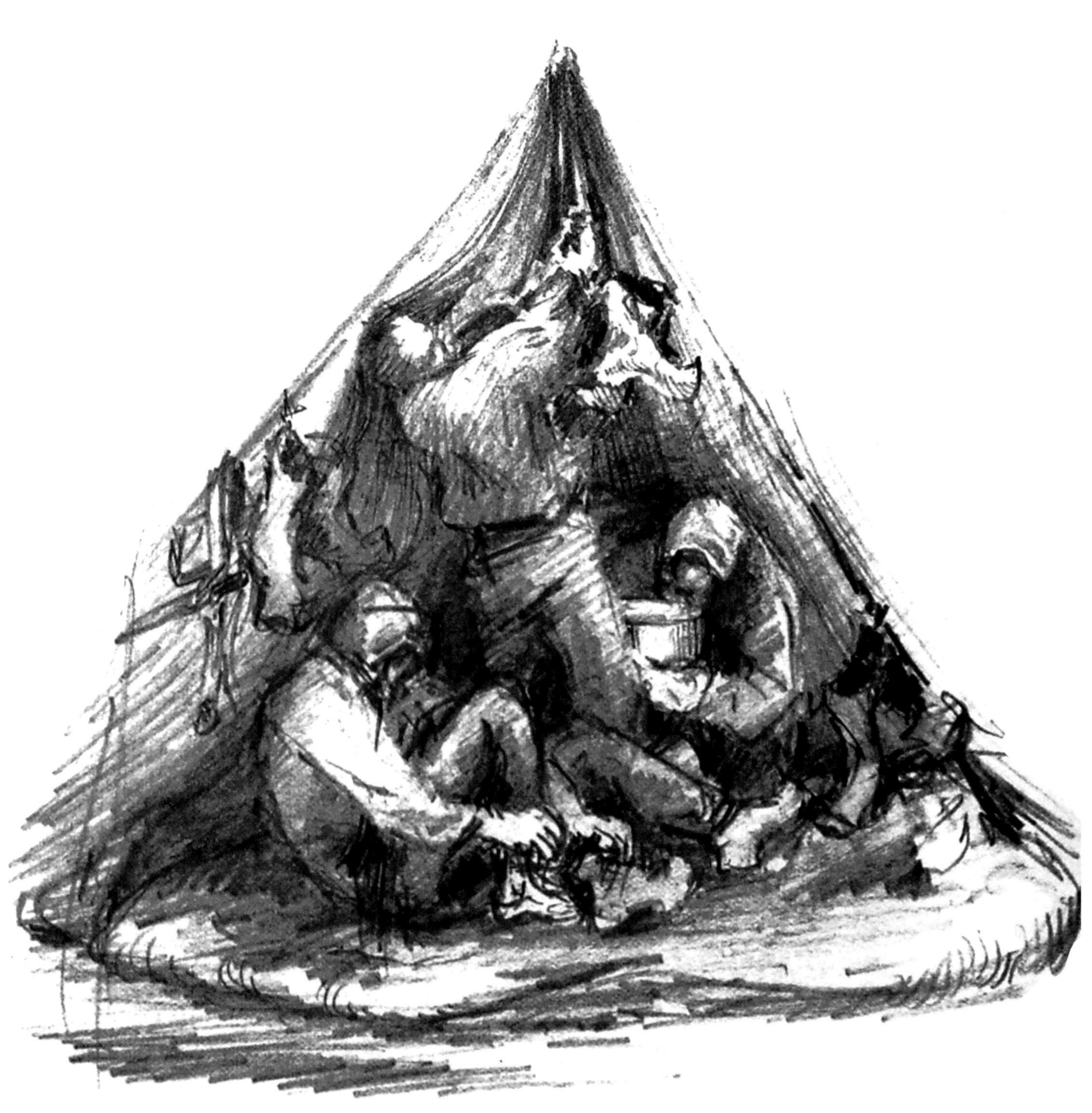

Edward Wilson – Camping after dark.

calm sea between the ice, which varied from burnished copper to salmon pink; bergs and pack to the north had a pale greenish hue with deep purple shadows, the sky shaded to saffron and pale green. We gazed long at these beautiful effects.

He drew the tents the polar group slept in, and painted the treacherous coast of Ross Island.

> When setting up a camp, there is usually an 'outside man' and an 'inside man' after erecting the tent.
> The outside man passes in equipment that will be needed and secures, dogs, sledges and the tent while the inside man will arrange the interior while there is a little more room and gets the stove going for a hot drink.

Scott was to write a last letter to Wilson's wife:

> I should like you to know how splendid he was at the end – everlastingly cheerful and ready to sacrifice himself for others … I can do no more to comfort you than to tell you that he died as he lived, a brave, true man – the best of comrades and staunchest of friends.

Wilson, in his diary, expressed his elation at the vision of the Antarctic which he was the first to record:

> Brilliant sunshine all night and the sea as smooth as glass and the pack all loose enough to make a way through. These days are with one for all time – they are never to be forgotten – they are found nowhere else in all the world but at the poles. One wishes to convey even a glimpse of its unimaginable beauty.

Indeed, his legacy was to be the pictures of extraordinary sunsets, great icebergs and the daunting effort of sledging across the snow, as well as the most meticulous paintings of the birds and wildlife he encountered.

Scott and the *Discovery* team had trekked as far as what is now known as the Polar Plateau, learning hard lessons about not only their own survival but also that of the dog teams on which they had hoped to rely. Many of the dogs died, and the rest were kept alive only by eating their slaughtered fellows.

It was a decade before the team could put together the resource for their second and fatal expedition. But once again it was the artistic appreciation which Wilson left behind which was to fulfil his ambitions to show this new frozen world to the people back home. On the point of death, Wilson wrote a farewell letter to his wife:

Today may be the last effort. Birdie and I are going to try and reach the Depot 11 miles north of us and return to this tent where Captain Scott is lying with a frozen foot if I don't make it, I shall simply fall and go to sleep in the snow and I have your little books, (the testament and prayer book) with me in my breast pocket … Don't be unhappy – all is for the best. We are playing a good part in the great scheme arranged by God himself and all is well … I am only sorry I couldn't have seen your loving letters and Mother's and Dad's and the Smith's and all the happy news I had hoped to see – but all these things are easily seen later, I expect … God be with you – my love is as living for you as ever … we will meet after death and death had no terrors … my own dear wife, good-bye for the present … I do not cease to pray for you – to the very last.

*　*　*

Edward Wilson kept a diary of the expedition:

Wed 17 Jan
We camped on the Pole itself at 6.30 p.m. this evening. In the morning we were up 13 m geog at 5 a.m. and got away on Amundsen's tracks going S.S.W. for 3 hours, passing two small snow cairns and then finding his tracks too much snowed up to follow we made our own bee line for the Pole, camped for lunch at 12.30 and off again from 3 to 6.30 p.m. It blew force 4–6 all day in our teeth with temp. –22°, the coldest march I ever remember. It was difficult to keep one's hands from freezing in double woollen and fur mitts. Oates, Evans, and Bowers all have pretty severe frost-bitten noses and cheeks, and we had to camp early for lunch on account of Evans' hands. It was a very bitter day. Sun was out now and again – observations taken at lunch and before and after supper and at night at 7 p.m. and at 2 a.m. by our time. The weather was not clear, the air was full of crystals driving towards us as we came south making the horizon grey and thick and hazy. We could see no sign of cairn or flag and from Amundsen's direction of tracks this morning he has probably hit a point about 3 miles off. We hope for clear weather tomorrow, but in any case are all agreed that he can claim prior right to the Pole itself. He has beaten us in so far as he made a race of it. We have done what we came for all the same and as our programme was made out. From his tracks we think there were only 2 men on skis with plenty of dogs on rather low diet.

They seem to have had an oval tent. We sleep one night at the Pole and have had a
double hoosh with some last bits of chocolate, and Ber's cigarettes have been much
appreciated by Scott and Oates and Evans. A tiring day – now turning in to a somewhat
starchy frozen bag. Tomorrow we start for home and shall do our utmost to get back in
time to send the news to the ship.

Thurs 18 Jan
Sights were taken in the night and at about 5 a.m. we turned out and marched from
this night camp about 32 miles back in a S. E. direction to a spot which we 33 m
geog judged from last night's sights to be the Pole. Here we lunched, camp – built a
cairn – took photos, flew the Queen Mother's Union Jack and all our own flags. We
call this the Pole, though as a matter of fact we went half a mile further on in a S. E.
direction after taking further sights to the actual final spot and here we left the Union
Jack flying. During the forenoon we passed the Norwegians' last southerly camp. They
called it Polheim and left here a small tent with Norwegian and Fram flags flying and
a considerable amount of gear in the tent, half reindeer sleeping bags, sleeping socks,
reinskin trowsers 2 pair, a sextant and artificial horizon, a hypsometer with all the
thermometers broken etc. I took away the spirit lamp of it which I have wanted for
sterilizing and making disinfectant lotion of snow. There were also letters there. One
from Amundsen to King Haakon with a request that Scott should send it to him. There
was also a list of the 5 men who made up their party, but no news as to what they had
done. I made some sketches here but it was blowing very cold -22. Birdie took some
photos. We found no sledge there though they said there was one. It may have been
been buried in drift. The tent was a funny little thing for 2 men, pegged out with white
line and tent pegs of yellow wood. I took some strips of blue grey silk off the tent seams.
It was perished. The Norskies had got to the Pole on December 16 and were here from
15th to 17th. At our lunch South Pole camp we saw a sledge runner with a black flag
about half a mile away bearing from it. Scott sent me on ski to fetch it and I found
a note tied to it showing that this was the Norskies' actual final Pole position. I was
given the flag and the note with Amundsen's signature and I got a piece of the sledge
runner as well. The small chart of our wanderings shows best how all these things lie.
After lunch we made 6.2 miles from the Pole camp to the north again and here we are
camped for the night.

Chapter 12

The Moon

Neil Armstrong's first steps on the moon in 1969 inspired a host of artistic dreams about what he would find and what space vehicles and extraterrestrial human colonies would look like.

America's National Aeronautics and Space Administration (NASA) had already commissioned a number of artists to help them think about what the future might hold and how it could be created, and Rick Guidice was to produce his spectacular 'Cylinder Colony'. Within its rocket shapes were fields of vegetation, even windmills, expressing the confident assertion that man could live happily in sight of the adjacent stars. There are giant windows; living space is above and around; the colony is contained in a 16-kilometre sphere of air.

Don Davis, too, imagined a verdant colony with the inhabitants flying around in little space taxis.

NASA had commissioned a Princeton professor, Gerard O'Neill, to lead a team to explore ideas about architecture for humans in space. Working with architects, researchers, engineers and scientists in Mountain View, California, O'Neill assessed whether his ideas were feasible, eventually drawing up three concepts to present to NASA: the Bernal Sphere, the Toroidal Colony and the Cylindrical Colony.

Each used centrifugal force to generate artificial gravity, reflected in their circular designs and vast solar arrays to power their rotation. Inside, verdant landscapes offered comfortable living in Modernist homes. Bauhaus structures popped up among lakes and forests; elsewhere, whitewashed villas and terracotta patios brought an Ionian charm to the cold vacuum of space.

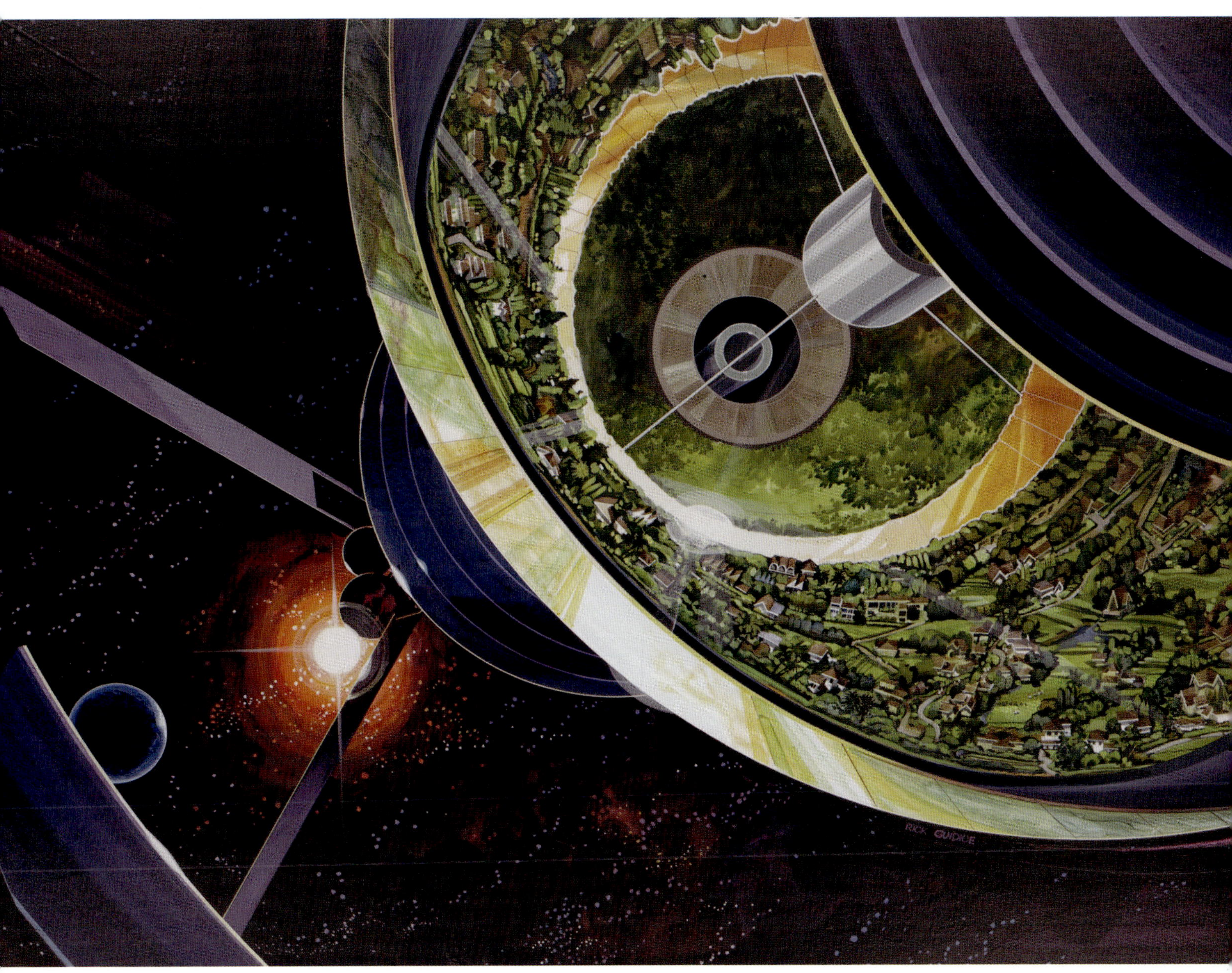

Rick Guidice – Space Colonization, Bernal Sphere.

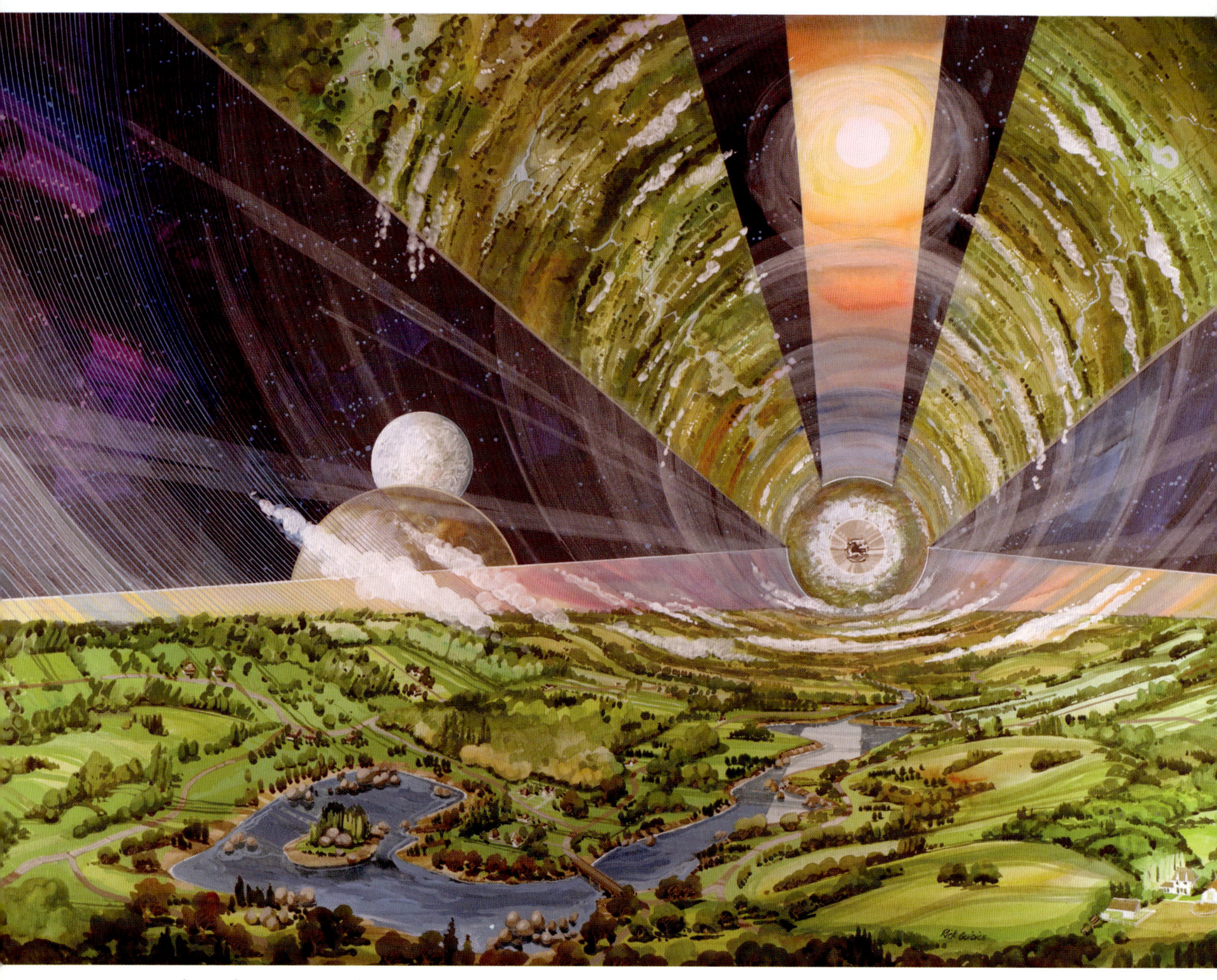

Rick Guidice – Space Colonization, interior of Torus wheel (L-5).

Opposite: Don Davis – Bernal sphere colony.

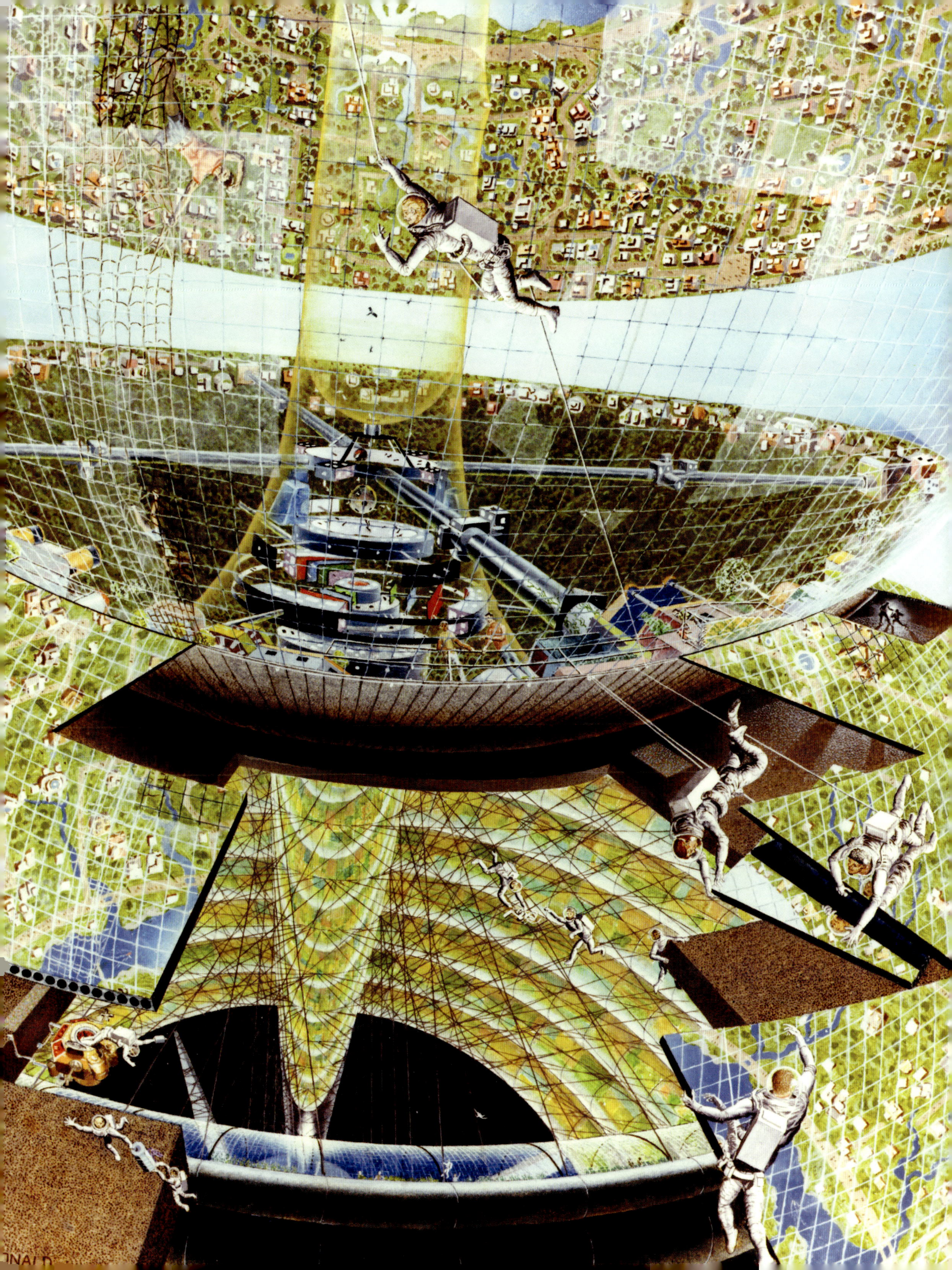

Picture Credits

Front cover, main: National Library of Australia
Front cover, inset: Pictorial Press Ltd/Alamy Stock Photo
Back cover, top: Canadian Museum of History
Back cover, bottom: © National Maritime Museum, Greenwich, London
P.viii: © National Maritime Museum, Greenwich, London
P.ix: Alexander Turnbull Library, Wellington, New Zealand
P.x: Hocken Collections Uare Taoka o Hakena, University of Otago, 7,444
P.xi: Alexander Turnbull Library, Wellington, New Zealand
P.xii: Auckland Art Gallery Toi o Tāmaki, gift of Rear Admiral F. Burgess-Watson, 1935
Pp.2–3, 6–8: © The Trustees of the British Museum
P.10: © The Trustees of the Natural History Museum, London
Pp.11–16: © National Maritime Museum, Greenwich, London
P.18: Captain Cook Memorial Museum, Whitby
P.19: © National Maritime Museum, Greenwich, London
P.20: Wellcome Collection
P.21: © National Maritime Museum, Greenwich, London
P.23: Captain Cook Memorial Museum, Whitby
P.24: Dixson Galleries, State Library of New South Wales
Pp.25, 27: © National Maritime Museum, Greenwich, London
P.30: Pictorial Press Ltd/Alamy Stock Photo
P.31: The Natural History Museum/Alamy Stock Photo
P.32: The Picture Art Collection/Alamy Stock Photo
P.33: National Library of Australia
P.34: With permission of The Royal Green Jackets (Rifles) Museum, Winchester
P.35: The Picture Art Collection/Alamy Stock Photo
P.36: Museum Africa
P.44: State Library Victoria
P.45: Art Gallery of South Australia, Morgan Thomas Bequest Fund 1951
P.46: National Library of Australia
P.47: Art Gallery of New South Wales, purchased with assistance from Mr and Mrs J.K. Bain 1985.
   Image © Art Gallery of New South Wales
P.48: Dixson Library, State Library of New South Wales
P.50: © The Board of Trustees of the Royal Botanic Gardens, Kew
P.52: Iziko Social History – William Fehr Collection, Iziko Museums of South Africa
P.53: Iziko South African National Gallery

P.55: Alexander Turnbull Library, Wellington, New Zealand

Pp.56, 59–60, 62: National Library of Australia

Pp.64, 69: Alexander Turnbull Library, Wellington, New Zealand

P.70: National Library of Australia

P.71: Dixson Library, State Library of New South Wales

P.72: Art Gallery of New South Wales, commissioned by the Trustees and purchased 1874. Image © Art Gallery of New South Wales

P.73: Art Gallery of New South Wales, gift of the Corry Family 1946. Image © Art Gallery of New South Wales

P.75: Alexander Turnbull Library, Wellington, New Zealand

P.77: Fletcher Trust Collection, Auckland

P.78: Dixson Library, State Library of New South Wales

P.79: Hocken Collections Uare Taoka o Hakena, University of Otago, 13,382

P.82: Alexander Turnbull Library, Wellington, New Zealand

P.87: Image Courtesy of the National Army Museum, London

P.88: Library and Archives Canada/William Molson Macpherson fonds/e008300427

P.89: National Gallery of Canada, Ottawa. Photo: NGC

P.92: Royal Holloway, University of London

P.93: Photo: Tate

P.94: Royal Holloway, University of London

P.95: Sotheby's

P.96: National Gallery of Canada, Ottawa. Photo: NGC

P.97: Canadian Museum of History, 2011.156.1

P.100: Historic Collection/Alamy Stock Photo

P.101: Art Gallery of Greater Victoria

P.102: National Gallery of Canada, Ottawa. Photo: NGC

P.103: Library and Archives Canada/George Heriot collection/c012768k

Pp. 106–107, 109–10: Historic Illustrations/Alamy Stock Photo

P.115: Courtesy National Museums Liverpool, Walker Art Gallery

P.118: Museum Purchase from the estate of John Heard, Augustine Heard Collection, 1931, M3810.79A

P.119: Hong Kong Museum of Art Collection

P.120: Courtesy of the National Army Museum, London

P.121: © British Library Board

P.122: Photo: Tate

P.124: Royal Armouries Museum

P.126: Photo: Tate

P.128: ART File F192, 21722, used by permission of the Folger Shakespeare Library

P.129: Shapero Rare Books

P.132: Historical Images Archive/Alamy Stock Photo

Pp.133, 135–6: © The Wilson/Bridgeman Images

Pp.134, 137: The Print Collector/Alamy Stock Photo

P.138: The History Collection/Alamy Stock Photo

Pp.143–5: NASA